Mathematics

COORDINATING AUTHOR
Ernest R. Duncan

W. G. Quast
Charles E. Allen
Lelon R. Capps
Frank Ebos
Mary Ann Hater Haubner

Houghton Mifflin Company • BOSTON

Atlanta • Dallas • Geneva, Ill. • Hopewell, N.J. • Palo Alto • Toronto

Authors

COORDINATING AUTHOR

Ernest R. Duncan
Rutgers University
New Brunswick, New Jersey

W. G. Quast
Slippery Rock State College
Slippery Rock, Pennsylvania

Charles E. Allen
Los Angeles Public Schools
Los Angeles, California

Frank Ebos
University of Toronto
Toronto, Canada

Lelon R. Capps
University of Kansas
Lawrence, Kansas

Mary Ann Hater Haubner
Mount Saint Joseph College
Cincinnati, Ohio

Editorial Advisers

Mary P. Dolciani
Hunter College
City University of New York
New York, New York

Andrew Gleason
Harvard University
Cambridge, Massachusetts

Consultants

Louella B. Tapo
Teacher
Olde Orchard Elementary School
Columbus, Ohio

Heyward M. Thomas
Coordinator of Mathematics
Atlanta Public Schools
Atlanta, Georgia

Contents

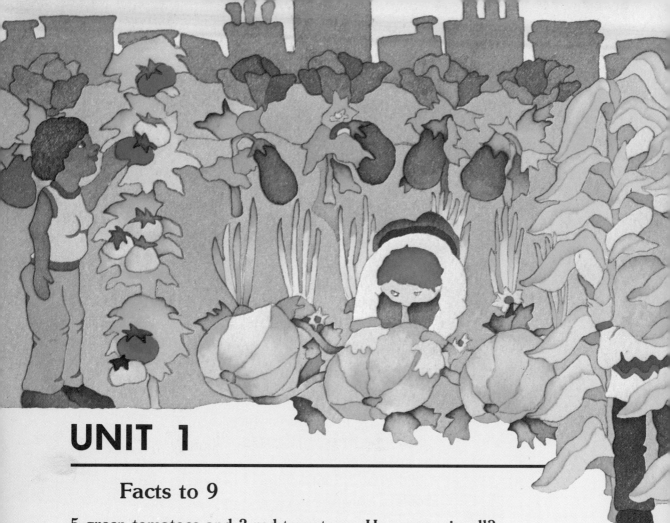

UNIT 1

Facts to 9

5 green tomatoes and 3 red tomatoes. How many in all?
To answer, add 5 and 3.

5 <u>plus</u> 3 <u>equals</u> 8.

$5 + 3 = 8$

The <u>sum</u> is 8.

$$\begin{array}{r} 5 \\ +3 \\ \hline 8 \end{array}$$

8 tomatoes. Take away 3. How many are left?
To answer, subtract 3 from 8.

8 <u>minus</u> 3 <u>equals</u> 5.

$8 - 3 = 5$

The <u>difference</u> is 5.

$$\begin{array}{r} 8 \\ -3 \\ \hline 5 \end{array}$$

2

Addition and Subtraction

a Add or subtract.

1. 4 + 1   2. 5 + 1   3. 6 + 1   4. 7 + 1   5. 8 + 1

6. 3 + 1   7. 3 + 2   8. 3 + 3   9. 3 + 4   10. 3 + 5

11. 7 − 1   12. 6 − 1   13. 5 − 1   14. 4 − 1   15. 3 − 1

16. 8 − 1   17. 8 − 2   18. 8 − 3   19. 8 − 4   20. 8 − 5

21. 2   22. 2   23. 2   24. 2   25. 2   26. 2
    +1   +2   +3   +5   +6   +7

27. 7   28. 7   29. 7   30. 9   31. 9   32. 9
    −7   −6   −5   −0   −1   −2

33. 0   34. 1   35. 2   36. 9   37. 9   38. 9
    +4   +4   +4   −9   −8   −7

3

Facts to 13

9 + 1 = 10

9 + 2 = 11

9 + 3 = 12

9 + 4 = 13

a Add or subtract.

1. 9 + 1	2. 9 + 2	3. 9 + 3	4. 9 + 4
5. 8 + 2	6. 8 + 3	7. 8 + 4	8. 8 + 5
9. 7 + 3	10. 7 + 4	11. 7 + 5	12. 7 + 6
13. 6 + 4	14. 6 + 5	15. 6 + 6	16. 6 + 7
17. 5 + 5	18. 10 − 5	19. 3 + 7	20. 10 − 7
21. 4 + 6	22. 10 − 6	23. 2 + 8	24. 10 − 8
25. 11 − 9	26. 11 − 8	27. 11 − 7	28. 11 − 6
29. 11 − 2	30. 11 − 3	31. 11 − 4	32. 11 − 5
33. 12 − 9	34. 12 − 8	35. 12 − 7	36. 12 − 6
37. 13 − 9	38. 13 − 8	39. 13 − 7	40. 13 − 6

b Add or subtract.

41. 8 +5	**42.** 6 +6	**43.** 4 +9	**44.** 5 +7	**45.** 9 +3	**46.** 4 +6
47. 11 − 6	**48.** 13 − 4	**49.** 12 − 5	**50.** 11 − 7	**51.** 13 − 6	**52.** 11 − 4
53. 6 +5	**54.** 10 − 7	**55.** 12 − 6	**56.** 5 +8	**57.** 4 +7	**58.** 10 − 5
59. 13 − 8	**60.** 12 − 7	**61.** 8 +4	**62.** 10 − 6	**63.** 6 +7	**64.** 3 +7

Picture graph

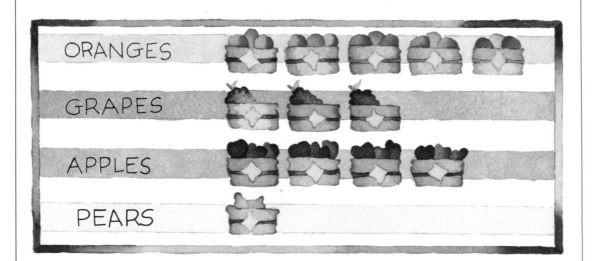

The picture graph shows how many boxes of fruit the corner store sold one day.

1. How many boxes of grapes and pears in all?
2. How many boxes of oranges and apples in all?
3. How many boxes of fruit in all?
4. Were more oranges sold than grapes and pears together?

5

Facts to 18

The table shows all
the facts you need for
addition and subtraction.

$$\boxed{6} + \boxed{8} = \boxed{14}$$

$$\boxed{14} - \boxed{8} = \boxed{6}$$

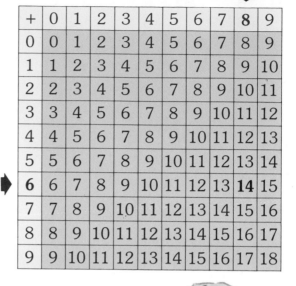

+	0	1	2	3	4	5	6	7	8	9
0	0	1	2	3	4	5	6	7	8	9
1	1	2	3	4	5	6	7	8	9	10
2	2	3	4	5	6	7	8	9	10	11
3	3	4	5	6	7	8	9	10	11	12
4	4	5	6	7	8	9	10	11	12	13
5	5	6	7	8	9	10	11	12	13	14
6	6	7	8	9	10	11	12	13	14	15
7	7	8	9	10	11	12	13	14	15	16
8	8	9	10	11	12	13	14	15	16	17
9	9	10	11	12	13	14	15	16	17	18

a Add or subtract.

1. $1 + 1$	2. $3 + 1$	3. $5 + 1$	4. $7 + 1$	5. $9 + 1$
6. $1 + 2$	7. $3 + 2$	8. $5 + 2$	9. $7 + 2$	10. $9 + 2$
11. $3 + 3$	12. $5 + 3$	13. $7 + 3$	14. $9 + 3$	15. $4 + 4$
16. $6 + 4$	17. $8 + 4$	18. $5 + 5$	19. $7 + 5$	20. $9 + 5$
21. $6 + 6$	22. $7 + 6$	23. $8 + 6$	24. $9 + 6$	25. $7 + 7$
26. $8 + 7$	27. $9 + 7$	28. $8 + 8$	29. $9 + 8$	30. $9 + 9$

31.	32.	33.	34.	35.	36.
$\begin{array}{r} 12 \\ -\ 3 \\ \hline \end{array}$	$\begin{array}{r} 12 \\ -\ 4 \\ \hline \end{array}$	$\begin{array}{r} 12 \\ -\ 5 \\ \hline \end{array}$	$\begin{array}{r} 12 \\ -\ 7 \\ \hline \end{array}$	$\begin{array}{r} 12 \\ -\ 8 \\ \hline \end{array}$	$\begin{array}{r} 12 \\ -\ 9 \\ \hline \end{array}$

37.	38.	39.	40.	41.	42.
$\begin{array}{r} 13 \\ -\ 8 \\ \hline \end{array}$	$\begin{array}{r} 14 \\ -\ 8 \\ \hline \end{array}$	$\begin{array}{r} 15 \\ -\ 8 \\ \hline \end{array}$	$\begin{array}{r} 16 \\ -\ 9 \\ \hline \end{array}$	$\begin{array}{r} 17 \\ -\ 9 \\ \hline \end{array}$	$\begin{array}{r} 18 \\ -\ 9 \\ \hline \end{array}$

43.	44.	45.	46.	47.	48.
$\begin{array}{r} 9 \\ +5 \\ \hline \end{array}$	$\begin{array}{r} 5 \\ +9 \\ \hline \end{array}$	$\begin{array}{r} 14 \\ -\ 5 \\ \hline \end{array}$	$\begin{array}{r} 14 \\ -\ 9 \\ \hline \end{array}$	$\begin{array}{r} 7 \\ +7 \\ \hline \end{array}$	$\begin{array}{r} 14 \\ -\ 7 \\ \hline \end{array}$

b Add or subtract.

49. 8 +8	**50.** 7 +9	**51.** 15 − 6	**52.** 6 +8	**53.** 16 − 8	**54.** 15 − 7
55. 8 +9	**56.** 15 − 9	**57.** 17 − 8	**58.** 8 +7	**59.** 16 − 7	**60.** 9 +9

c Write A, B, C, or D to match the story with the fact.

61. 6 pails are full of berries.
8 more pails are filled.
14 pails in all are full.

62. 17 berry pickers are working.
8 leave.
9 berry pickers are left.

63. We bake 8 pies.
We put 6 into the freezer.
2 pies are left out.

64. I have 8 jars full of jam.
I have 8 empty jars.
I have 16 jars in all.

A. 8 − 6 = 2
B. 8 + 8 = 16
C. 6
+ 8
‾‾‾
14

D. 17
− 8
‾‾‾
9

Addition-Subtraction Facts

Number patterns help you memorize addition-subtraction facts.

5 + 5 = 10	10 − 5 = 5	1 + 0 = 1
6 + 5 = 11	11 − 5 = 6	2 + 0 = 2
7 + 5 = 12	12 − 5 = 7	3 + 0 = 3
8 + 5 = 13	13 − 5 = 8	4 + 0 = 4

a Add or subtract.

1. 2 + 8	2. 10 − 8	3. 3 + 7	4. 10 − 7
3 + 8	11 − 8	4 + 7	11 − 7
4 + 8	12 − 8	5 + 7	12 − 7
5 + 8	13 − 8	6 + 7	13 − 7
5. 0 + 5	6. 5 − 5	7. 6 + 0	8. 6 − 0
0 + 6	6 − 6	7 + 0	7 − 0
0 + 7	7 − 7	8 + 0	8 − 0
0 + 8	8 − 8	9 + 0	9 − 0

9. 4 +6	10. 5 +6	11. 6 +6	12. 7 +6	13. 8 +6	14. 9 +6
15. 10 − 6	16. 11 − 6	17. 12 − 6	18. 13 − 6	19. 14 − 6	20. 15 − 6

8

b Add or subtract.

21. | 6 | 7 | 8 | 9 |
|---|---|---|---|
| +4 | +3 | +2 | +1 |

22. | 6 | 7 | 8 | 9 |
|---|---|---|---|
| +6 | +5 | +4 | +3 |

23. | 11 | 11 | 11 | 11 |
|---|---|---|---|
| − 5 | − 4 | − 3 | − 2 |

24. | 13 | 13 | 13 | 13 |
|---|---|---|---|
| − 6 | − 7 | − 8 | − 9 |

25. | 6 | 8 | 14 | 14 |
|---|---|---|---|
| +8 | +6 | − 8 | − 6 |

26. | 5 | 9 | 14 | 14 |
|---|---|---|---|
| +9 | +5 | − 9 | − 5 |

27. | 7 | 9 | 16 | 16 |
|---|---|---|---|
| +9 | +7 | − 9 | − 7 |

28. | 9 | 8 | 17 | 17 |
|---|---|---|---|
| +8 | +9 | − 8 | − 9 |

c 29. Is the sum of 7 and 8 the same as the sum of 8 and 7?

30. Is the sum of 5 and 7 the same as the sum of 7 and 5?

31. What subtraction facts can you state if you know
that 4 + 5 = 9?

Review A (pages 2–9)

1. 5 + 4

2. 3 + 3

3. 7 − 3

4. 8 − 7

5. 4 + 6

6. 7 + 5

7. 11 − 9

8. 13 − 6

9. | 7 |
|---|
| +8 |

10. | 8 |
|---|
| +9 |

11. | 16 |
|---|
| − 7 |

12. | 18 |
|---|
| − 9 |

13. | 0 |
|---|
| +5 |

14. | 9 |
|---|
| +0 |

15. | 7 |
|---|
| −0 |

16. | 8 |
|---|
| −8 |

Extra practice on p. 310

Addition to 20

See what happens when you add ten.

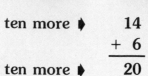

4	ten more ➧	14		4	ten more ➧	14
+5		+ 5		+6		+ 6
9	ten more ➧	19		10	ten more ➧	20

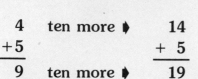

a Add.

1. 0
    +1

2. 10
    + 1

3. 0
    +4

4. 10
    + 4

5. 0
    +9

6. 10
    + 9

7. 3
    +3

8. 13
    + 3

9. 4
    +5

10. 14
     + 5

11. 6
     +2

12. 16
     + 2

13. 1
     +7

14. 11
     + 7

15. 4
     +4

16. 14
     + 4

17. 2
     +3

18. 12
     + 3

19. 3
     +4

20. 13
     + 4

21. 5
     +2

22. 15
     + 2

23. 7
     +2

24. 17
     + 2

25. 5
     +5

26. 15
     + 5

27. 7
     +3

28. 17
     + 3

29. 2
     +8

30. 12
     + 8

31. 1
     +9

32. 11
     + 9

33. 6
     +4

34. 16
     + 4

35. 3
     +7

36. 13
     + 7

b Add.

37. 10 + 5	**38.** 14 + 2	**39.** 18 + 2	**40.** 11 + 4	**41.** 16 + 3	**42.** 13 + 2
43. 15 + 4	**44.** 11 + 3	**45.** 13 + 5	**46.** 10 + 6	**47.** 12 + 5	**48.** 14 + 3
49. 11 + 8	**50.** 10 + 2	**51.** 19 + 1	**52.** 13 + 6	**53.** 15 + 3	**54.** 12 + 7

c Answer the question.

55. 12 ears of corn sold
8 more sold
How many sold in all?

56. 15 cents paid
5 cents more paid
How much paid in all?

57. 11 bags used
2 more used
How many used in all?

58. 10 crows in the field
5 more crows flying in
How many crows in all?

11

Addition to 28

4	ten more ▶	14
+6		+ 6
10	ten more ▶	20

4	ten more ▶	14
+7		+ 7
11	ten more ▶	21

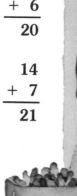

a Add.

1. 6 +6	2. 16 + 6	3. 4 +8	4. 14 + 8	5. 7 +5	6. 17 + 5
7. 5 +8	8. 15 + 8	9. 7 +6	10. 17 + 6	11. 9 +4	12. 19 + 4
13. 7 +7	14. 17 + 7	15. 9 +5	16. 19 + 5	17. 6 +8	18. 16 + 8
19. 6 +9	20. 16 + 9	21. 8 +7	22. 18 + 7	23. 9 +6	24. 19 + 6
25. 13 + 4	26. 13 + 5	27. 13 + 6	28. 13 + 7	29. 13 + 8	30. 13 + 9
31. 18 + 1	32. 18 + 2	33. 18 + 3	34. 18 + 4	35. 18 + 5	36. 18 + 6

12

b Add.

37. 17 + 8	38. 19 + 3	39. 18 + 8	40. 12 + 9	41. 16 + 7
42. 19 + 8	43. 16 + 5	44. 15 + 7	45. 14 + 9	46. 17 + 9
47. 14 + 7	48. 19 + 2	49. 18 + 9	50. 17 + 4	51. 19 + 9

Secret code

L	N	T	I	U	H	E	M	C
20	21	22	23	24	25	26	27	28

Use the sums and the code to complete the message.

1. 18 + 2   2. 15 + 9   3. 13 + 8   4. 19 + 9   5. 17 + 8
6. 16 + 6   7. 14 + 9   8. 19 + 8   9. 17 + 9

1   2   3   4   5   6   7   8   9

Adding Three or More Numbers

Step 1   To add 9, 4, and 8,
first add 9 and 4.

Step 2   Keep the sum 13 in
your mind and add 8.

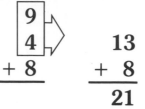

$$\begin{array}{r} 9 \\ 4 \\ + 8 \\ \hline \end{array} \qquad \begin{array}{r} 13 \\ + 8 \\ \hline 21 \end{array}$$

9 big planters
7 hangers
4 small planters
= 20 items

9 small pots
4 medium pots
8 large pots
———
21 pots

4 carrot seed pkt.
6 corn seed pkt.
3 okra seed pkt.
13 seed pkt.

3 pkg. fertilizer
2 pkg. loam
1 pkg. mulch
6 pkg.

a   Add.

1. $\begin{array}{r} 3 \\ 1 \\ + 4 \\ \hline \end{array}$ 4

2. $\begin{array}{r} 6 \\ 2 \\ + 1 \\ \hline \end{array}$ 8

3. $\begin{array}{r} 2 \\ 0 \\ + 3 \\ \hline \end{array}$ 2

4. $\begin{array}{r} 4 \\ 3 \\ + 2 \\ \hline \end{array}$ 7

5. $\begin{array}{r} 7 \\ 2 \\ + 4 \\ \hline \end{array}$ 9

6. $\begin{array}{r} 3 \\ 4 \\ + 5 \\ \hline \end{array}$ 7

7. $\begin{array}{r} 6 \\ 3 \\ + 7 \\ \hline \end{array}$ 9

8. $\begin{array}{r} 4 \\ 4 \\ + 5 \\ \hline \end{array}$ 8

9. $\begin{array}{r} 8 \\ 4 \\ + 5 \\ \hline \end{array}$ 12

10. $\begin{array}{r} 7 \\ 7 \\ + 3 \\ \hline \end{array}$ 14

11. $\begin{array}{r} 6 \\ 9 \\ + 4 \\ \hline \end{array}$ 15

12. $\begin{array}{r} 5 \\ 8 \\ + 4 \\ \hline \end{array}$ 13

13. $\begin{array}{r} 7 \\ 5 \\ + 8 \\ \hline \end{array}$ 12

14. $\begin{array}{r} 9 \\ 6 \\ + 5 \\ \hline \end{array}$ 15

15. $\begin{array}{r} 8 \\ 6 \\ + 6 \\ \hline \end{array}$ 14

16. $\begin{array}{r} 6 \\ 5 \\ + 9 \\ \hline \end{array}$ 11

17. $\begin{array}{r} 7 \\ 6 \\ + 9 \\ \hline \end{array}$ 13

18. $\begin{array}{r} 8 \\ 9 \\ + 7 \\ \hline \end{array}$ 17

19. $\begin{array}{r} 7 \\ 5 \\ + 9 \\ \hline \end{array}$ 12

20. $\begin{array}{r} 6 \\ 8 \\ + 8 \\ \hline \end{array}$ 14

ⓑ Add.

21.	22.	23.	24.	25.	26.
4	5	7	8	5	6
4	4	3	6	8	9
+3	+6	+8	+4	+7	+6

27.	28.	29.	30.	31.	32.
7	3	4	5	6	4
6	8	9	7	2	5
4	2	3	4	4	3
+2	+5	+6	2	6	2
			+3	+7	+9

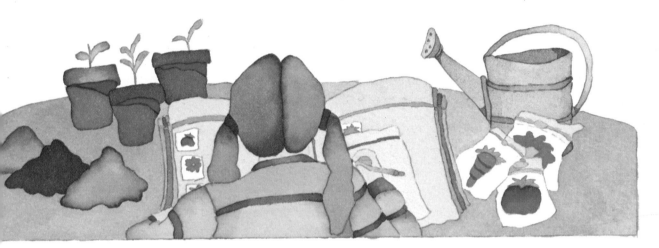

Review B   (pages 10–15)

1.	2.	3.	4.
10	17	15	12
+ 3	+ 2	+ 4	+ 8

5.	6.	7.	8.
16	18	15	19
+ 5	+ 6	+ 7	+ 9

9.	10.	11.	12.
8	7	3	8
1	7	9	8
+5	+5	+8	+8

Extra practice on p. 311

Problem Solving   Problem • Plan • Arithmetic • Answer

The class needs milk cartons for planting seeds.
They save 7 cartons on Monday and 9 more on Tuesday.
How many is that in all?

You solve a problem by answering the question it asks.
You may think and work like this:

1	Understand the problem.	What do you know? What do you want to know?	7 cartons 9 more cartons How many in all?
2	Make a plan.	What do you do to solve the problem?	Add 7 and 9.
3	Do the arithmetic.	Show your work.	7 + 9 = 16
4	Give the answer.	How many cartons in all?	16 cartons

1. Mario brings 2 packets of seeds to class. Mimi brings 3 more. How many packets is that in all?

2. Joe has 13 seeds. He gives 5 to Carla. How many does Joe have left?

3. The teacher gives Carla 7 seeds. Joe gives Carla 5 seeds. How many seeds is that in all?

4. Mimi has 6 seedlings. She puts 2 in a dark corner. She puts the rest in the sun. How many does she put in the sun?

5. Jane earns 5¢ for the class by selling plants. Mario earns 10¢. How much do they earn together?

16

Unit Test

Add or subtract.   (pages 2–5)

1.	3	2.	8	3.	7	4.	9	5.	5
	+4		−6		+2		−8		+3

6.	5	7.	7	8.	13	9.	11	10.	12
	+5		+6		− 9		− 4		− 8

Add or subtract.   (pages 6–9)

11.	18	12.	6	13.	9	14.	17	15.	8
	− 9		+8		+7		− 9		−0

Add.   (pages 10–13)

16.	10	17.	13	18.	12	19.	19	20.	19
	+ 8		+ 6		+ 8		+ 2		+ 9

Add.   (pages 14–15)

21.	5	22.	7	23.	9	24.	7	25.	9
	3		5		9		8		4
	+6		+4		+2		+6		+8

Solve.   (page 16)

26. Ann and Jim put 11 plants in the school yard.
    Only 8 are blooming. How many are not blooming?

27. There was 1 rainy day last week.
    There were 3 rainy days this week.
    How many rainy days is that in all?

Taking Another Look

Pages 2–5

```
  7        13
 +6       −6
 ──       ──
 13        7
```

Add or subtract.

1. 3
   +1

2. 3
   +2

3. 5
   −1

4. 5
   −2

5. 8
   +2

6. 8
   +3

7. 13
   − 5

8. 13
   − 6

9. 5
   +4

10. 4
    +2

11. 9
    −7

12. 8
    −3

13. 6
    +5

14. 9
    +3

15. 12
    − 8

16. 11
    − 4

Pages 6–9

```
  9        16
 +7       −7
 ──       ──
 16        9
```

Add or subtract.

1. 8
   +6

2. 8
   +7

3. 8
   +8

4. 8
   +9

5. 15
   − 9

6. 15
   − 8

7. 15
   − 7

8. 15
   − 6

9. 9
   +5

10. 7
    +9

11. 14
    − 7

12. 17
    − 9

13. 6
    +4

14. 8
    +0

15. 16
    − 8

16. 14
    − 8

17. 9
    +9

18. 7
    +5

19. 13
    − 4

20. 10
    − 2

Pages 10–13

$$\begin{array}{r} 5 \\ + 8 \\ \hline 13 \end{array} \text{ten more} \rightarrow \begin{array}{r} 15 \\ + 8 \\ \hline 23 \end{array}$$

Add.

1.
$$\begin{array}{r} 0 \\ +3 \\ \hline \end{array}$$

2.
$$\begin{array}{r} 10 \\ + 3 \\ \hline \end{array}$$

3.
$$\begin{array}{r} 7 \\ +2 \\ \hline \end{array}$$

4.
$$\begin{array}{r} 17 \\ + 2 \\ \hline \end{array}$$

5.
$$\begin{array}{r} 4 \\ +6 \\ \hline \end{array}$$

6.
$$\begin{array}{r} 14 \\ + 6 \\ \hline \end{array}$$

7.
$$\begin{array}{r} 6 \\ +8 \\ \hline \end{array}$$

8.
$$\begin{array}{r} 16 \\ + 8 \\ \hline \end{array}$$

9.
$$\begin{array}{r} 19 \\ + 1 \\ \hline \end{array}$$

10.
$$\begin{array}{r} 12 \\ + 6 \\ \hline \end{array}$$

11.
$$\begin{array}{r} 10 \\ + 5 \\ \hline \end{array}$$

12.
$$\begin{array}{r} 11 \\ + 7 \\ \hline \end{array}$$

13.
$$\begin{array}{r} 19 \\ + 7 \\ \hline \end{array}$$

14.
$$\begin{array}{r} 18 \\ + 4 \\ \hline \end{array}$$

15.
$$\begin{array}{r} 15 \\ + 7 \\ \hline \end{array}$$

16.
$$\begin{array}{r} 19 \\ + 9 \\ \hline \end{array}$$

Pages 14–15

$$\begin{array}{r} 6 \\ 7 \\ + 8 \\ \hline \end{array} \rightarrow \begin{array}{r} 13 \\ + 8 \\ \hline 21 \end{array}$$

Add.

1.
$$\begin{array}{r} \boxed{\begin{array}{r}3\\2\end{array}} \rightarrow 5 \\ + 4 \\ \hline \end{array}$$

2.
$$\begin{array}{r} \boxed{\begin{array}{r}6\\1\end{array}} \rightarrow 7 \\ + 5 \\ \hline \end{array}$$

3.
$$\begin{array}{r} \boxed{\begin{array}{r}8\\9\end{array}} \rightarrow 17 \\ + 5 \\ \hline \end{array}$$

4.
$$\begin{array}{r} 2 \\ 4 \\ +7 \\ \hline \end{array}$$

5.
$$\begin{array}{r} 9 \\ 6 \\ +8 \\ \hline \end{array}$$

6.
$$\begin{array}{r} 9 \\ 4 \\ +5 \\ \hline \end{array}$$

Page 16

1. **Problem**
2. **Plan**
3. **Arithmetic**
4. **Answer**

Solve.

1. Amy has 3 coins. Roberto has 5 coins. How many coins do they have in all?

2. Vera has 9 baseball cards. She gives 6 to her brother. How many does she have left?

Something Extra • MAGIC SQUARES

This is a magic square. Each row, column, and diagonal has the same sum.

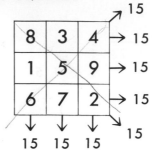

Are these magic squares?

1.

7	0	5
2	4	6
3	8	1

2.

6	1	8
2	9	4
7	5	3

3.

10	5	6
3	7	11
8	9	4

4. Make a 3-by-3 square. Add 2 to each member of square A. Put the sums in your square.

Do you have a magic square?

A

2	9	4
7	5	3
6	1	8

+2 →

4	?	?
?	?	?
?	?	?

5. Copy and complete square C.

A

8	1	6
3	5	7
4	9	2

+

B

2	4	0
0	2	4
4	0	2

→

C

10	5	?
?	?	?
?	?	?

6. Are A, B, and C magic squares?

Reviewing Needed Skills

Add or subtract.

1. $1 + 1$ 2. $2 + 1$ 3. $7 + 1$ 4. $8 + 1$

5. $9 + 1$ 6. $5 + 5$ 7. $7 + 3$ 8. $6 + 4$

9. $10 + 1$ 10. $10 + 3$ 11. $10 + 7$ 12. $10 + 9$

13. $\begin{array}{r} 9 \\ +2 \\ \hline \end{array}$ 14. $\begin{array}{r} 9 \\ +7 \\ \hline \end{array}$ 15. $\begin{array}{r} 9 \\ +4 \\ \hline \end{array}$ 16. $\begin{array}{r} 9 \\ +8 \\ \hline \end{array}$ 17. $\begin{array}{r} 9 \\ +5 \\ \hline \end{array}$ 18. $\begin{array}{r} 9 \\ +9 \\ \hline \end{array}$

19. $\begin{array}{r} 11 \\ -\ 5 \\ \hline \end{array}$ 20. $\begin{array}{r} 12 \\ -\ 3 \\ \hline \end{array}$ 21. $\begin{array}{r} 13 \\ -\ 6 \\ \hline \end{array}$ 22. $\begin{array}{r} 14 \\ -\ 8 \\ \hline \end{array}$ 23. $\begin{array}{r} 15 \\ -\ 7 \\ \hline \end{array}$ 24. $\begin{array}{r} 16 \\ -\ 9 \\ \hline \end{array}$

25. $\begin{array}{r} 19 \\ +\ 1 \\ \hline \end{array}$ 26. $\begin{array}{r} 11 \\ +\ 9 \\ \hline \end{array}$ 27. $\begin{array}{r} 17 \\ +\ 3 \\ \hline \end{array}$ 28. $\begin{array}{r} 15 \\ +\ 5 \\ \hline \end{array}$ 29. $\begin{array}{r} 12 \\ +\ 8 \\ \hline \end{array}$ 30. $\begin{array}{r} 16 \\ +\ 4 \\ \hline \end{array}$

31. $\begin{array}{r} 16 \\ +\ 7 \\ \hline \end{array}$ 32. $\begin{array}{r} 19 \\ +\ 8 \\ \hline \end{array}$ 33. $\begin{array}{r} 13 \\ +\ 8 \\ \hline \end{array}$ 34. $\begin{array}{r} 17 \\ +\ 7 \\ \hline \end{array}$ 35. $\begin{array}{r} 18 \\ +\ 6 \\ \hline \end{array}$ 36. $\begin{array}{r} 19 \\ +\ 9 \\ \hline \end{array}$

37. $\begin{array}{r} 8 \\ 5 \\ +9 \\ \hline \end{array}$ 38. $\begin{array}{r} 9 \\ 1 \\ +7 \\ \hline \end{array}$ 39. $\begin{array}{r} 5 \\ 0 \\ +8 \\ \hline \end{array}$ 40. $\begin{array}{r} 7 \\ 4 \\ +8 \\ \hline \end{array}$ 41. $\begin{array}{r} 8 \\ 9 \\ +9 \\ \hline \end{array}$ 42. $\begin{array}{r} 6 \\ 3 \\ +2 \\ \hline \end{array}$

43. $\begin{array}{r} 2¢ \\ 2¢ \\ +1¢ \\ \hline \end{array}$ 44. $\begin{array}{r} 5¢ \\ 3¢ \\ +2¢ \\ \hline \end{array}$ 45. $\begin{array}{r} 4¢ \\ 6¢ \\ +5¢ \\ \hline \end{array}$ 46. $\begin{array}{r} 8¢ \\ 4¢ \\ +8¢ \\ \hline \end{array}$ 47. $\begin{array}{r} 2¢ \\ 7¢ \\ +6¢ \\ \hline \end{array}$ 48. $\begin{array}{r} 9¢ \\ 7¢ \\ +9¢ \\ \hline \end{array}$

Write the missing numbers.

49. 6, 7, 8, ▢, ▢, 11 50. 16, 17, 18, ▢, ▢, 21

51. 46, 47, 48, ▢, ▢, 51 52. 66, 67, 68, ▢, ▢, 71

Write the number.

53. thirteen 54. seventeen 55. thirty 56. seventy

57. eighteen 58. fourteen 59. eighty 60. forty

21

UNIT 2

Numbers in Order

0 1 2 3 4 5 6 7 8 9 10

These numbers are in order from least to greatest.

5 is to the left of 8.

5 is less than 8.

$5 < 8$

8 is to the right of 5.

8 is greater than 5.

$8 > 5$

6 and 7 are *between* 5 and 8.

22

Numbers and Measurement

a Write the missing numbers.

1. 7 ___ 9 10 ___

2. 17 18 ___ ___ 21

3. 59 60 ___ ___ 63

4. ___ 77 78 79 ___

b Write < or > for ▓.

5. 20 ▓ 30
24 ▓ 34

6. 40 ▓ 30
45 ▓ 35

7. 20 ▓ 70
27 ▓ 70

8. 60 ▓ 30
60 ▓ 37

9. 40 ▓ 90
48 ▓ 93

10. 50 ▓ 70
56 ▓ 72

11. 70 ▓ 40
71 ▓ 49

12. 80 ▓ 10
81 ▓ 18

Numbers to 999

2 hundreds   4 tens   3 ones

200   +   40   +   3   =   243

The digit **2** in **243** is in the **hundreds' place**.
The digit **4** in **243** is in the **tens' place**.
The digit **3** in **243** is in the **ones' place**.

243 is the **standard form**.
We read **243** as *two hundred forty-three*.

a Write the standard form.

1. 40 + 9   2. 200 + 40 + 9   3. 600 + 40 + 9

4. 70 + 8   5. 300 + 70 + 8   6. 700 + 70 + 8

7. 90 + 5   8. 800 + 90 + 5   9. 800 + 90 + 9

10. 6 tens 5 ones   11. 3 hundreds 6 tens 5 ones

12. 8 tens 9 ones   13. 4 hundreds 8 tens 9 ones

14. 7 tens 3 ones   15. 6 hundreds 7 tens 3 ones

16. 5 tens   17. 9 hundreds 5 tens

24

b Write the standard form.

18. 4 hundreds 5 tens 6 ones

19. 700 + 30 + 6

20. two hundred twenty-eight

21. 3 hundreds 4 tens

22. one hundred four

23. 600 + 5

24. 4 hundreds 3 ones

25. seven hundred sixty

Write the missing numbers.

26.

124 125 126

27.

347 348 349

28.

497 498   501

29.

410   412 413

c Write < or > for .

30. 400 ▨ 200

420 ▨ 220

31. 300 ▨ 500

327 ▨ 527

32. 300 ▨ 200

320 ▨ 260

33. 300 ▨ 400

350 ▨ 410

34. 500 ▨ 600

529 ▨ 641

35. 700 ▨ 400

715 ▨ 468

Numbers to 9999

thousands	hundreds	tens	ones
3	5	2	7
3	0	2	7

We read 3527 as *three thousand five hundred twenty-seven.*
3027 has **0** hundreds.
We read 3027 as *three thousand twenty-seven.*

a Write the digit that is in the hundreds' place.

   1. 1234   **2.** 6512   **3.** 6058   **4.** 4275   **5.** 3197

Write the digit that is in the thousands' place.

   6. 8170   **7.** 1695   **8.** 5320   **9.** 3907   **10.** 6075

Write the standard form.

11. 400 + 60 + 7   **12.** 9000 + 400 + 60 + 7

13. 2 hundreds 9 tens   **14.** 6 thousands 2 hundreds 9 tens

15. 6 hundreds 5 tens   **16.** 9 thousand 650

17. 8 hundreds 6 ones   **18.** 3 thousand 806

b Write the numbers that are between the given numbers.

19. 999 ▦ ▦ 1002
20. 5400 ▦ ▦ 5403
21. 2364 ▦ ▦ 2367
22. 6308 ▦ ▦ 6311
23. 8019 ▦ ▦ 8022
24. 1378 ▦ ▦ 1381
25. 7299 ▦ ▦ 7302
26. 4998 ▦ ▦ 5001

c Write A, B, C, or D to match.

27. three thousand three
28. three thousand thirty
29. three thousand three hundred thirty
30. three thousand three hundred three

   A. 3330   B. 3003   C. 3303   D. 3030

Numbers to 1,000,000

millions	hundred thousands	ten thousands	thousands	hundreds	tens	ones
	3	5	2	6	8	9
1	0	0	0	0	0	0

We read 352,689 as *352 thousand, 689*.
We read 1,000,000 as *one million*.

a Write the digit that is in the ten thousands' place.

1. 32,675   2. 140,562   3. 610,325   4. 804,739

Write the digit that is in the hundred thousands' place.

5. 638,500   6. 183,205   7. 209,371   8. 1,000,000

Write the standard form.

9. 52 thousand   10. 52 thousand, 784

11. 60 thousand   12. 60 thousand, 500

13. 145 thousand   14. 145 thousand, 286

15. 999 thousand   16. 999 thousand, 999

17. ten thousand   18. ten thousand, ten

19. fifty thousand   20. fifty thousand, five

21. one hundred thousand   22. one million

28

b Write the numbers that are between the given numbers.

23. 9999 ▨ ▨ 10,002

24. 13,074 ▨ ▨ 13,077

25. 52,300 ▨ ▨ 52,303

26. 75,268 ▨ ▨ 75,271

27. 39,999 ▨ ▨ 40,002

28. 99,998 ▨ ▨ 100,001

29. 250,009 ▨ ▨ 250,012

30. 182,332 ▨ ▨ 182,335

31. 699,990 ▨ ▨ 699,993

32. 734,197 ▨ ▨ 734,200

33. 199,009 ▨ ▨ 199,012

34. 999,997 ▨ ▨ 1,000,000

Digital clocks

A digital clock shows the hour and the number of minutes past the hour.

12 o'clock

1 minute later ▶

1 minute past 12

59 minutes past 12

1 minute later ▶

1 o'clock

Hours are shown in order from 1 to 12.
Minutes past the hour are shown in order from 1 to 59.

Show the time one minute later.

1. 2:01   2. 5:06   3. 9:30   4. 11:29   5. 12:00   6. 12:59

7. 12:34   8. 10:10   9. 7:09   10. 9:42   11. 3:55   12. 2:59

Rounding

The town issued *exactly* 627 dog tags. That is *about* 630.

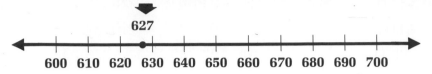

627

```
  600  610  620  630  640  650  660  670  680  690  700
```

627 rounded to the nearest ten is 630.

627 rounded to the nearest hundred is 600.

625 is in the middle between 620 and 630.
Round 625 *up* to 630. Round 650 *up* to 700.

a Round to the nearest ten.

```
  40  41  42  43  44  45  46  47  48  49  50
```

1. 44   2. 41   3. 46   4. 43   5. 48   6. 45

Round to the nearest hundred.

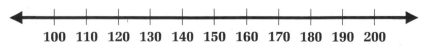

```
  100  110  120  130  140  150  160  170  180  190  200
```

7. 120   8. 190   9. 160   10. 110   11. 130   12. 150

b Round to the nearest ten.

13. 71	**14.** 88	**15.** 67	**16.** 55	**17.** 14	**18.** 47
19. 83	**20.** 94	**21.** 17	**22.** 264	**23.** 321	**24.** 118
25. 435	**26.** 782	**27.** 649	**28.** 156	**29.** 222	**30.** 906

Round to the nearest hundred.

31. 482	**32.** 591	**33.** 833	**34.** 647	**35.** 754	**36.** 230
37. 850	**38.** 142	**39.** 98	**40.** 652	**41.** 909	**42.** 333
43. 249	**44.** 774	**45.** 105	**46.** 150	**47.** 943	**48.** 582

c Round to the nearest ten dollars.

49. $24	**50.** $39	**51.** $15	**52.** $11	**53.** $86	**54.** $93
55. $138	**56.** $233	**57.** $209	**58.** $516	**59.** $149	**60.** $435

Review A   (pages 22–31)

Write < or > for ▓.

1. 30 ▓ 40	**2.** 36 ▓ 46	**3.** 80 ▓ 50	**4.** 81 ▓ 59

Write the standard form.

5. 100 + 10 + 1	**6.** 200 + 70 + 6	**7.** 300 + 20	**8.** 900 + 8

Write the numbers that are between the given numbers.

9. 2130 ▓ ▓ 2133   **10.** 998 ▓ ▓ 1001

11. 89,999 ▓ ▓ 90,002   **12.** 749,998 ▓ ▓ 750,001

Round to the nearest ten.

13. 36	**14.** 65	**15.** 174	**16.** 206

Money

penny
1¢

nickel
5¢

dime
10¢

quarter
25¢

half dollar
50¢

one dollar
100¢

Ways to Show Amounts of Money			
Amount	1 dollar and 25 cents	2 dollars and 5 cents	65 cents
Dollar sign and point	$1.25	$2.05	$.65
Cent sign	125¢	205¢	65¢

a Use a dollar sign and a point to show the amount.

1. 3 dollars and 35 cents

2. 18 dollars and 10 cents

3. 1 dollar 1 quarter

4. 5 dollars 1 nickel

5. 186¢

6. 207¢

Show the amount in cents.

7. 1 nickel 4 pennies

8. 1 quarter 2 pennies

9. 2 dimes 1 nickel

10. 1 half dollar 1 dime

11. 1 dollar

12. 1 dollar 1 quarter

13. $1.75

14. $2.10

b Write A, B, C, D, or E to match the
amount with the nearest dollar.
Round 50 cents or more to a dollar.

15: $2.98   A. $15
16: $2.15   B. $14
17: $14.75   C. $3
18: $.97   D. $2
19: $14.49   E. $1

c What is the cost to the
nearest dollar?

20. hamster house $23.39
21. gerbil food $.98
22. water bottle $1.89
23. shavings $2.57
24. exercise wheels $4.19

Some Metric Units

A <u>centimeter</u> (cm) is this long.
1 cm

This hot dog is about 12 cm long.

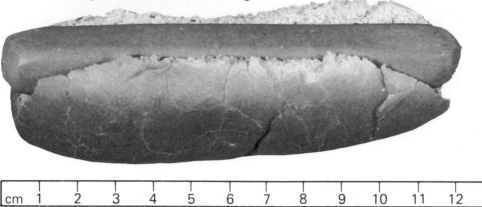

| cm | 1 | 2 | 3 | 4 | 5 | 6 | 7 | 8 | 9 | 10 | 11 | 12 |

A <u>meter</u> (m) is **100 cm.**
A kitchen counter is about one meter high.

A <u>kilometer</u> (km) is **1000 m.**
You can walk one kilometer in about **10 minutes.**

a Write the length in centimeters.

1.

2.

3.

4.

34

b Write cm, m, or km for ▦.

5. The monkey's banana is 15 ▦ long.

6. My popcorn box is 20 ▦ tall.

7. The tiger cub is 1 ▦ long.

8. An ostrich can run 1 ▦ in about a minute.

9. The peacock feather is 90 ▦ long.

10. The alligator's pool is 1 ▦ deep.

11. There are 5 ▦ of roads in the animal park.

12. The fence is 250 ▦ high around the bears.

Measuring up

The giraffe's neck is 275 cm long. How long is your neck?

The elephant's trunk is 200 cm long. How long is your nose?

The gorilla is 180 cm tall. How tall are you?

More Metric Units

A piece of popcorn is about one **gram** (g). A hot dog is about **50** g.

A **kilogram** (kg) is 1000 g. 20 hot dogs are about 1 kg. A 9-year-old is about 35 kg.

a Choose the best answer. Write a, b, or c.

1.

a. 1 g   b. 1 kg   c. 100 kg

2.

a. 2 g   b. 20 g   c. 20 kg

3.

a. 200 g   b. 2 kg   c. 200 kg

4.

a. 2 g   b. 200 g   c. 2 kg

b Write g or kg to name the best unit to measure each.

5. an ostrich

6. a peanut

7. a hamburger

8. a straw

9. a zebra

10. a zookeeper

c The graph shows the amounts of some foods needed for City Zoo animals yearly.

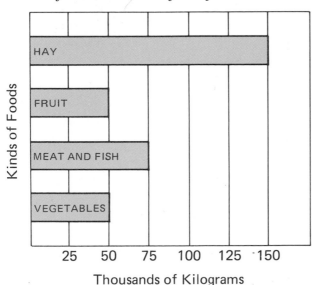

11. How much hay?

12. How much fruit?

13. How much meat and fish?

14. What two kinds of foods are needed in about equal amounts?

Some United States Units

Length

|—————————————|
   1 inch

1 foot (ft) is 12 inches (in.).
1 yard (yd) is 3 feet.
1 mile (mi) is 5280 feet.

Weight

1 pound (lb) is 16 ounces (oz).
1 ton is 2000 pounds.

You can walk one mile in about fifteen minutes.
One pound is the weight of four sticks of butter.

a Choose the best answer. Write a, b, or c.

1. egg's length: ▦ inches
   a. 2   b. 20   c. 200

2. cow's weight: ▦ pounds
   a. 10   b. 1000   c. 100,000

3. truck's weight: ▦ tons
   a. 2   b. 200   c. 2000

4. butter in cake: ▦ ounces
   a. 8   b. 80   c. 800

5. pail's height: ▦ feet
   a. 1   b. 10   c. 100

6. distance to town: ▦ miles
   a. 5   b. 5000   c. 500,000

b Name the best United States unit to measure each.

7. weight of a freight train   8. length of a train route

9. length of my thumb   10. weight of a farmer

11. weight of an egg   12. height of a cow

Review B   (pages 32–39)

Use a dollar sign and a point to show the amount.

1. 1 dollar   1 dime   2. 3 dollars and 5 cents   3. 50¢   4. 150¢

Write cm, m, or km to name the best unit to measure each.

5. coin   6. bus   7. bus route   8. zoo ticket

Write g or kg to name the best unit to measure each.

9. flea   10. dog   11. dog tag   12. dog house

Name the best United States unit to measure each.

13. weight of a dog   14. weight of a flea

15. length of a worm   16. distance between cities

Extra practice on p. 313

Problem Solving Problem • Plan • Arithmetic • Answer

A whale is 14 m long.
A boat is 6 m long.
The whale is longer than the boat.
How much longer?

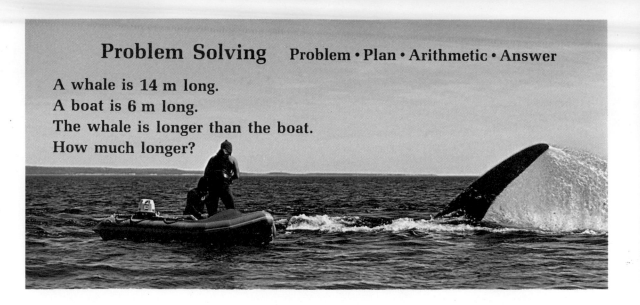

	Understand the problem.	What do you know? What do you want to know?	14 m 6 m How many meters longer?
	Make a plan.	What do you do to solve the problem?	Subtract 6 from 14.
	Do the arithmetic.	Show your work.	$\begin{array}{r} 14 \\ -\ 6 \\ \hline 8 \end{array}$
	Give the answer.	How many meters longer?	8 m

1. A whale is 14 m long. A boat is 5 m long.
   How much shorter is the boat?

2. The little fish is 4 kg. The big fish is 13 kg.
   How many more kilograms is the big fish?

3. Brian got 8 nibbles on his line. His mother got
   15 on hers. How many more nibbles did his mother get?

4. On Saturday 17 fish were caught. On Sunday 9 fish
   were caught. How many more were caught on Saturday?

Unit Test

Write < or > for ▦.   (pages 22-25)

1. 70 ▦ 50   **2.** 72 ▦ 52   **3.** 30 ▦ 90   **4.** 39 ▦ 93

5. 400 ▦ 300   **6.** 436 ▦ 336   **7.** 700 ▦ 900   **8.** 784 ▦ 924

Write the numbers that are between the given
numbers.   (pages 26-29)

9. 6255 ▦ ▦ 6258   **10.** 999 ▦ ▦ 1002

11. 29,998 ▦ ▦ 30,001   **12.** 689,999 ▦ ▦ 690,002

Round to the nearest ten.   (pages 30-31)

13. 47   **14.** 35   **15.** 763   **16.** 509

Use a dollar sign and a point to show
the amount.   (pages 32-33)

17. 2 dollars 1 quarter   **18.** 1 dollar and 1 cent   **19.** 40¢   **20.** 250¢

Write cm, m, or km to name the best unit
to measure each.   (pages 34-35)

21. distance across an ocean   **22.** a pen

23. a pad of paper   **24.** a football field

Write g or kg to name the best unit to
measure each.   (pages 36-37)

25. a student   **26.** a pen

27. a coin   **28.** a horse

Solve.   (page 40)

29. A tuna is 3 m long. A boat is 11 m long.
How much shorter is the tuna?

30. 18 fish are in a big tank. 9 fish are in a small tank.
How many more fish are in the big tank?

Taking Another Look

Pages 22–25

50 < 60

53 < 65

400 > 200

430 > 290

Write < or > for ■.

1. 30 ■ 40   2. 36 ■ 46   3. 50 ■ 20

4. 52 ■ 28   5. 600 ■ 500   6. 610 ■ 570

7. 21 ■ 12   8. 18 ■ 8   9. 39 ■ 51

10. 101 ■ 98   11. 323 ■ 233   12. 267 ■ 289

13. 617 ■ 521   14. 852 ■ 925   15. 409 ■ 490

16. 905 ■ 650   17. 781 ■ 879   18. 549 ■ 944

Pages 26–29

Count to write numbers between 9999 and 10,002.

9999
10,000
10,001
10,002

Write the numbers that are between the given numbers.

1. 999 ■ ■ 1002   2. 4127 ■ ■ 4130

3. 7008 ■ ■ 7011   4. 1546 ■ ■ 1549

5. 6255 ■ ■ 6258   6. 29,998 ■ ■ 30,001

7. 689,999 ■ ■ 690,002

8. 938,500 ■ ■ 938,503

9. 209,371 ■ ■ 209,374

10. 999,997 ■ ■ 1,000,000

11. 450,623 ■ ■ 450,626

12. 700,098 ■ ■ 700,101

Pages 30–31

538 is between 530 and 540. Nearest ten: 540

538 is between 500 and 600. Nearest hundred: 500

Round to the nearest ten.

1. 32   2. 81   3. 75   4. 67

5. 23   6. 218   7. 455   8. 712

Round to the nearest hundred.

9. 112   10. 940   11. 635   12. 777

13. 854   14. 96   15. 450   16. 286

Pages 32–33

1 dollar and
2 dimes
$1.20
120¢

Use a dollar sign and a point to show the amount.

1. 35¢
2. 4 dollars and 15 cents
3. 18 dollars 1 dime
4. 125¢
5. 3 dollars 1 quarter
6. 1 dollar 1 nickel
7. 309¢
8. 7 dollars and 60 cents

Pages 34–35

|— 1 cm —|

1 m is 100 cm.
1 km is 1000 m.
A baseball bat
is about a
meter.

Write cm, m, or km for ▨.

1. My pencil is 19 ▨ long.
2. The diving board is 1 ▨ high.
3. We drove 15 ▨ to the beach.
4. The swimming pool is 25 ▨ long.
5. My brother is 152 ▨ tall.

Pages 36–37

1 kg is 1000 g.
Measure a bug
in grams.
Measure a
student in
kilograms.

Write g or kg to name the best unit to measure each.

1. a needle
2. a stove
3. a person
4. a wagon
5. a feather
6. a dime
7. a leaf
8. a motorcycle
9. a match
10. a desk
11. an envelope
12. a dog

Page 40

1. Problem
2. Plan
3. Arithmetic
4. Answer

Solve.

1. Sherri drove 17 km. Arthur drove 8 km. How much farther did Sherri drive?

2. My house is 10 m long. My room is 4 m long. How much longer is the house?

Something Extra • ROMAN NUMERALS

A different way to name numbers is to use Roman Numerals.

I is 1.   V is 5.   X is 10.

VIII means 5 + 1 + 1 + 1, or 8.
IX means 10 − 1, or 9.

Write the standard form.

1. II   2. VII   3. XII   4. IV   5. XIV
6. XV   7. VI   8. XVI   9. IX   10. XIX

Write the Roman numeral.

11. 3   12. 4   13. 6   14. 7   15. 9
16. 11   17. 14   18. 15   19. 18   20. 19

L is 50.   C is 100.   D is 500.   M is 1000.

Count by tens in Roman numerals.

21.

10	20	30	40	50	60	70	80	90
X	?	?	XL	?	LX	?	?	XC

Count by hundreds in Roman numerals.

22.

100	200	300	400	500	600	700	800	900
C	?	?	CD	?	DC	?	?	CM

Write the standard form.

23. XXI   24. XXIX   25. XXXV   26. XXXIV   27. LV
28. LXII   29. CXX   30. CCL   31. MD   32. MCM

Write the Roman numeral.

33. 22   34. 24   35. 31   36. 39   37. 56
38. 61   39. 130   40. 350   41. 1600   42. 1400

Reviewing Needed Skills

Add or subtract.

1. 8 $+6$	2. 6 $+7$	3. 15 -7	4. 18 -9	5. 9 $+5$	6. 8 $+9$

7. 15 -9	8. 14 -8	9. 5 $+8$	10. 7 $+4$	11. 16 -9	12. 13 -4

13. 19 $+7$	14. 16 $+9$	15. 17 $+3$	16. 14 $+6$	17. 15 $+7$	18. 18 $+8$

19. 12 $+9$	20. 13 $+8$	21. 11 $+8$	22. 15 $+4$	23. 16 $+6$	24. 17 $+7$

25. 9 4 $+7$	26. 8 4 $+9$	27. 5 1 $+4$	28. 2 3 $+6$	29. 9 9 $+8$	30. 7 3 $+6$

Write the standard form.

31. 1 ten 8 ones

32. 6 tens 5 ones

33. 1 hundred 2 tens 3 ones

34. 8 hundreds 5 tens

35. 9 thousand, 436

36. 16 thousand, 705

Round to the nearest ten.

37. 22   38. 67   39. 35   40. 74   41. 38¢   42. $19

Round to the nearest hundred.

43. 305   44. 272   45. 695   46. 414   47. 152   48. 749

Use a dollar sign and a point to show the amount.

49. 3 dollars 1 dime   50. 75¢   51. 212¢   52. 105¢

Round to the nearest dollar.

53. $19.95   54. $2.19   55. $13.50   56. $5.88

UNIT 3

Two-place Addition

There are 23 walkers, 34 riders, and 12 bikers.

	Add the ones.	Add the tens.
23 +34	2 3 + 3 4 7	2 3 + 3 4 5 7

	Add the ones.	Add the tens.
23 34 +12	2 3 3 4 + 1 2 9	2 3 3 4 + 1 2 6 9

46

Addition and Subtraction

a Add.

1. 10 +10	**2.** 30 +10	**3.** 10 +70	**4.** 20 +40	**5.** 50 +30	**6.** 40 +40
7. 35 +10	**8.** 23 +40	**9.** 42 +50	**10.** 10 +25	**11.** 40 +37	**12.** 60 +23
13. 34 +42	**14.** 15 +23	**15.** 22 +44	**16.** 63 +26	**17.** 71 +18	**18.** 53 +24
19. 10 10 +10	**20.** 26 50 +20	**21.** 42 33 +10	**22.** 26 51 +12	**23.** 22 23 +14	**24.** 44 22 +33

47

Two-place Addition

How many are here today? Add 26 and 28.

Add the ones.

$$\begin{array}{r} 2\,6 \\ +\ 2\,8 \\ \hline 14 \end{array}$$ ▶ 1 ten 4 ones

Give the ten
to the tens.

$$\begin{array}{r} 1 \\ 2\,6 \\ +\ 2\,8 \\ \hline 4 \end{array}$$

Add the tens.

$$\begin{array}{r} 1 \\ 2\,6 \\ +\ 2\,8 \\ \hline 5\,4 \end{array}$$

a Add.

1. 6 +4	2. 36 +54	3. 56 +24	4. 7 +3	5. 27 +13	6. 47 +33
7. 8 +2	8. 18 +22	9. 68 +12	10. 8 +3	11. 38 +53	12. 68 +23
13. 26 +34	14. 26 +35	15. 26 +36	16. 26 +39	17. 26 +38	18. 26 +37
19. 53 +17	20. 54 +17	21. 55 +17	22. 59 +27	23. 58 +27	24. 57 +27

b Add.

25. 27 +65	26. 42 +18	27. 39 +26	28. 78 +13
29. 37 +44	30. 25 +28	31. 13 +77	32. 46 +36
33. 12 26 +32	34. 42 23 +24	35. 25 34 +31	36. 45 15 +21

c Add.

37. 26 +94	38. 83 +84	39. 77 +32	40. 65 +39
41. 43 +78	42. 88 +59	43. 42 +78	44. 75 +25
45. 63 23 +54	46. 36 52 +37	47. 72 21 +43	48. 32 33 +35

No pencils needed

You may add 14, 13, and 17 in any order. To add in your head, you may first add the two numbers whose ones make a ten.

$$13 + 17 = 30 \qquad 30 + 14 = 44$$

Add in your head.

1. 26 + 14 + 21   2. 25 + 36 + 25   3. 11 + 27 + 33

Two-place Addition

Compare these examples.

3	23	93		3	53	93		3	63	93
+6	+ 6	+ 6		+7	+ 7	+ 7		+9	+ 9	+ 9
9	29	99		10	60	100		12	72	102

a Add.

1. 6	**2.** 16	**3.** 36	**4.** 5	**5.** 35	**6.** 95
+3	+ 3	+ 3	+2	+ 2	+ 2

7. 6	**8.** 16	**9.** 36	**10.** 7	**11.** 27	**12.** 97
+4	+ 4	+ 4	+3	+ 3	+ 3

13. 8	**14.** 48	**15.** 58	**16.** 9	**17.** 39	**18.** 99
+3	+ 3	+ 3	+4	+ 4	+ 4

19. 26	**20.** 26	**21.** 26	**22.** 45	**23.** 45	**24.** 45
+ 3	+ 4	+ 5	+ 2	+ 5	+ 8

25. 8	**26.** 18	**27.** 38	**28.** 7	**29.** 37	**30.** 47
+7	+ 7	+ 7	+9	+ 9	+ 9

b Add.

31. 65 + 9	**32.** 52 + 8	**33.** 37 + 6	**34.** 43 + 9	**35.** 78 + 4	**36.** 39 + 7

37. 74 + 7	**38.** 38 + 6	**39.** 91 + 9	**40.** 48 + 3	**41.** 56 + 9	**42.** 35 + 8

43. 39 6 + 5	**44.** 68 3 + 4	**45.** 52 9 + 4	**46.** 63 6 + 8	**47.** 28 9 + 6	**48.** 43 9 + 8

49. 27 6 5 + 8	**50.** 36 3 8 + 5	**51.** 27 2 9 + 4	**52.** 63 8 5 + 6	**53.** 22 9 4 + 5	**54.** 51 8 7 + 6

Using coins

You can make 44¢ with 1 quarter, 1 dime, 1 nickel, and 4 pennies, or with 4 dimes and 4 pennies.

Name two ways to make the amount. Do not use all pennies.

1. 27¢   **2.** 33¢   **3.** 61¢   **4.** 49¢   **5.** 76¢   **6.** 58¢

Three-place Addition

Add **287** and **134**.

Add the ones.
Add the tens.

```
    1
  2 8 7
+ 1 3 4
 12 1
```

↓

1 hundred 2 tens

Give the hundred to
the hundreds.

```
  1 1
  2 8 7
+ 1 3 4
  2 1
```

Add the hundreds.

```
  1 1
  2 8 7
+ 1 3 4
  4 2 1
```

a Add.

1. 24
   +53

2. 324
   +453

3. 64
   +25

4. 164
   +425

5. 38
   +21

6. 538
   +421

7. 24
   +56

8. 424
   +256

9. 67
   +23

10. 467
    +123

11. 28
    +52

12. 328
    +452

13. 520
    +160

14. 528
    +162

15. 430
    +250

16. 437
    +255

17. 610
    +270

18. 616
    +278

19. 570
    +160

20. 572
    +164

21. 380
    +290

22. 381
    +294

23. 270
    +490

24. 271
    +494

25. 260
    +480

26. 265
    +487

27. 360
    +570

28. 368
    +574

29. 470
    +430

30. 476
    +438

b Add.

31. 356 +279	32. 101 +809	33. 127 +373	34. 567 + 7	35. 365 +824	36. 853 +108

37. 723 +657	38. 238 +794	39. 388 + 76	40. 632 +154	41. 899 + 5	42. 475 +525

43. 203 317 +468	44. 172 653 +134	45. 333 333 +333	46. 528 308 +158	47. 121 385 208 +168	48. 353 276 194 +215

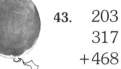

c Solve.

49. 150 balloons are red, 150 are blue, and 150 are green. How many balloons in all?

50. Rosa's group tags 123 balloons. Tim's group tags 109 balloons. How many are tagged in all?

51. Tina's balloon beats last year's record distance by 2 km. Last year's record was 368 km. What is Tina's record distance?

52. Luis's balloon lands in a tree 5 km from school. Someone sets it free. It travels 116 km farther. How far does it travel in all?

Four-place Addition

We add thousands as we did ones, tens, and hundreds.

Example 1
```
  2647
+ 3251
------
  5898
```

Example 2
```
     1
  2647
+ 3138
------
  5785
```

Example 3
```
  1 1 1
  2647
+ 8658
------
11,305
```

a Add.

1. 647
  +132

2. 2647
  +3132

3. 7647
  +5132

4. 389
  +274

5. 2389
  +5274

6. 3900
  +5900

7. 3940
  +5940

8. 3940
  +5980

9. 3942
  +5984

10. 3942
  +5989

11. 7000
  +2000

12. 7002
  +2004

13. 7042
  +2094

14. 7048
  +2096

15. 7648
  +2296

16. 4009
  +5008

17. 4039
  +5028

18. 4039
  +5088

19. 4239
  +5188

20. 4239
  +5988

b Add.

21. 2637
+3489

22. 5746
+4343

23. 6053
+2084

24. 2674
+5313

25. 3582
+4209

26. 9999
+9999

27. 6341
+2257

28. 2398
+1499

29. 1775
+2925

30. 8307
+3087

c Solve.

31. 2845 hot lunches
3520 box lunches
How many lunches in all?

32. 1250 milk cartons for March
1250 milk cartons for April
How many in all?

Review A   (pages 46–55)

1. 50
+40

2. 67
+20

3. 35
+42

4. 31
20
+45

5. 42
+28

6. 36
+27

7. 75
+25

8. 58
+69

9. 34
+ 5

10. 42
+ 8

11. 65
+ 7

12. 96
+ 4

13. 352
+517

14. 336
+354

15. 463
+275

16. 278
+159

17. 3065
+4923

18. 2563
+3398

19. 5682
+2679

20. 5395
+5716

Two-place Subtraction

Subtract the ones.

```
  68        6 8
- 26      - 2 6
          -----
              2
```

Subtract the tens.

```
          6 8
        - 2 6
        -----
          4 2
```

Take a ten to make 12 ones.

```
            5 12
  62        6̸ 2̸
- 26      - 2  6
```

Subtract the ones.

```
            5 12
            6̸ 2̸
          - 2  6
          ------
               6
```

Subtract the tens.

```
            5 12
            6̸ 2̸
          - 2  6
          ------
            3  6
```

a Subtract.

1. 56	2. 56	3. 56	4. 67	5. 67	6. 67
−30	−24	−51	−20	−41	−62

7. 60	8. 60	9. 60	10. 70	11. 70	12. 70
−30	−24	−43	−42	−28	−65

13. 83	14. 83	15. 83	16. 92	17. 92	18. 92
−27	−36	−54	−38	−18	−84

b Subtract.

19. 56 −35	20. 41 −26	21. 80 −45	22. 67 −30	23. 25 − 4	24. 67 −59
25. 72 −36	26. 38 − 9	27. 99 −88	28. 22 −19	29. 31 −20	30. 46 −42
31. 94 −26	32. 53 −38	33. 80 −21	34. 51 − 8	35. 72 −65	36. 78 −24

c Solve.

37. 85 students are putting on a play. 16 of them will act. The rest are helpers. How many are helpers?

38. 36 paper flowers are needed for props in the play. The students have made 17. How many more are needed?

39. Bob and Janet together have 96 programs to hand out. Janet takes 48 to hand out. How many are left for Bob?

Three-place Subtraction

Subtract 267 from 845.

Subtract the ones.

```
   3 15
 8 4̷ 5̷
-2 6 7
       8
```

Take 1 hundred to make 13 tens.

```
 7 13 15
 8̷ 4̷ 5̷
-2 6  7
       8
```

Subtract the tens and hundreds.

```
 7 13 15
 8̷ 4̷ 5̷
-2 6  7
 5 7  8
```

Add 578 and 267 to check the subtraction.

```
  578
+ 267
  845 ✓
```

a Subtract.

1. 32 −21	2. 432 −121	3. 42 −18	4. 642 −518	5. 50 −24	6. 750 −324
7. 64 −31	8. 640 −310	9. 646 −310	10. 646 −312	11. 646 −319	12. 646 −339
13. 52 −18	14. 520 −180	15. 526 −180	16. 526 −184	17. 526 −189	18. 596 −189
19. 600 − 10	20. 603 − 7	21. 602 − 8	22. 602 − 28	23. 602 − 48	24. 605 − 37

b Subtract and check.

25. $\begin{array}{r} 319 \\ -138 \\ \hline \end{array}$	26. $\begin{array}{r} 309 \\ -138 \\ \hline \end{array}$	27. $\begin{array}{r} 707 \\ -245 \\ \hline \end{array}$	28. $\begin{array}{r} 803 \\ -510 \\ \hline \end{array}$	29. $\begin{array}{r} 507 \\ -185 \\ \hline \end{array}$
30. $\begin{array}{r} 316 \\ -138 \\ \hline \end{array}$	31. $\begin{array}{r} 306 \\ -138 \\ \hline \end{array}$	32. $\begin{array}{r} 803 \\ -478 \\ \hline \end{array}$	33. $\begin{array}{r} 605 \\ -129 \\ \hline \end{array}$	34. $\begin{array}{r} 902 \\ -667 \\ \hline \end{array}$
35. $\begin{array}{r} 310 \\ -138 \\ \hline \end{array}$	36. $\begin{array}{r} 300 \\ -138 \\ \hline \end{array}$	37. $\begin{array}{r} 500 \\ -275 \\ \hline \end{array}$	38. $\begin{array}{r} 800 \\ -648 \\ \hline \end{array}$	39. $\begin{array}{r} 900 \\ -339 \\ \hline \end{array}$

A magic square

In this magic square the
sum of any three numbers
in a line is the same.
Copy and complete the square.

72	9	54
?	45	?
?	?	?

59

Four-place Subtraction

We subtract thousands as we did ones, tens, and hundreds.

Example 1

$$\begin{array}{r} 5689 \\ -2568 \\ \hline 3121 \end{array}$$

Example 2

$$\begin{array}{r} {}^{4\ \ 12\ 14\ 16} \\ \cancel{5}\ \cancel{3}\ \cancel{5}\ \cancel{6} \\ -2\ 5\ 6\ 8 \\ \hline 2\ 7\ 8\ 8 \end{array}$$

Example 3

$$\begin{array}{r} {}^{4\ 9\ 9\ 10} \\ \cancel{5}\ \cancel{0}\ \cancel{0}\ \cancel{0} \\ -2\ 5\ 6\ 8 \\ \hline 2\ 4\ 3\ 2 \end{array}$$

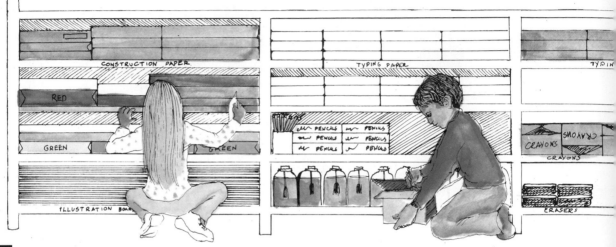

a Subtract.

1. $\begin{array}{r}845\\-143\\\hline\end{array}$	2. $\begin{array}{r}6845\\-5143\\\hline\end{array}$	3. $\begin{array}{r}768\\-294\\\hline\end{array}$	4. $\begin{array}{r}9768\\-3294\\\hline\end{array}$	5. $\begin{array}{r}9768\\-9294\\\hline\end{array}$
6. $\begin{array}{r}7000\\-5000\\\hline\end{array}$	7. $\begin{array}{r}7800\\-5400\\\hline\end{array}$	8. $\begin{array}{r}7860\\-5420\\\hline\end{array}$	9. $\begin{array}{r}7869\\-5422\\\hline\end{array}$	10. $\begin{array}{r}7862\\-5429\\\hline\end{array}$
11. $\begin{array}{r}7000\\-4000\\\hline\end{array}$	12. $\begin{array}{r}7200\\-4800\\\hline\end{array}$	13. $\begin{array}{r}7288\\-4826\\\hline\end{array}$	14. $\begin{array}{r}7288\\-4829\\\hline\end{array}$	15. $\begin{array}{r}7288\\-4896\\\hline\end{array}$
16. $\begin{array}{r}1200\\-\ \ 700\\\hline\end{array}$	17. $\begin{array}{r}1264\\-\ \ 725\\\hline\end{array}$	18. $\begin{array}{r}1264\\-\ \ 783\\\hline\end{array}$	19. $\begin{array}{r}1264\\-789\\\hline\end{array}$	20. $\begin{array}{r}3264\\-1789\\\hline\end{array}$
21. $\begin{array}{r}6734\\-3287\\\hline\end{array}$	22. $\begin{array}{r}6730\\-3287\\\hline\end{array}$	23. $\begin{array}{r}6700\\-3287\\\hline\end{array}$	24. $\begin{array}{r}6000\\-3287\\\hline\end{array}$	25. $\begin{array}{r}6000\\-3087\\\hline\end{array}$

b Subtract and check.

26. 4779
    −1674

27. 7056
    −3427

28. 5563
    −4038

29. 8306
    −1624

30. 6392
    −4815

31. 8244
    −6938

32. 6948
    −3712

33. 9604
    −3587

34. 5000
    −1234

35. 3224
    −1859

c Read the list of supplies.

36. How much more ruled paper than plain?

37. How much more plain paper than squared?

38. How much less typing paper than ruled?

Supplies
- ✓ plain paper   8000 sheets
- ✓ ruled paper   9500 sheets
- ✓ squared paper   2440 sheets
- ✓ typing paper   4500 sheets
- rulers
- crayon boxes
- chalk
- erasers

61

Addition and Subtraction with Money

I have $3.25.　　　**I spend $3.19.**　　　**My change is 6¢.**

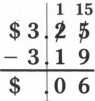

$$
\begin{array}{r}
1\ 15 \\
\$\,3.\overset{}{2}\,5 \\
-\ 3.1\ 9 \\
\hline
\$\ \ .0\ 6 \\
\end{array}
$$

Keep the points in line.

a Add or subtract. Keep the points in line.

1. $.25
　　　 + .50

2. $.75
　　　 + .25

3. $.95
　　　 − .43

4. $.50
　　　 − .47

5. $2.35
　　　 + .75

6. $2.07
　　　 + .89

7. $3.75
　　　 − .68

8. $1.37
　　　 − .99

9. $3.88
　　　 +2.12

10. $5.05
　　　 +1.98

11. $7.75
　　　 −2.32

12. $5.00
　　　 −3.67

13. $24.49
　　　 +18.44

14. $10.99
　　　 +14.99

15. $23.62
　　　 −11.98

16. $10.00
　　　 − 5.99

b Answer.

17. Which book costs the least? Which costs the most?

18. What do the game and puzzle books cost together?

19. How much more does the moon book cost than the rock book?

20. Pam buys *Games, Turtles,* and *Rocks.* How much is that?

21. Jane has 3 quarters. Can she buy *Games?*

22. Julio has $3. Can he buy *History of Canada* and *France?*

23. Mr. Li buys *101 Stories.* What is his change from $5?

Figuring change

I pay for a 63¢ pad with $1. The clerk can figure my change
by giving me coins to build 63¢ up to 100¢.

   63¢ + 2¢ = 65¢   65¢ + 10¢ = 75¢   75¢ + 25¢ = 100¢

My change is 2 pennies, 1 dime, and 1 quarter.

Figure the change from $1 for each using the fewest coins.

1. 54¢ pad   2. 79¢ jump rope   3. 43¢ pen   4. 88¢ crayons

Estimating

About how much do
these cost together?

Round 47¢ to 50¢. ▶   **50¢**
Round 42¢ to 40¢. ▶ **+40¢**
    Estimated sum ▶   **90¢**

When you shop, estimate to answer these questions.
Do I have about enough money?
Is my bill about right?
Is my change about right?

a Round each number. Then estimate the answer.

1. 37 +22	**2.** 53 +62	**3.** 25 +87	**4.** 49¢ +22¢	**5.** 38¢ +38¢
6. 87 −23	**7.** 75 −59	**8.** 83 −21	**9.** 35¢ −29¢	**10.** 25¢ −13¢

Round to the nearest dollar. Then estimate the answer.

11. $2.98 +3.88	**12.** $4.19 +2.87	**13.** $12.97 + 5.59	**14.** $5.00 −2.99	**15.** $14.29 −13.88
16. $1.99 2.19 +3.78	**17.** $2.08 .98 +1.88	**18.** $12.88 3.11 + 1.97	**19.** $19.95 12.19 + 8.75	**20.** $11.08 12.98 +13.87

b Estimate the answer.

21. Swing repairs $15.26
    New ball . . . . $ 3.98
    Total cost to the
    nearest dollar?

22. Class 1 . . . . . .295 students
    Class 2 . . . . . .272 students
    Class 3 . . . . . .305 students
    Class 4 . . . . . .314 students
    About how many hundred
    students in all?

Review B   (pages 56–65)

1. 38	2. 51	3. 82	4. 68
−23	−27	− 8	−59
5. 795	6. 632	7. 207	8. 900
−542	−456	−163	−288
9. 2875	10. 6154	11. 7875	12. 3000
−1304	−2386	−6952	−1275
13. $.25	14. $12.39	15. $.95	16. $5.00
+.75	+ 5.99	− .89	−2.19

Round each number. Then estimate the answer.

17. 67	18. 45	19. 51	20. 75
+72	+53	−22	−39

Extra practice on p. 315

Problem Solving   Problem • Plan • Arithmetic • Answer

Sometimes an estimate is as useful as an exact answer.

A class of 26 students is having a party with a class of 28 students. *About* how many cups are needed?

1	**Understand the problem.**	What do you know? What do you want to know?	26 students 28 students *About* how many?
2	**Make a plan.**	What do you do to solve the problem?	Round 26 to 30. Round 28 to 30. Add 30 and 30.
3	**Do the arithmetic.**	Show your work.	$\begin{array}{r} 30 \\ +30 \\ \hline 60 \end{array}$
4	**Give the answer.**	*About* how many cups are needed?	About 60 cups

26 students and 28 students are exactly 54 students, but it is best to plan for extra cups at a party.

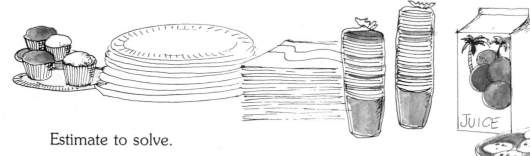

Estimate to solve.

1. 26 students and 52 parents are having refreshments. About how many plates are needed?

2. We spend 76¢ for cups, 53¢ for napkins, and 89¢ for juice. About how much do we spend in all?

3. We have 12 cupcakes, 36 cookies, and 24 brownies. About how many people can have one treat?

Unit Test

Add.   (pages 46–51)

1. 52
   +47

2. 38
   +26

3. 47
   + 9

4. 27
    32
   +56

Add.   (pages 52–55)

5. 325
   +423

6. 648
   +277

7. 2374
   +6523

8. 3394
   +3759

Subtract.   (pages 56–61)

9. 58
   −33

10. 62
    −26

11. 32
    − 8

12. 68
    −59

13. 823
    −576

14. 500
    −243

15. 3254
    −1867

16. 7000
    −3268

Add or subtract.   (pages 62–63)

17. $.89
    +.99

18. $13.75
    + 8.25

19. $.85
    −.69

20. $3.00
    −1.99

Round each number. Then estimate the answer.   (pages 64–65)

21. 54
    +69

22. 32
    +35

23. 82
    −34

24. 65
    −48

Solve.   (page 66)

25. 31 cups, 26 cups, and 28 cups.
    About how many in all?

26. 79¢, 42¢, 67¢, and 35¢.
    About how much in all?

Taking Another Look

Pages 46–51

Add the ones.

```
  2 5
+ 3 6
-----
    11
```

**Give the ten
to the tens.
Add the tens.**

```
  1
  2 5
+ 3 6
-----
  6 1
```

Add.

1. 40 +20	2. 43 +25	3. 60 +20	4. 62 +24
5. 5 +6	6. 55 + 6	7. 55 +26	8. 55 +46
9. 67 +21	10. 33 +14	11. 38 +22	12. 17 +69
13. 15 + 3	14. 26 + 9	15. 44 + 2	16. 64 + 8
17. 57 +32	18. 79 +15	19. 68 +27	20. 49 + 6

Pages 52–55

```
1 1 1
4 9 2 8
+ 3 2 7 3
---------
8 2 0 1
```

Add.

1. 354 +235	2. (1) 354 +237	3. (1) 384 +235	4. (11) 384 +237
5. 4546 +4231	6. (11) 4546 +4257	7. (111) 4546 +4857	8. (111) 5546 +6857
9. 156 +654	10. 426 +365	11. 329 +294	12. 408 +313
13. 645 +857	14. 178 +365	15. 7178 +2365	16. 5467 +3859
17. 8143 +1489	18. 6008 +2993	19. 3658 +9847	20. 5136 +8976

Take a ten to make 13 ones. Subtract the ones.

```
    4 13
  9 5̸ 3̸
− 2 6 8
        5
```

Take 1 hundred to make 14 tens. Subtract the tens and hundreds.

```
  8 14 13
  9̸ 5̸ 3̸
− 2 6 8
  6 8 5
```

Subtract.

1. 76 − 34	2. 976 − 634	3. 6976 − 6634	4. 6976 − 4634
5. 952 − 636	6. 952 − 656	7. 6926 − 4837	8. 6926 − 4937
9. 81 − 43	10. 54 − 26	11. 487 − 369	12. 521 − 184
13. 620 − 308	14. 792 − 398	15. 4385 − 2196	16. 7672 − 3894
17. 8062 − 5378	18. 9537 − 5849	19. 6000 − 1234	20. 5020 − 3624

```
        7 17
  $ 5 . 8̸ 7̸
  − 5 . 6 9
  $   . 1 8
```

Add or subtract.

1. $.75 + .49	2. $.84 − .36	3. $2.59 +3.26	4. $6.54 − 5.79

```
$.38 ▶ $ .40
+.69 ▶ + .70
        $1.10
```

Round to the nearest dollar to estimate the answer.

1. $6.23 +5.89	2. $4.98 − 3.12	3. $8.09 + .91	4. $24.13 − 16.79

---

1. **Problem**
2. **Plan**
3. **Arithmetic**
4. **Answer**

Estimate to solve.

1. 38 band members, 22 scouts, and 56 people on floats are in a parade. About how many in all?

2. The cookies cost 89¢ and the crackers cost 52¢. About how much more do the cookies cost?

Something Extra • A.M. and P.M.

The clock shows 15 minutes after 4, or 4:15.
4:15 A.M. is between midnight and noon.
4:15 P.M. is between noon and midnight.

Write A.M. or P.M. to show the correct time period.

1. Breakfast is at 7:45.

2. School is out at 3:00.

3. The movie opens at 1:30.

4. The sun rose at 6:21.

5. Bedtime is at 8:30.

6. Gym is at 10:40.

7. Lunch is at 12:15.

8. The moon is bright at 12:30.

What time is it? Write A.M. or P.M. with your answer.

9. 4 hours after 7:30 A.M.

10. 4 hours after 10:45 P.M.

11. 7 hours after 11:00 P.M.

12. 12 hours after 11:00 P.M.

13. 30 minutes after 10:30 A.M.

14. 15 minutes after 6:45 P.M.

15. 30 minutes after 11:45 P.M.

16. 20 minutes after 11:50 A.M.

Solve.

17. Dan works at a diner from 8:30 P.M. to 1:30 A.M.
    How many hours is that?

18. Joan works the night shift from 11:00 P.M. to 7:00 A.M.
    How many hours long is the night shift?

19. The computer operator comes to work at 5:00 P.M.
    She leaves at midnight. How many hours is she at work?

20. Miguel is a bank clerk with a 9-to-5 job. If he takes an
    hour off for lunch, how many hours is he on the job?

21. Justina leaves home at 8:15 A.M. She returns at 6:20 P.M.
    How long is she away from home?

22. It is now 9:00 A.M. on Monday. School will be over for the
    week 3:00 P.M. on Friday. How many hours from now is that?

Reviewing Needed Skills

Add.

1. 2 + 2   2. 3 + 3   3. 2 + 2 + 2   4. 3 + 3 + 3

5. 2 + 2 + 2 + 2   6. 3 + 3 + 3 + 3   7. 4 + 4   8. 4 + 4 + 4

9.	10.	11.	12.	13.	14.
2	4	6	8	10	12
+2	+2	+2	+2	+ 2	+ 2

15.	16.	17.	18.	19.	20.
14	16	3	6	9	12
+ 2	+ 2	+3	+3	+3	+ 3

21.	22.	23.	24.	25.	26.
15	18	21	24	4	8
+ 3	+ 3	+ 3	+ 3	+4	+4

27.	28.	29.	30.	31.	32.
12	16	20	24	28	32
+ 4	+ 4	+ 4	+ 4	+ 4	+ 4

33.	34.	35.	36.	37.	38.
2	2	3	3	4	4
2	2	3	3	4	4
2	2	3	3	4	4
2	2	3	3	4	4
+2	2	+3	3	+4	4
	+2		+3		+4

Count to list the missing numbers.

39. 1, ▦, 3, ▦, 5, ▦   40. 1, 2, 3, ▦, 5, 6, 7, ▦, 9, 10, 11, ▦

41. 1, 2, ▦, 4, 5, ▦   42. 1, 2, 3, 4, ▦, 6, 7, 8, 9, ▦

Show the amount in dollars.

43. 3 hundred cents   44. 4 hundred cents

45. 4 quarters   46. 4 quarters 100 pennies

UNIT 4

Meaning of Multiplication

How many cars in all? 3 twos.

Add. $2 + 2 + 2 = 6$
Multiply. $3 \times 2 = 6$

3 <u>times</u> 2 <u>equals</u> 6. The <u>product</u> of 3 and 2 is 6.

Multiplication and Division

a Add or multiply.

1. 2 + 2	2. 2 × 2	3. 3 + 3	4. 2 × 3
5. 4 + 4	6. 2 × 4	7. 5 + 5	8. 2 × 5
9. 6 + 6	10. 2 × 6	11. 7 + 7	12. 2 × 7
13. 8 + 8	14. 2 × 8	15. 9 + 9	16. 2 × 9
17. 3 + 3 + 3	18. 3 × 3	19. 4 + 4 + 4	20. 3 × 4
21. 5 + 5 + 5	22. 3 × 5	23. 6 + 6 + 6	24. 3 × 6
25. 7 + 7 + 7	26. 3 × 7	27. 8 + 8 + 8	28. 3 × 8
29. 1 + 1 + 1 + 1	30. 4 × 1	31. 2 + 2 + 2 + 2	32. 4 × 2
33. 3 + 3 + 3 + 3	34. 4 × 3	35. 4 + 4 + 4 + 4	36. 4 × 4
37. 5 + 5 + 5 + 5	38. 4 × 5	39. 6 + 6 + 6 + 6	40. 4 × 6
41. 7 + 7 + 7 + 7	42. 4 × 7	43. 8 + 8 + 8 + 8	44. 4 × 8

Meaning of Multiplication

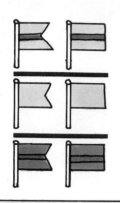

3 twos

$3 \times 2 = 6$

$$\begin{array}{r} 2 \\ \times 3 \\ \hline 6 \end{array}$$

2 threes

$2 \times 3 = 6$

$$\begin{array}{r} 3 \\ \times 2 \\ \hline 6 \end{array}$$

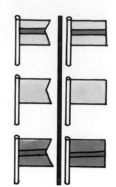

a Add or multiply.

1. $2 + 2 + 2 + 2$
3. $4 + 4$

2. 4×2
4. 2×4

5. $4 + 4 + 4$
7. $3 + 3 + 3 + 3$

6. 3×4
8. 4×3

9. $6 + 6$
11. $2 + 2 + 2 + 2 + 2 + 2$
13. $3 + 3 + 3$

10. 2×6
12. 6×2
14. 3×3

b Multiply.

15. 3
    ×2

16. 2
    ×3

17. 2
    ×2

18. 4
    ×2

19. 2
    ×4

20. 2
    ×5

21. 5
    ×3

22. 3
    ×5

23. 3
    ×3

24. 3
    ×4

25. 4
    ×3

26. 4
    ×4

c How many packages do I need for 6 road signs?

27.

28.

How many packages do I need for 12 model trees?

29.

30.

Meaning of Division

Six cards. Take away 2 cards. Do it 3 times.
None are left. There are 3 twos in 6.
6 divided by 2 equals 3. The quotient is 3.

$$6 \div 2 = 3 \qquad 2\overline{)6}^{\,3}$$

a Divide.

1. 4 ÷ 2   **2.** 8 ÷ 2   **3.** 10 ÷ 2

4. 6 ÷ 3   **5.** 9 ÷ 3   **6.** 12 ÷ 3

7. 12 ÷ 2   **8.** 12 ÷ 6   **9.** 12 ÷ 4

Multiply or divide.

10.   3
    ×2

11. 3)6

12.   2
    ×3

13. 2)6

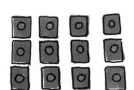

14.   4
    ×2

15. 4)8

16.   2
    ×4

17. 2)8

18.   4
    ×3

19. 4)12

20.   3
    ×4

21. 3)12

22.   5
    ×2

23. 5)10

24.   2
    ×5

25. 2)10

c Eight rabbits are in a hat. Lisa pulls out 4.
Pepe pulls out 4 more.

26. How many rabbits are left in the hat?

27. 8 *minus* 2 fours *equals* ▩.

28. How many fours are in 8?

29. 8 ÷ 4 = ▩

Two

We may count the shells by twos.

2   4   6   8   10   12   14   16   18

9 twos = 18   9 twos are in 18.

9 × 2 = 18   18 ÷ 2 = 9

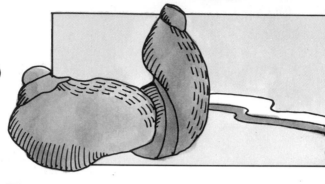

 Multiply or divide.

1. 1 × 2	2. 2 × 2
3. 3 × 2	4. 2 × 3
5. 4 × 2	6. 2 × 4
7. 5 × 2	8. 2 × 5
9. 6 × 2	10. 12 ÷ 2
11. 2 × 6	12. 12 ÷ 6
13. 7 × 2	14. 14 ÷ 2
15. 2 × 7	16. 14 ÷ 7
17. 8 × 2	18. 16 ÷ 2
19. 2 × 8	20. 16 ÷ 8
21. 9 × 2	22. 18 ÷ 2
23. 2 × 9	24. 18 ÷ 9
25. 8 ÷ 2	26. 8 ÷ 4
27. 6 ÷ 2	28. 6 ÷ 3
29. 2 ÷ 2	30. 2 ÷ 1

b Multiply or divide.

31. $\begin{array}{r} 5 \\ \times 2 \\ \hline \end{array}$	**32.** $\begin{array}{r} 9 \\ \times 2 \\ \hline \end{array}$	**33.** $\begin{array}{r} 2 \\ \times 7 \\ \hline \end{array}$	**34.** $\begin{array}{r} 3 \\ \times 2 \\ \hline \end{array}$	**35.** $\begin{array}{r} 6 \\ \times 2 \\ \hline \end{array}$
36. $\begin{array}{r} 2 \\ \times 8 \\ \hline \end{array}$	**37.** $\begin{array}{r} 4 \\ \times 2 \\ \hline \end{array}$	**38.** $\begin{array}{r} 2 \\ \times 9 \\ \hline \end{array}$	**39.** $\begin{array}{r} 2 \\ \times 5 \\ \hline \end{array}$	**40.** $\begin{array}{r} 1 \\ \times 2 \\ \hline \end{array}$
41. $\begin{array}{r} 2 \\ \times 3 \\ \hline \end{array}$	**42.** $\begin{array}{r} 8 \\ \times 2 \\ \hline \end{array}$	**43.** $\begin{array}{r} 2 \\ \times 6 \\ \hline \end{array}$	**44.** $\begin{array}{r} 2 \\ \times 4 \\ \hline \end{array}$	**45.** $\begin{array}{r} 7 \\ \times 2 \\ \hline \end{array}$

46. $2\overline{)4}$ **47.** $2\overline{)16}$ **48.** $2\overline{)2}$ **49.** $3\overline{)6}$ **50.** $2\overline{)12}$

51. $4\overline{)8}$ **52.** $2\overline{)10}$ **53.** $6\overline{)12}$ **54.** $2\overline{)14}$ **55.** $2\overline{)18}$

56. $7\overline{)14}$ **57.** $9\overline{)18}$ **58.** $8\overline{)16}$ **59.** $2\overline{)8}$ **60.** $5\overline{)10}$

c Solve.

61. 2 kinds of sea shells
4 of each kind
How many sea shells in all?

62. 12 clam shells to share
2 friends to share them
How many clam shells for each?

Three

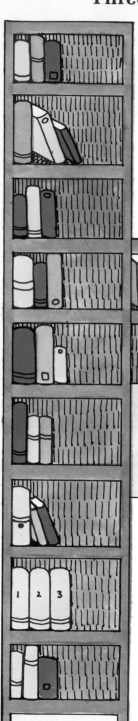

3   6   9   12   15   18   21   24   27

27 books

9 threes   3 nines

27 ÷ 3 = 9   27 ÷ 9 = 3

a Multiply or divide.

1. 1×3	**2.** $3 \div 3$	**3.** 3×1	**4.** $3 \div 1$
5. 2×3	**6.** $6 \div 3$	**7.** 3×2	**8.** $6 \div 2$
9. 4×3	**10.** $12 \div 3$	**11.** 3×4	**12.** $12 \div 4$
13. 5×3	**14.** $15 \div 3$	**15.** 3×5	**16.** $15 \div 5$
17. 6×3	**18.** $18 \div 3$	**19.** 3×6	**20.** $18 \div 6$
21. 7×3	**22.** $21 \div 3$	**23.** 3×7	**24.** $21 \div 7$
25. 8×3	**26.** $24 \div 3$	**27.** 3×8	**28.** $24 \div 8$
29. 9×3	**30.** $27 \div 3$	**31.** 3×9	**32.** $27 \div 9$

b Multiply or divide.

33. 3 ×5	**34.** 3 ×9	**35.** 3 ×7	**36.** 6 ×3	**37.** 3 ×8	**38.** 3 ×3

39. 4 ×3	**40.** 3 ×6	**41.** 5 ×3	**42.** 1 ×3	**43.** 8 ×3	**44.** 7 ×3

45. 3$\overline{)9}$ **46.** 3$\overline{)24}$ **47.** 3$\overline{)3}$ **48.** 4$\overline{)12}$ **49.** 7$\overline{)21}$ **50.** 3$\overline{)15}$

51. 3$\overline{)21}$ **52.** 3$\overline{)27}$ **53.** 5$\overline{)15}$ **54.** 3$\overline{)18}$ **55.** 8$\overline{)24}$ **56.** 9$\overline{)27}$

c What is the cost of 3 books at each price?

57. $1 each   **58.** $5 each   **59.** $2 each

60. $3 each   **61.** $6 each   **62.** $4 each

How many $3 books can I buy with each amount?

63. $9   **64.** 3 hundred cents   **65.** 12 quarters

66. $12   **67.** 6 hundred cents   **68.** 8 quarters 100 pennies

---

Review A   (pages 72–81)

1. 3 + 3	**2.** 2 × 3	**3.** 2 + 2 + 2 + 2	**4.** 4 × 2
5. 5 × 2	**6.** 2 × 5	**7.** 6 × 2	**8.** 2 × 6

9. 2 ×3	**10.** 2$\overline{)6}$	**11.** 3 ×4	**12.** 3$\overline{)12}$

13. 8 × 2	**14.** 7 × 2	**15.** 12 ÷ 2	**16.** 18 ÷ 2
17. 7 × 3	**18.** 9 × 3	**19.** 3$\overline{)15}$	**20.** 3$\overline{)24}$

Extra practice on p. 316

Four

We may count the cross-stitches by fours.

4
8
12
16
20
24
28
32
36

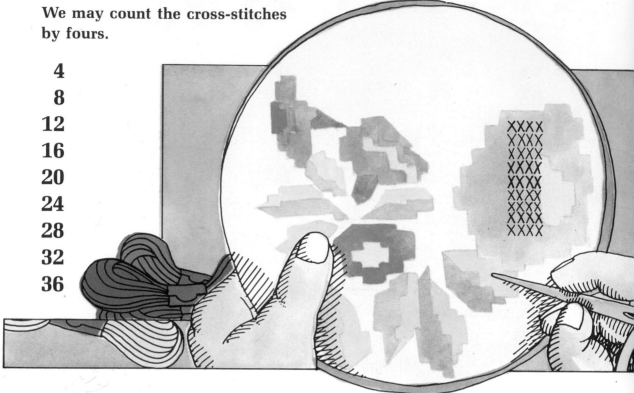

a Multiply or divide.

1. 1×4	2. 2×4	3. 3×4	4. 4×4
5. 5×4	6. 4×5	7. 6×4	8. 4×6
9. 7×4	10. $28 \div 4$	11. 4×7	12. $28 \div 7$
13. 8×4	14. $32 \div 4$	15. 4×8	16. $32 \div 8$
17. 9×4	18. 4×9	19. $36 \div 4$	20. $36 \div 9$

21. 5×4	22. 6×4	23. 3×4	24. 2×4
4×5	4×6	4×3	4×2
$20 \div 4$	$24 \div 4$	$12 \div 4$	$8 \div 4$
$20 \div 5$	$24 \div 6$	$12 \div 3$	$8 \div 2$

25. $20 \div 4$	26. $8 \div 4$	27. 1×4	28. 4×4
$24 \div 4$	$16 \div 4$	$4 \div 4$	$16 \div 4$
$28 \div 4$	$32 \div 4$	$4 \div 1$	

b Multiply or divide.

29.	30.	31.	32.	33.	34.
5 ×4	4 ×1	6 ×4	9 ×4	4 ×2	3 ×4

35.	36.	37.	38.	39.	40.
4 ×9	7 ×4	4 ×5	8 ×4	4 ×6	4 ×4

41. 4)16   42. 4)4   43. 5)20   44. 2)8   45. 6)24   46. 4)36

47. 8)32   48. 3)12   49. 7)28   50. 4)24   51. 9)36   52. 4)12

c Solve.

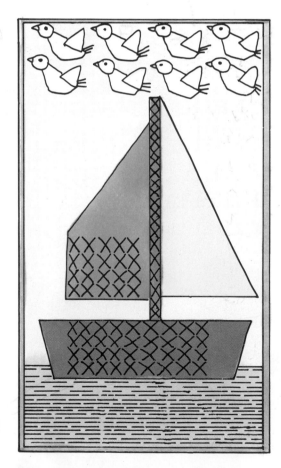

53. Jim drew the pattern for the sail. He put 4 rows of 5 cross-stitches in it. How many cross-stitches in all?

54. There are 2 rows of 4 birds. How many birds in all?

55. Four rows of 9 cross-stitches make the boat. How many cross-stitches in all?

56. Sofia can sew a bird in 4 minutes. How many can she sew in 20 minutes?

57. Blue, black, and red thread. Four packages of each color. How many packages in all?

58. How many waves 4 cm long fit in a space 16 cm across?

83

Two, Three, Four

$$4 \times 2 = 8 \qquad 4 \times 3 = 12 \qquad 4 \times 4 = 16$$

a List the numbers and multiply.

1. 2, 4, 6, ▨, ▨
2. 4 × 2
3. 5 × 2
4. 6, 8, 10, ▨, ▨
5. 6 × 2
6. 7 × 2
7. 10, 12, 14, ▨, ▨
8. 8 × 2
9. 9 × 2

10. 3, 6, 9, ▨, ▨
11. 4 × 3
12. 5 × 3
13. 9, 12, 15, ▨, ▨
14. 6 × 3
15. 7 × 3
16. 15, 18, 21, ▨, ▨
17. 8 × 3
18. 9 × 3

19. 4, 8, 12, ▨, ▨
20. 4 × 4
21. 5 × 4
22. 12, 16, 20, ▨, ▨
23. 6 × 4
24. 7 × 4
25. 20, 24, 28, ▨, ▨
26. 8 × 4
27. 9 × 4

b Multiply or divide.

28. $\begin{array}{r} 2 \\ \times 7 \\ \hline \end{array}$	29. $\begin{array}{r} 3 \\ \times 8 \\ \hline \end{array}$	30. $\begin{array}{r} 4 \\ \times 3 \\ \hline \end{array}$	31. $\begin{array}{r} 2 \\ \times 9 \\ \hline \end{array}$	32. $\begin{array}{r} 3 \\ \times 2 \\ \hline \end{array}$	33. $\begin{array}{r} 4 \\ \times 5 \\ \hline \end{array}$
34. $\begin{array}{r} 3 \\ \times 6 \\ \hline \end{array}$	35. $\begin{array}{r} 4 \\ \times 8 \\ \hline \end{array}$	36. $\begin{array}{r} 4 \\ \times 4 \\ \hline \end{array}$	37. $\begin{array}{r} 3 \\ \times 7 \\ \hline \end{array}$	38. $\begin{array}{r} 2 \\ \times 8 \\ \hline \end{array}$	39. $\begin{array}{r} 4 \\ \times 9 \\ \hline \end{array}$

40. $4\overline{)20}$ 41. $2\overline{)18}$ 42. $4\overline{)28}$ 43. $3\overline{)21}$ 44. $2\overline{)16}$ 45. $4\overline{)16}$

46. $2\overline{)14}$ 47. $4\overline{)24}$ 48. $3\overline{)18}$ 49. $3\overline{)27}$ 50. $4\overline{)32}$ 51. $2\overline{)6}$

52. $4\overline{)36}$ 53. $3\overline{)15}$ 54. $2\overline{)10}$ 55. $3\overline{)24}$ 56. $2\overline{)12}$ 57. $3\overline{)12}$

c Use the code to read the word.

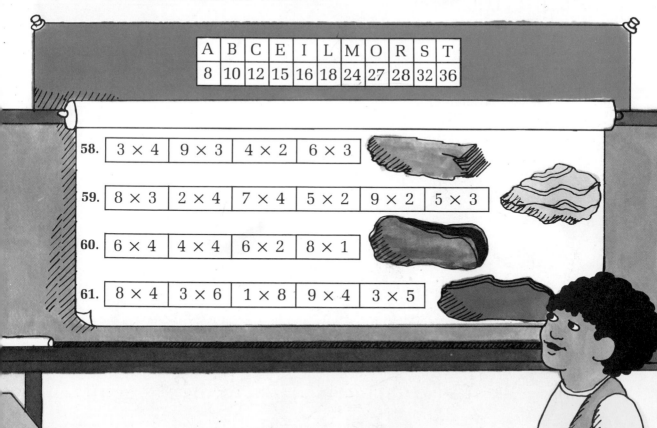

A	B	C	E	I	L	M	O	R	S	T
8	10	12	15	16	18	24	27	28	32	36

58. | 3 × 4 | 9 × 3 | 4 × 2 | 6 × 3 |

59. | 8 × 3 | 2 × 4 | 7 × 4 | 5 × 2 | 9 × 2 | 5 × 3 |

60. | 6 × 4 | 4 × 4 | 6 × 2 | 8 × 1 |

61. | 8 × 4 | 3 × 6 | 1 × 8 | 9 × 4 | 3 × 5 |

Multiplication Table, 0–4

Memorize the facts in the table.
Look for patterns to help you.

$0 \times 0 = 0$ $5 \times 0 = 0$
$0 \times 1 = 0$ $5 \times 1 = 5$
$0 \times 2 = 0$ $5 \times 2 = 10$
$0 \times 3 = 0$ $5 \times 3 = 15$
$0 \times 4 = 0$ $5 \times 4 = 20$

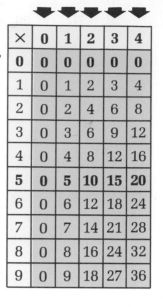

×	0	1	2	3	4
0	0	0	0	0	0
1	0	1	2	3	4
2	0	2	4	6	8
3	0	3	6	9	12
4	0	4	8	12	16
5	0	5	10	15	20
6	0	6	12	18	24
7	0	7	14	21	28
8	0	8	16	24	32
9	0	9	18	27	36

a Multiply or divide.

1. 1×4	**2.** $9 \div 1$	**3.** $4 \div 4$	**4.** 2×4
3×4	$8 \div 1$	$3 \div 3$	4×4
5×4	$7 \div 1$	$2 \div 2$	6×4
7×4	$6 \div 1$	$1 \div 1$	8×4

5. 6×0	**6.** $3 \div 3$	**7.** $24 \div 4$	**8.** 6×3
3×0	$6 \div 3$	$28 \div 4$	7×3
2×0	$9 \div 3$	$32 \div 4$	8×3
1×0	$12 \div 3$	$36 \div 4$	9×3

9. $\begin{array}{r} 0 \\ \times 2 \\ \hline \end{array}$	**10.** $\begin{array}{r} 1 \\ \times 2 \\ \hline \end{array}$	**11.** $\begin{array}{r} 2 \\ \times 2 \\ \hline \end{array}$	**12.** $\begin{array}{r} 2 \\ \times 7 \\ \hline \end{array}$	**13.** $\begin{array}{r} 2 \\ \times 8 \\ \hline \end{array}$	**14.** $\begin{array}{r} 2 \\ \times 9 \\ \hline \end{array}$

15. $3\overline{)0}$	**16.** $3\overline{)3}$	**17.** $3\overline{)6}$	**18.** $3\overline{)21}$	**19.** $3\overline{)24}$	**20.** $3\overline{)27}$
21. $4\overline{)8}$	**22.** $4\overline{)4}$	**23.** $4\overline{)0}$	**24.** $4\overline{)28}$	**25.** $4\overline{)24}$	**26.** $4\overline{)20}$

b Multiply or divide.

27. $\begin{array}{r}4\\ \times 9\\ \hline\end{array}$ 28. $\begin{array}{r}9\\ \times 4\\ \hline\end{array}$ 29. $4\overline{)36}$ 30. $9\overline{)36}$ 31. $\begin{array}{r}1\\ \times 1\\ \hline\end{array}$ 32. $1\overline{)1}$

33. $\begin{array}{r}3\\ \times 8\\ \hline\end{array}$ 34. $\begin{array}{r}8\\ \times 3\\ \hline\end{array}$ 35. $3\overline{)24}$ 36. $8\overline{)24}$ 37. $\begin{array}{r}2\\ \times 2\\ \hline\end{array}$ 38. $2\overline{)4}$

39. $\begin{array}{r}3\\ \times 5\\ \hline\end{array}$ 40. $\begin{array}{r}5\\ \times 3\\ \hline\end{array}$ 41. $3\overline{)15}$ 42. $5\overline{)15}$

43. $\begin{array}{r}4\\ \times 8\\ \hline\end{array}$ 44. $\begin{array}{r}8\\ \times 4\\ \hline\end{array}$ 45. $4\overline{)32}$ 46. $8\overline{)32}$

Review B   (pages 82–87)

1. 3×4 2. 6×4 3. $4\overline{)20}$ 4. $4\overline{)4}$

5. $\begin{array}{r}2\\ \times 3\\ \hline\end{array}$ 6. $\begin{array}{r}4\\ \times 7\\ \hline\end{array}$ 7. $2\overline{)14}$ 8. $3\overline{)24}$

9. 6×3 10. 3×6 11. $18 \div 3$ 12. $18 \div 6$

Extra practice on p. 317

Problem Solving   Problem • Plan • Arithmetic • Answer

2 Make a plan.	What do you do to solve the problem?	Add? Subtract? Multiply? Divide?

8 stamps
2 stamps
How many stamps in all?

Plan: Add

8 stamps
2 stamps sold
How many stamps are left?

Plan: Subtract

8 stamps in a package
2 packages
How many stamps in all?

Plan: Multiply

8 stamps to share
2 friends
How many stamps for each?

Plan: Divide

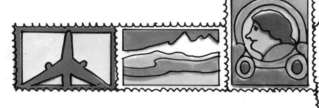

Write your plan and then solve.

1. 20 postage stamps
   8 mailed on letters
   How many are left?

2. 16 stamps about music
   4 friends to share them
   How many stamps for each?

3. 3 rows of Air Mail stamps
   6 stamps in a row
   How many stamps in all?

4. 16 stamps about music
   9 stamps about sports
   How many more about music?

5. 24 stamps on a page
   4 rows
   How many stamps in a row?

6. 4 stamps from Canada
   3 stamps from France
   8 stamps from Mexico
   How many stamps in all?

Unit Test

Add or multiply. (pages 72–75)

1. 5 + 5   **2.** 2 × 5   **3.** 4 + 4 + 4   **4.** 3 × 4

5. 4 × 2   **6.** 2 × 4

7. $\begin{array}{r} 3 \\ \times 5 \\ \hline \end{array}$ **8.** $\begin{array}{r} 5 \\ \times 3 \\ \hline \end{array}$

Multiply or divide. (pages 76–77)

9. 4 × 3   **10.** 12 ÷ 3   **11.** 3 × 3   **12.** $3\overline{)9}$

Multiply or divide. (pages 78–81)

13. $\begin{array}{r} 2 \\ \times 7 \\ \hline \end{array}$ **14.** $\begin{array}{r} 2 \\ \times 9 \\ \hline \end{array}$ **15.** $2\overline{)12}$ **16.** $2\overline{)16}$

17. $\begin{array}{r} 3 \\ \times 6 \\ \hline \end{array}$ **18.** $\begin{array}{r} 3 \\ \times 8 \\ \hline \end{array}$ **19.** $3\overline{)21}$ **20.** $3\overline{)27}$

Multiply or divide. (pages 82–83)

21. $\begin{array}{r} 4 \\ \times 5 \\ \hline \end{array}$ **22.** $\begin{array}{r} 4 \\ \times 7 \\ \hline \end{array}$ **23.** $4\overline{)16}$ **24.** $4\overline{)32}$

Multiply or divide. (pages 84–87)

25. 3 × 2   **26.** 6 ÷ 2   **27.** $\begin{array}{r} 4 \\ \times 6 \\ \hline \end{array}$ **28.** $4\overline{)24}$

Write your plan and then solve. (page 88)

29. 6 letters
2 stamps on each
How many stamps in all?

30. 6 stamps to share
2 stamp collectors
How many stamps for each?

Taking Another Look

Pages 72–75

3 fours = 12
4 + 4 + 4 = 12
3 × 4 = 12

Add or multiply.

1. $2 + 2 + 2$ 2. 3×2 3. $4 + 4$ 4. 2×4

5. $5 + 5 + 5$ 6. 3×5 7. $3 + 3 + 3$ 8. 3×3

9. $6 + 6 + 6$ 10. 3×6 11. $1 + 1 + 1$ 12. 3×1

13. 2×5 14. 5×2 15. 4×1 16. 1×4

17. $\begin{array}{r} 6 \\ \times 2 \\ \hline \end{array}$ 18. $\begin{array}{r} 2 \\ \times 6 \\ \hline \end{array}$ 19. $\begin{array}{r} 4 \\ \times 3 \\ \hline \end{array}$ 20. $\begin{array}{r} 3 \\ \times 4 \\ \hline \end{array}$

Pages 76–77

3 fours are in 12.
12 divided by 4
equals 3.

$12 \div 4 = 3$

$4\overline{)12}$ with quotient 3

Multiply or divide.

1. $\begin{array}{r} 4 \\ \times 2 \\ \hline \end{array}$ 2. $4\overline{)8}$ 3. $\begin{array}{r} 2 \\ \times 4 \\ \hline \end{array}$ 4. $2\overline{)8}$

5. $\begin{array}{r} 3 \\ \times 2 \\ \hline \end{array}$ 6. $6 \div 3$ 7. $\begin{array}{r} 2 \\ \times 5 \\ \hline \end{array}$ 8. $10 \div 2$

Pages 78–81

21 pencils
7 threes
or
3 sevens
21 ÷ 3 = 7
21 ÷ 7 = 3

Multiply or divide.

1. $\begin{array}{r} 2 \\ \times 7 \\ \hline \end{array}$ 2. $\begin{array}{r} 7 \\ \times 2 \\ \hline \end{array}$ 3. $\begin{array}{r} 2 \\ \times 8 \\ \hline \end{array}$ 4. $\begin{array}{r} 8 \\ \times 2 \\ \hline \end{array}$

5. $2\overline{)14}$ 6. $7\overline{)14}$ 7. $2\overline{)16}$ 8. $8\overline{)16}$

9. $\begin{array}{r} 3 \\ \times 8 \\ \hline \end{array}$ 10. $\begin{array}{r} 3 \\ \times 3 \\ \hline \end{array}$ 11. $\begin{array}{r} 6 \\ \times 3 \\ \hline \end{array}$ 12. $\begin{array}{r} 5 \\ \times 3 \\ \hline \end{array}$

13. $9\overline{)27}$ 14. $3\overline{)21}$ 15. $4\overline{)12}$ 16. $3\overline{)9}$

Pages 82–83

6 fours = 24
$$6 \times 4 = 24$$
6 fours are in 24.
$$24 \div 4 = 6$$

Multiply or divide.

1. 4
    ×4

2. 4
    ×5

3. 4$\overline{)16}$

4. 4$\overline{)20}$

5. 4
    ×8

6. 4
    ×6

7. 4$\overline{)36}$

8. 4$\overline{)28}$

Pages 84–87

2	3	4
4	6	8
6	9	12
8	12	16
10	15	20
12	18	24
14	21	28
16	24	32
18	27	36

Multiply or divide.

1. 3
    ×7

2. 2
    ×9

3. 4
    ×7

4. 3
    ×6

5. 3$\overline{)24}$

6. 2$\overline{)16}$

7. 3$\overline{)27}$

8. 2$\overline{)18}$

9. 3
    ×1

10. 4
     ×9

11. 3
     ×9

12. 2
     ×8

13. 3
     ×8

14. 2
     ×4

15. 5
     ×0

16. 4
     ×3

17. 4$\overline{)32}$

18. 3$\overline{)15}$

19. 4$\overline{)4}$

20. 4$\overline{)24}$

21. 2$\overline{)10}$

22. 2$\overline{)6}$

23. 3$\overline{)21}$

24. 4$\overline{)12}$

Page 88

Plan

Add?
Subtract?
Multiply?
Divide?

Write your plan and then solve.

1. 14 cookies
   8 cookies
   How many in all?

2. 12 plums to share
   4 friends
   How many plums for each?

3. 23 cookies
   7 eaten
   How many are left?

4. 2 plums for each child
   8 children
   How plums in all?

Something Extra • EVEN OR ODD

0 1 2 3 4 5 6 7 8 9 10 11 12 13 14 15 16 17 18 19

0, 2, 4, 6, 8, 10, 12, and so on are <u>even</u> <u>numbers</u>.
1, 3, 5, 7, 9, 11, 13, and so on are <u>odd</u> <u>numbers</u>.

1. List the next five even numbers after 18.

2. List the next five even numbers after 28.

3. The digit in the ones' place of an even number may be
   ▮, ▮, ▮, ▮, or ▮.

4. List the next five odd numbers after 19.

5. List the next five odd numbers after 29.

6. The digit in the ones' place of an odd number may be
   ▮, ▮, ▮, ▮, or ▮.

Is the number even or odd?

7. 30	8. 64	9. 57	10. 81
11. 333	12. 100	13. 685	14. 116
15. 2089	16. 3000	17. 578	18. 752
19. 50,000	20. 67,801	21. 99,999	22. 99,996
23. 806,587	24. 298,111	25. 672,354	26. one million

Multiply the number by 2. Is the answer even or odd?

27. 0	28. 1	29. 2	30. 3	31. 4
32. 5	33. 6	34. 7	35. 8	36. 9

37. Choose any even number. Add 1. Is the answer even or odd?

38. Choose any odd number. Add 1. Is the answer even or odd?

39. Choose any even number from 0 to 18. Can you divide it by 2 exactly?

40. Choose any odd number from 1 to 19. Can you divide it by 2 exactly?

Reviewing Needed Skills

Add.

1. $5 + 5$ 2. $6 + 6$ 3. $5 + 5 + 5$ 4. $6 + 6 + 6$

5. $5 + 5 + 5 + 5$ 6. $6 + 6 + 6 + 6$ 7. $7 + 7$ 8. $8 + 8$

9. $7 + 7 + 7$ 10. $8 + 8 + 8$ 11. $9 + 9$ 12. $9 + 9 + 9$

13. $\begin{array}{r} 15 \\ + 5 \\ \hline \end{array}$	14. $\begin{array}{r} 15 \\ +10 \\ \hline \end{array}$	15. $\begin{array}{r} 15 \\ +15 \\ \hline \end{array}$	16. $\begin{array}{r} 30 \\ + 5 \\ \hline \end{array}$	17. $\begin{array}{r} 35 \\ + 5 \\ \hline \end{array}$	18. $\begin{array}{r} 40 \\ + 5 \\ \hline \end{array}$
19. $\begin{array}{r} 18 \\ + 6 \\ \hline \end{array}$	20. $\begin{array}{r} 18 \\ +12 \\ \hline \end{array}$	21. $\begin{array}{r} 18 \\ +18 \\ \hline \end{array}$	22. $\begin{array}{r} 36 \\ + 6 \\ \hline \end{array}$	23. $\begin{array}{r} 42 \\ + 6 \\ \hline \end{array}$	24. $\begin{array}{r} 48 \\ + 6 \\ \hline \end{array}$
25. $\begin{array}{r} 21 \\ + 7 \\ \hline \end{array}$	26. $\begin{array}{r} 21 \\ +14 \\ \hline \end{array}$	27. $\begin{array}{r} 21 \\ +21 \\ \hline \end{array}$	28. $\begin{array}{r} 42 \\ + 7 \\ \hline \end{array}$	29. $\begin{array}{r} 49 \\ + 7 \\ \hline \end{array}$	30. $\begin{array}{r} 56 \\ + 7 \\ \hline \end{array}$
31. $\begin{array}{r} 24 \\ + 8 \\ \hline \end{array}$	32. $\begin{array}{r} 24 \\ +16 \\ \hline \end{array}$	33. $\begin{array}{r} 24 \\ +24 \\ \hline \end{array}$	34. $\begin{array}{r} 48 \\ + 8 \\ \hline \end{array}$	35. $\begin{array}{r} 56 \\ + 8 \\ \hline \end{array}$	36. $\begin{array}{r} 64 \\ + 8 \\ \hline \end{array}$
37. $\begin{array}{r} 27 \\ + 9 \\ \hline \end{array}$	38. $\begin{array}{r} 27 \\ +18 \\ \hline \end{array}$	39. $\begin{array}{r} 27 \\ +27 \\ \hline \end{array}$	40. $\begin{array}{r} 54 \\ + 9 \\ \hline \end{array}$	41. $\begin{array}{r} 63 \\ + 9 \\ \hline \end{array}$	42. $\begin{array}{r} 72 \\ + 9 \\ \hline \end{array}$

Multiply or divide.

43. $\begin{array}{r} 1 \\ \times 5 \\ \hline \end{array}$	44. $\begin{array}{r} 2 \\ \times 5 \\ \hline \end{array}$	45. $\begin{array}{r} 3 \\ \times 5 \\ \hline \end{array}$	46. $\begin{array}{r} 4 \\ \times 5 \\ \hline \end{array}$	47. $\begin{array}{r} 1 \\ \times 6 \\ \hline \end{array}$	48. $\begin{array}{r} 2 \\ \times 6 \\ \hline \end{array}$
49. $\begin{array}{r} 3 \\ \times 6 \\ \hline \end{array}$	50. $\begin{array}{r} 4 \\ \times 6 \\ \hline \end{array}$	51. $\begin{array}{r} 1 \\ \times 7 \\ \hline \end{array}$	52. $\begin{array}{r} 2 \\ \times 7 \\ \hline \end{array}$	53. $\begin{array}{r} 3 \\ \times 7 \\ \hline \end{array}$	54. $\begin{array}{r} 4 \\ \times 7 \\ \hline \end{array}$
55. $\begin{array}{r} 2 \\ \times 8 \\ \hline \end{array}$	56. $\begin{array}{r} 3 \\ \times 8 \\ \hline \end{array}$	57. $\begin{array}{r} 4 \\ \times 8 \\ \hline \end{array}$	58. $\begin{array}{r} 2 \\ \times 9 \\ \hline \end{array}$	59. $\begin{array}{r} 3 \\ \times 9 \\ \hline \end{array}$	60. $\begin{array}{r} 4 \\ \times 9 \\ \hline \end{array}$

61. $2\overline{)10}$ 62. $3\overline{)18}$ 63. $2\overline{)18}$ 64. $4\overline{)24}$ 65. $3\overline{)24}$ 66. $4\overline{)28}$

UNIT 5

Five

Count the marchers by fives.

| 5 | 10 | 15 | 20 | 25 | 30 |

6 fives = 30   6 fives are in 30.

$6 \times 5 = 30$ $30 \div 5 = 6$

94

Multiplication and Division

a Multiply or divide.

1. 1×5	2. 2×5	3. 3×5	4. 4×5	5. 6×5
6. 5×1	7. 5×2	8. 5×3	9. 5×4	10. 5×6
11. $5 \div 5$	12. $10 \div 5$	13. $15 \div 5$	14. $20 \div 5$	15. $30 \div 5$
16. $5 \div 1$	17. $10 \div 2$	18. $15 \div 3$	19. $20 \div 4$	20. $30 \div 6$

b How many marchers?

21. 2 rows of 5   22. 6 rows of 5   23. 5 rows of 5

How many rows with 5 marchers in a row?

24. 30 marchers   25. 20 marchers   26. 15 marchers

27. 25 marchers   28. 10 marchers   29. 5 marchers

95

Five

We count the minutes past the hour in fives.

8 fives = 40   8 fives are in 40.

$$\begin{array}{r} 5 \\ \times 8 \\ \hline 40 \end{array}$$

$$5\overline{)40}^{\,8}$$

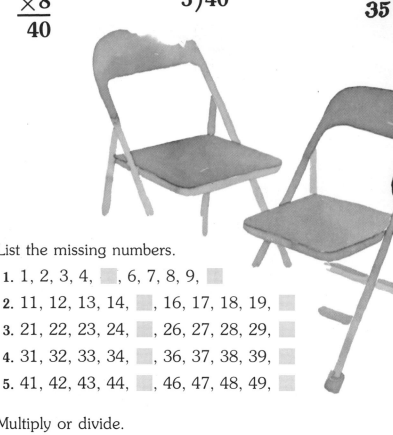

 List the missing numbers.

1. 1, 2, 3, 4, ▨, 6, 7, 8, 9, ▨
2. 11, 12, 13, 14, ▨, 16, 17, 18, 19, ▨
3. 21, 22, 23, 24, ▨, 26, 27, 28, 29, ▨
4. 31, 32, 33, 34, ▨, 36, 37, 38, 39, ▨
5. 41, 42, 43, 44, ▨, 46, 47, 48, 49, ▨

Multiply or divide.

6. 1×5
3×5
5×5
7×5

7. 2×5
4×5
6×5
8×5

8. $5 \div 5$
$10 \div 5$
$15 \div 5$
$20 \div 5$

9. 9×5
5×9
$45 \div 5$
$45 \div 9$

10. $\begin{array}{r} 5 \\ \times 3 \\ \hline \end{array}$

11. $\begin{array}{r} 3 \\ \times 5 \\ \hline \end{array}$

12. $\begin{array}{r} 5 \\ \times 6 \\ \hline \end{array}$

13. $\begin{array}{r} 6 \\ \times 5 \\ \hline \end{array}$

14. $\begin{array}{r} 5 \\ \times 7 \\ \hline \end{array}$

15. $\begin{array}{r} 7 \\ \times 5 \\ \hline \end{array}$

16. $5\overline{)15}$

17. $3\overline{)15}$

18. $5\overline{)30}$

19. $6\overline{)30}$

20. $5\overline{)35}$

21. $7\overline{)35}$

b Multiply or divide.

22.	5 ×5	23.	4 ×5	24.	9 ×5	25.	5 ×7	26.	2 ×5	27.	5 ×6

28.	5 ×8	29.	6 ×5	30.	5 ×1	31.	8 ×5	32.	7 ×5	33.	5 ×9

34. 5)‾5‾   35. 4)‾20‾   36. 5)‾25‾   37. 5)‾40‾   38. 6)‾30‾   39. 1)‾5‾

40. 5)‾10‾   41. 9)‾45‾   42. 5)‾35‾   43. 5)‾15‾   44. 2)‾10‾   45. 5)‾45‾

c Solve.

46. 5 music books
$2 each
Total cost?

47. 45 minutes to practice
5 songs
Number of minutes per song?

48. 10 players
One stand for 2 players
How many music stands?

49. $20 band uniform
4 people give $5 each
Enough money?

Six

1 for 6¢
2 for 12¢
3 for 18¢
4 for 24¢
5 for 30¢
6 for 36¢
7 for 42¢
8 for 48¢
9 for 54¢

CLOSE-OUT SALE
ONLY 6¢ EACH

 List the missing numbers.

1. 1, 2, 3, 4, 5, ▨, 7, 8, 9, 10, 11, ▨
2. 13, 14, 15, 16, 17, ▨, 19, 20, 21, 22, 23, ▨
3. 25, 26, 27, 28, 29, ▨, 31, 32, 33, 34, 35, ▨
4. 37, 38, 39, 40, 41, ▨, 43, 44, 45, 46, 47, ▨
5. 49, 50, 51, 52, 53, ▨, 55, 56, 57, 58, 59, ▨

Multiply or divide.

6. 2 × 6	7. 6 × 2	8. 3 × 6	9. 6 × 3	10. 6 × 6
11. 12 ÷ 6	12. 12 ÷ 2	13. 18 ÷ 6	14. 18 ÷ 3	15. 36 ÷ 6

16. 4 × 6	17. 5 × 6	18. 7 × 6	19. 8 × 6	20. 9 × 6
6 × 4	6 × 5	6 × 7	6 × 8	6 × 9
24 ÷ 6	30 ÷ 6	42 ÷ 6	48 ÷ 6	54 ÷ 6
24 ÷ 4	30 ÷ 5	42 ÷ 7	48 ÷ 8	54 ÷ 9

21. 1 × 6	22. 4 × 6	23. 7 × 6	24. 12 ÷ 2	25. 6 × 1
2 × 6	5 × 6	8 × 6	24 ÷ 4	6 ÷ 1
3 × 6	6 × 6	9 × 6	48 ÷ 8	6 ÷ 6

b Multiply or divide.

26.	27.	28.	29.	30.	31.
6 ×5	3 ×6	7 ×6	6 ×6	2 ×6	6 ×9

32.	33.	34.	35.	36.	37.
6 ×3	6 ×4	6 ×8	9 ×6	6 ×7	5 ×6

38. 6)36 39. 6)48 40. 7)42 41. 6)30 42. 4)24 43. 6)54

44. 6)6 45. 2)12 46. 9)54 47. 8)48 48. 6)18 49. 6)42

c How many 6-cent whistles can you buy with your pennies?

50. 24 pennies   51. 36 pennies

52. 18 pennies   53. 42 pennies

54. 30 pennies   55. 12 pennies

56. 54 pennies   57. 48 pennies

What is the cost of one bell?

58. 6 bells for 48¢

59. 9 bells for 54¢

60. 7 bells for 42¢

61. 6 bells for 30¢

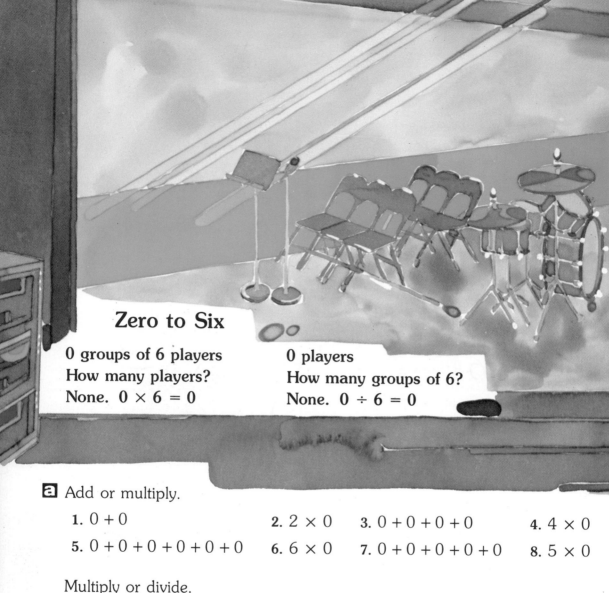

Zero to Six

0 groups of 6 players
How many players?
None. $0 \times 6 = 0$

0 players
How many groups of 6?
None. $0 \div 6 = 0$

a Add or multiply.

1. $0 + 0$

2. 2×0

3. $0 + 0 + 0 + 0$

4. 4×0

5. $0 + 0 + 0 + 0 + 0 + 0$

6. 6×0

7. $0 + 0 + 0 + 0 + 0$

8. 5×0

Multiply or divide.

9. 0×1
0×2
0×3
0×4

10. $0 \div 6$
$0 \div 5$
$0 \div 4$
$0 \div 3$

11. 0×5
2×5
4×5
6×5

12. $0 \div 4$
$4 \div 4$
$8 \div 4$
$12 \div 4$

13. $0 \div 1$
$1 \div 1$
$2 \div 1$
$3 \div 1$

14. 0×6
1×6
2×6
3×6

15. 0×1
1×1
2×1
3×1

16. $6 \div 6$
$5 \div 5$
$4 \div 4$
$3 \div 3$

17. $12 \div 1$
$12 \div 2$
$12 \div 3$
$12 \div 4$

18. 1×5
3×5
5×5
7×5

b Multiply or divide.

19.	20.	21.	22.	23.	24.
6 ×0	5 ×6	0 ×9	1 ×4	4 ×3	5 ×5

25.	26.	27.	28.	29.	30.
4 ×4	6 ×1	3 ×6	5 ×9	3 ×0	6 ×7

31. 5)0   32. 6)6   33. 5)35   34. 4)36   35. 3)24   36. 4)28

37. 2)16   38. 1)5   39. 3)27   40. 5)40   41. 4)0   42. 4)24

c Solve.

43. The group practices 3 hours every day for 5 days before making a record. How many hours in all do they practice?

44. Their record has 18 minutes of songs on one side. How many songs about 3 minutes long fit on this side?

45. Each of the 6 players spends $2 for sandwiches and cold drinks at lunch. What is the total cost of lunch for all?

46. The group will do 4 shows every week for the next 8 weeks. How many shows will they do in all?

Seven

1 week	....	7 days
2 weeks	....	14 days
3 weeks	....	21 days
4 weeks	....	28 days
5 weeks	....	35 days
6 weeks	....	42 days
7 weeks	....	49 days
8 weeks	....	56 days
9 weeks	....	63 days

a List the missing numbers.

1. 1, 2, 3, 4, 5, 6, ▮, 8, 9, 10, 11, 12, 13, ▮
2. 15, 16, 17, 18, 19, 20, ▮, 22, 23, 24, 25, 26, 27, ▮
3. 29, 30, 31, 32, 33, 34, ▮, 36, 37, 38, 39, 40, 41, ▮
4. 43, 44, 45, 46, 47, 48, ▮, 50, 51, 52, 53, 54, 55, ▮
5. 57, 58, 59, 60, 61, 62, ▮, 64, 65, 66, 67, 68, 69, ▮

Multiply or divide.

6. 5×7	7. 7×5	8. 6×7	9. 7×6	10. 7×7
11. $35 \div 7$	12. $35 \div 5$	13. $42 \div 7$	14. $42 \div 6$	15. $49 \div 7$

16. 2×7	17. 3×7	18. 4×7	19. 8×7	20. 9×7
7×2	7×3	7×4	7×8	7×9
$14 \div 7$	$21 \div 7$	$28 \div 7$	$56 \div 7$	$63 \div 7$
$14 \div 2$	$21 \div 3$	$28 \div 4$	$56 \div 8$	$63 \div 9$

21. 1×7	22. 4×7	23. 7×7	24. $14 \div 2$	25. 7×1
2×7	5×7	8×7	$28 \div 4$	$7 \div 1$
3×7	6×7	9×7	$56 \div 8$	$7 \div 7$

Multiply or divide.

26. $\begin{array}{r} 7 \\ \times 6 \\ \hline \end{array}$	27. $\begin{array}{r} 7 \\ \times 3 \\ \hline \end{array}$	28. $\begin{array}{r} 5 \\ \times 7 \\ \hline \end{array}$	29. $\begin{array}{r} 7 \\ \times 4 \\ \hline \end{array}$
30. $\begin{array}{r} 2 \\ \times 7 \\ \hline \end{array}$	31. $\begin{array}{r} 7 \\ \times 7 \\ \hline \end{array}$	32. $\begin{array}{r} 9 \\ \times 7 \\ \hline \end{array}$	33. $\begin{array}{r} 1 \\ \times 7 \\ \hline \end{array}$
34. $\begin{array}{r} 7 \\ \times 8 \\ \hline \end{array}$	35. $\begin{array}{r} 6 \\ \times 7 \\ \hline \end{array}$	36. $\begin{array}{r} 7 \\ \times 5 \\ \hline \end{array}$	37. $\begin{array}{r} 7 \\ \times 9 \\ \hline \end{array}$

38. $7\overline{)49}$ 39. $7\overline{)14}$ 40. $3\overline{)21}$ 41. $7\overline{)56}$

42. $9\overline{)63}$ 43. $7\overline{)28}$ 44. $6\overline{)42}$ 45. $7\overline{)7}$

46. $7\overline{)35}$ 47. $7\overline{)63}$ 48. $4\overline{)28}$ 49. $8\overline{)56}$

Review A   (pages 94–103)

1. 1×5 2. 6×5 3. $25 \div 5$ 4. $15 \div 5$

5. $\begin{array}{r} 5 \\ \times 9 \\ \hline \end{array}$ 6. $\begin{array}{r} 5 \\ \times 8 \\ \hline \end{array}$ 7. $5\overline{)35}$ 8. $5\overline{)40}$

9. $\begin{array}{r} 6 \\ \times 7 \\ \hline \end{array}$ 10. $\begin{array}{r} 6 \\ \times 9 \\ \hline \end{array}$ 11. $6\overline{)36}$ 12. $6\overline{)48}$

13. $\begin{array}{r} 6 \\ \times 0 \\ \hline \end{array}$ 14. $\begin{array}{r} 0 \\ \times 5 \\ \hline \end{array}$ 15. $6\overline{)0}$ 16. $6\overline{)6}$

17. $\begin{array}{r} 7 \\ \times 4 \\ \hline \end{array}$ 18. $\begin{array}{r} 7 \\ \times 7 \\ \hline \end{array}$ 19. $7\overline{)63}$ 20. $7\overline{)42}$

Eight

| 0 | 8 | 16 | 24 | 32 | 40 | 48 | 56 | 64 | 72 |

9 eights

$$\begin{array}{r} 8 \\ \times\ 9 \\ \hline 72 \end{array}$$

$$8\overline{)72}\ ^{9}$$

$$9 \times 8 = 72 \qquad 72 \div 8 = 9$$

a List the missing numbers.

1. ▦, 1, 2, 3, 4, 5, 6, 7, ▦
2. ▦, 17, 18, 19, 20, 21, 22, 23, ▦
3. ▦, 33, 34, 35, 36, 37, 38, 39, ▦
4. ▦, 49, 50, 51, 52, 53, 54, 55, ▦
5. ▦, 65, 66, 67, 68, 69, 70, 71, ▦

Multiply or divide.

6. 0×8 7. 8×0 8. 1×8 9. 8×1 10. 8×8

11. 3×8 12. 4×8 13. 5×8 14. 6×8 15. 7×8
8×3 8×4 8×5 8×6 8×7
$24 \div 8$ $32 \div 8$ $40 \div 8$ $48 \div 8$ $56 \div 8$
$24 \div 3$ $32 \div 4$ $40 \div 5$ $48 \div 6$ $56 \div 7$

16. 1×8 17. 4×8 18. 7×8 19. $16 \div 2$ 20. 8×0
2×8 5×8 8×8 $32 \div 4$ 0×8
3×8 6×8 9×8 $64 \div 8$ $0 \div 8$

104

b Multiply or divide.

21. 1	22. 0	23. 8	24. 8	25. 8	26. 8
×8	×8	×7	×8	×5	×3

27. 8	28. 2	29. 8	30. 8	31. 7	32. 9
×9	×8	×6	×4	×8	×8

33. 8)16   34. 8)56   35. 3)24   36. 5)40   37. 8)72   38. 8)32

39. 6)48   40. 8)64   41. 8)8   42. 8)24   43. 7)56   44. 8)48

c Solve.

45. 8 albums
2 records in each album
How many records in all?

46. 48 records stacked up
6 stacks
How many in each stack?

47. 8 folk singers
4 songs by each singer
How many songs in all?

48. 3 drum solos
8 times as many piano solos
How many piano solos?

49. 8 albums
Each valued at $5
Total value of the albums?

50. 72 records
8 in each stack
How many stacks?

Zero to Eight

We may group facts for easy recall.
These facts are about 24.

6	4	8	3
× 4	× 6	× 3	× 8
24	24	24	24

$$6\overline{)24}=4 \qquad 4\overline{)24}=6 \qquad 8\overline{)24}=3 \qquad 3\overline{)24}=8$$

a Multiply or divide.

1. 4
   ×3

2. 3
   ×4

3. 4$\overline{)12}$

4. 3$\overline{)12}$

5. 2
   ×6

6. 6
   ×2

7. 2$\overline{)12}$

8. 6$\overline{)12}$

9. 2
   ×9

10. 9
    ×2

11. 2$\overline{)18}$

12. 9$\overline{)18}$

13. 3
    ×6

14. 6
    ×3

15. 3$\overline{)18}$

16. 6$\overline{)18}$

17. 2
    ×8

18. 4
    ×4

19. 2$\overline{)16}$

20. 4$\overline{)16}$

21. 4
    ×9

22. 6
    ×6

23. 4$\overline{)36}$

24. 6$\overline{)36}$

b Multiply or divide.

25. $\begin{array}{r} 8 \\ \times 2 \\ \hline \end{array}$	26. $\begin{array}{r} 7 \\ \times 4 \\ \hline \end{array}$	27. $\begin{array}{r} 3 \\ \times 8 \\ \hline \end{array}$
28. $\begin{array}{r} 0 \\ \times 8 \\ \hline \end{array}$	29. $\begin{array}{r} 7 \\ \times 7 \\ \hline \end{array}$	30. $\begin{array}{r} 6 \\ \times 5 \\ \hline \end{array}$
31. $\begin{array}{r} 7 \\ \times 8 \\ \hline \end{array}$	32. $\begin{array}{r} 8 \\ \times 9 \\ \hline \end{array}$	33. $\begin{array}{r} 6 \\ \times 6 \\ \hline \end{array}$
34. $\begin{array}{r} 4 \\ \times 5 \\ \hline \end{array}$	35. $\begin{array}{r} 1 \\ \times 8 \\ \hline \end{array}$	36. $\begin{array}{r} 7 \\ \times 0 \\ \hline \end{array}$

37. $8\overline{)16}$ 38. $7\overline{)42}$ 39. $4\overline{)32}$

40. $6\overline{)48}$ 41. $5\overline{)40}$ 42. $7\overline{)21}$

43. $3\overline{)27}$ 44. $8\overline{)64}$ 45. $5\overline{)35}$

46. $3\overline{)24}$ 47. $4\overline{)16}$ 48. $6\overline{)54}$

No pencils allowed

1. Add 2 and 6; multiply by 1; add 7; divide by 5; multiply by 4; divide by 3.

2. Multiply 2 by 8; add 4; divide by 4; multiply by 7; add 9.

3. Divide 24 by 6; add 3; multiply by 8; subtract 2; divide by 6.

4. Subtract 6 from 8; multiply by 8; divide by 8; multiply by 0; add 7.

Nine

Look at the patterns of the digits in the ones' place and the tens' place. Patterns can help you memorize these facts.

$1 \times 9 = $ | 9
$2 \times 9 = $ | 1 8
$3 \times 9 = $ | 2 7
$4 \times 9 = $ | 3 6
$5 \times 9 = $ | 4 5
$6 \times 9 = $ | 5 4
$7 \times 9 = $ | 6 3
$8 \times 9 = $ | 7 2
$9 \times 9 = $ | 8 1

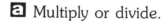 **a** Multiply or divide.

1. 7×9 2. 9×7 3. 8×9 4. 9×8 5. 9×9

6. $63 \div 9$ 7. $63 \div 7$ 8. $72 \div 9$ 9. $72 \div 8$ 10. $81 \div 9$

11. 2×9 12. 3×9 13. 4×9 14. 5×9 15. 6×9
    9×2 9×3 9×4 9×5 9×6
   $18 \div 9$ $27 \div 9$ $36 \div 9$ $45 \div 9$ $54 \div 9$
   $18 \div 2$ $27 \div 3$ $36 \div 4$ $45 \div 5$ $54 \div 6$

16. 1×9 17. $9 \div 9$ 18. 9×6 19. 9×1 20. 9×0
    2×9 $18 \div 9$ 9×7 1×9 0×9
    4×9 $36 \div 9$ 9×8 $9 \div 1$ $0 \div 9$
    8×9 $72 \div 9$ 9×9

b Multiply or divide.

21.	22.	23.	24.	25.	26.
9 ×3	2 ×9	9 ×6	9 ×4	5 ×9	7 ×9

27.	28.	29.	30.	31.	32.
9 ×9	9 ×8	1 ×9	9 ×7	0 ×9	3 ×9

33. 9)36 34. 9)9 35. 9)81 36. 5)45 37. 7)63 38. 9)72

39. 9)27 40. 9)54 41. 8)72 42. 9)18 43. 6)54 44. 9)63

c Solve.

45. 45 singers stand in 5 rows. How many are in each row?

46. The musical program is in 2 parts. There are 9 songs in each part. How many songs are in the program?

47. The youngest singer in the group is 9-year-old Janet. The oldest singer is 63-year-old Ben. Ben is how many times as old as Janet?

48. Organ music will be played in 9 shows each week for the next 6 weeks. How many shows is that in all?

49. Chairs are set up with 8 in each row. If a program is put on each chair, how many programs are needed for the last 9 rows?

Multiplication Table, 0-9

You must memorize the facts shown in the table.
The facts on one side match the facts on the other side.

$$\boxed{7} \times \boxed{6} = \boxed{42}$$

$$\boxed{6} \times \boxed{7} = \boxed{42}$$

×	0	1	2	3	4	5	6	7	8	9
0	0	0	0	0	0	0	0	0	0	0
1	0	1	2	3	4	5	6	7	8	9
2	0	2	4	6	8	10	12	14	16	18
3	0	3	6	9	12	15	18	21	24	27
4	0	4	8	12	16	20	24	28	32	36
5	0	5	10	15	20	25	30	35	40	45
6	0	6	12	18	24	30	36	42	48	54
7	0	7	14	21	28	35	42	49	56	63
8	0	8	16	24	32	40	48	56	64	72
9	0	9	18	27	36	45	54	63	72	81

a Multiply or divide.

1. 0×0 2. 1×1 3. 2×2 4. 3×3 5. 4×4

6. 7×6 7. 6×7 8. 7×3 9. 3×7 10. 7×7

11. $42 \div 6$ 12. $42 \div 7$ 13. $21 \div 3$ 14. $21 \div 7$ 15. $49 \div 7$

16. 4×8 17. 8×4 18. 9×8 19. 8×9 20. 8×8

21. $32 \div 8$ 22. $32 \div 4$ 23. $72 \div 8$ 24. $72 \div 9$ 25. $64 \div 8$

26. 1×5 27. 3×5 28. 5×5 29. 7×5 30. 9×5

31. $5 \overline{)0}$ 32. $5 \overline{)10}$ 33. $5 \overline{)20}$ 34. $5 \overline{)30}$ 35. $5 \overline{)40}$

36. $1 \overline{)4}$ 37. $1 \overline{)9}$ 38. $1 \overline{)5}$ 39. $1 \overline{)6}$ 40. $1 \overline{)0}$

41. $\begin{array}{r} 1 \\ \times 0 \\ \hline \end{array}$ 42. $\begin{array}{r} 2 \\ \times 0 \\ \hline \end{array}$ 43. $\begin{array}{r} 5 \\ \times 0 \\ \hline \end{array}$ 44. $\begin{array}{r} 8 \\ \times 0 \\ \hline \end{array}$ 45. $\begin{array}{r} 9 \\ \times 0 \\ \hline \end{array}$

b Multiply or divide.

46. 3×8	47. 4×4	48. 9×3	49. 4×8	50. 7×7	51. 8×9
52. 5×5	53. 4×6	54. 8×8	55. 9×9	56. 6×8	57. 6×6
58. 8×7	59. 3×6	60. 9×5	61. 7×4	62. 9×6	63. 7×5

64. $9\overline{)54}$ 65. $8\overline{)64}$ 66. $6\overline{)24}$ 67. $5\overline{)35}$ 68. $9\overline{)63}$ 69. $7\overline{)56}$

70. $3\overline{)21}$ 71. $6\overline{)36}$ 72. $7\overline{)49}$ 73. $4\overline{)32}$ 74. $5\overline{)30}$ 75. $9\overline{)45}$

76. $7\overline{)0}$ 77. $3\overline{)24}$ 78. $8\overline{)48}$ 79. $5\overline{)5}$ 80. $6\overline{)18}$ 81. $7\overline{)28}$

Review B   (pages 104–111)

1. 6×8 2. 5×8 3. $40 \div 8$ 4. $64 \div 8$

5. 4×6 6. 3×8 7. $24 \div 4$ 8. $24 \div 3$

9. 9×5 10. 9×7 11. $9\overline{)36}$ 12. $9\overline{)54}$

13. 6×7 14. 4×4 15. $8\overline{)48}$ 16. $3\overline{)27}$

Problem Solving   Problem • Plan • Arithmetic • Answer

 | **Make a plan.** | **What do you do to solve the problem?**

You can get 1 quarter
in trade for 5 nickels.
How many nickels do you
trade for 2 quarters?

Draw a picture to help you plan
how to solve the problem.

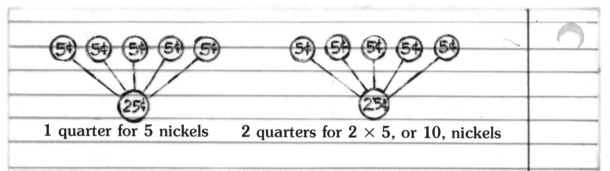

1 quarter for 5 nickels   **2 quarters for 2 × 5, or 10, nickels**

Complete the trade.

1 nickel for 5 pennies

1. 3 nickels for ▢ pennies   **2.** 5 nickels for ▢ pennies

3. 2 nickels for ▢ pennies   **4.** 4 nickels for ▢ pennies

1 dime for 2 nickels

5. 2 dimes for ▢ nickels   **6.** 5 dimes for ▢ nickels

7. 3 dimes for ▢ nickels   **8.** 7 dimes for ▢ nickels

1 dollar for 4 quarters

9. 2 dollars for ▢ quarters   **10.** 4 dollars for ▢ quarters

11. 3 dollars for ▢ quarters   **12.** 5 dollars for ▢ quarters

Unit Test

Multiply or divide.   (pages 94–99)

1. 5	2. 5	3. 5	4. 6	5. 3
×2	×5	×7	×8	×6

6. 5)‾30‾   7. 5)‾45‾   8. 6)‾42‾   9. 6)‾54‾   10. 5)‾40‾

Multiply or divide.   (pages 100–103)

11. 0	12. 4	13. 7	14. 5)‾0‾	15. 7)‾21‾	16. 7)‾56‾
×6	×0	×9			

Multiply or divide.   (pages 104–107)

17. 8	18. 8	19. 2	20. 8)‾16‾	21. 8)‾24‾	22. 4)‾12‾
×4	×7	×9			

Multiply or divide.   (pages 108–111)

23. 9	24. 9	25. 4	26. 9)‾63‾	27. 9)‾81‾	28. 7)‾49‾
×6	×3	×7			

Complete the trade.   (page 112)

29. 1 quarter for 5 nickels
    4 quarters for ▨ nickels

30. 1 half dollar for 2 quarters
    6 half dollars for ▨ quarters

Taking Another Look

Pages 94–99

○   ○   ○
○   ○   ○
○   ○   ○
○   ○   ○
○   ○   ○
○   ○   ○

.6   12   18

3 sixes = 18
3 × 6 = 18

3 sixes are in 18.

$$6\overline{)18} \quad 3$$

Multiply or divide.

1. 2 × 5   2. 10 ÷ 5   3. 2 × 6   4. 12 ÷ 6

5. 5 × 6   6. 6 × 5   7. 30 ÷ 6   8. 30 ÷ 5

9. 5   10. 6   11. 6   12. 5
   ×7   ×6   ×9   ×4

13. 6   14. 5   15. 5   16. 6
   ×7   ×9   ×5   ×3

17. 5   18. 6   19. 6   20. 5
   ×8   ×4   ×8   ×3

21. 5)45   22. 6)24   23. 5)20   24. 6)36

25. 5)40   26. 5)25   27. 6)48   28. 6)54

Pages 100–103

2 sevens = 14

   7
  ×2
 ─────
  14

2 sevens are in 14.

$$7\overline{)14} \quad 2$$

Multiply or divide.

1. 5 × 7   2. 35 ÷ 7   3. 3 × 7   4. 21 ÷ 7

5. 0   6. 7   7. 0   8. 6
  ×7   ×0   ×6   ×0

9. 7   10. 7   11. 7   12. 9
  ×8   ×4   ×6   ×0

13. 0   14. 7   15. 7   16. 7
  ×5   ×9   ×7   ×8

17. 7)0   18. 7)42   19. 7)63   20. 6)0

21. 7)28   22. 5)0   23. 7)7   24. 7)56

114

Pages 104–107

4 eights = 32

$$\begin{array}{r} 8 \\ \times 4 \\ \hline 32 \end{array}$$

4 eights are in 32.

$$8\overline{)32}^{\,4}$$

Multiply or divide.

1. $\begin{array}{r} 8 \\ \times 1 \\ \hline \end{array}$
2. $\begin{array}{r} 8 \\ \times 2 \\ \hline \end{array}$
3. $\begin{array}{r} 8 \\ \times 3 \\ \hline \end{array}$
4. $\begin{array}{r} 8 \\ \times 4 \\ \hline \end{array}$

5. $8\overline{)8}$
6. $8\overline{)16}$
7. $8\overline{)24}$
8. $8\overline{)32}$

9. $\begin{array}{r} 8 \\ \times 7 \\ \hline \end{array}$
10. $\begin{array}{r} 7 \\ \times 6 \\ \hline \end{array}$
11. $\begin{array}{r} 4 \\ \times 5 \\ \hline \end{array}$
12. $\begin{array}{r} 8 \\ \times 6 \\ \hline \end{array}$

13. $\begin{array}{r} 8 \\ \times 8 \\ \hline \end{array}$
14. $\begin{array}{r} 5 \\ \times 5 \\ \hline \end{array}$
15. $\begin{array}{r} 8 \\ \times 9 \\ \hline \end{array}$
16. $\begin{array}{r} 0 \\ \times 8 \\ \hline \end{array}$

17. $4\overline{)32}$
18. $8\overline{)0}$
19. $7\overline{)56}$
20. $8\overline{)64}$

Pages 108–111

2 nines = 18

$$\begin{array}{r} 9 \\ \times 2 \\ \hline 18 \end{array}$$

2 nines are in 18.

$$9\overline{)18}^{\,2}$$

Multiply or divide.

1. $\begin{array}{r} 9 \\ \times 5 \\ \hline \end{array}$
2. $\begin{array}{r} 5 \\ \times 9 \\ \hline \end{array}$
3. $\begin{array}{r} 9 \\ \times 7 \\ \hline \end{array}$
4. $\begin{array}{r} 7 \\ \times 9 \\ \hline \end{array}$

5. $9\overline{)45}$
6. $5\overline{)45}$
7. $9\overline{)63}$
8. $7\overline{)63}$

9. $\begin{array}{r} 9 \\ \times 6 \\ \hline \end{array}$
10. $\begin{array}{r} 4 \\ \times 8 \\ \hline \end{array}$
11. $\begin{array}{r} 6 \\ \times 6 \\ \hline \end{array}$
12. $\begin{array}{r} 9 \\ \times 9 \\ \hline \end{array}$

13. $9\overline{)72}$
14. $1\overline{)9}$
15. $8\overline{)64}$
16. $4\overline{)36}$

Page 112

1 nickel for 5 pennies

Complete the trade.

1. 6 nickels for ▢ pennies
2. 9 nickels for ▢ pennies
3. 8 nickels for ▢ pennies

Something Extra • QUESTIONS FOR SHOPPERS

For each shopping list, answer these questions:

A. Do I have enough money? Estimate to answer Yes or No.
B. What is the exact total cost?
C. What is my change or how much more do I need?

1. $1.00 to spend
   39¢ roll of tape
   35¢ pen
   19¢ eraser

2. $1.00 to spend
   $ .69 ball
     .29 jacks
     .19 horn

3. $1.00 to spend
   $ .21 chalk
     .48 paints
     .29 pad

4. $1.00 to spend
   $ .49 mirror
     .18 comb
     .55 toothbrush
     .28 shoestrings

5. $1.50 to spend
   $ .79 bread
     .55 jam
     .29 nuts

6. $1.75 to spend
   2 cans 29¢ soup
   47¢ crackers
   59¢ cocoa

7. $5.00 to spend
   $1.76 doll dress
   1.19 doll shoes
   1.88 doll coat

8. $5.00 to spend
   $2.35 ball
     .96 net
   1.89 kite

9. $5.25 to spend
   $3.29 present
     .27 card
     .59 balloons
     .98 favors

You have a quarter. How many can you buy?

10. 6¢ lollipops

11. 4¢ mints

12. 9¢ nut bars

You have two quarters. How many can you buy?

13. 9¢ apples

14. 8¢ chocolates

15. 10¢ cookies

16. What Mr. Spendit bought
    $1.93 fishing hat
    $1.49 lure
    $ .68 hooks
    $ .47 sinkers

Mr. Spendit's change
1 quarter, 3 nickels,
3 pennies

How much money did Mr. Spendit give the clerk?

Reviewing Needed Skills

Add.

1. $\begin{array}{r} 8 \\ 5 \\ +6 \\ \hline \end{array}$
2. $\begin{array}{r} 9 \\ 4 \\ +5 \\ \hline \end{array}$
3. $\begin{array}{r} 36 \\ 42 \\ +27 \\ \hline \end{array}$
4. $\begin{array}{r} 62 \\ 21 \\ +33 \\ \hline \end{array}$
5. $\begin{array}{r} 53 \\ 64 \\ +85 \\ \hline \end{array}$

6. $\begin{array}{r} 5 \\ 5 \\ 1 \\ +6 \\ \hline \end{array}$
7. $\begin{array}{r} 9 \\ 3 \\ 6 \\ +8 \\ \hline \end{array}$
8. $\begin{array}{r} 23 \\ 54 \\ 37 \\ +42 \\ \hline \end{array}$
9. $\begin{array}{r} 59 \\ 63 \\ 18 \\ +25 \\ \hline \end{array}$
10. $\begin{array}{r} 74 \\ 23 \\ 36 \\ +51 \\ \hline \end{array}$

Subtract.

11. $\begin{array}{r} 68 \\ -26 \\ \hline \end{array}$
12. $\begin{array}{r} 70 \\ -42 \\ \hline \end{array}$
13. $\begin{array}{r} 92 \\ -38 \\ \hline \end{array}$
14. $\begin{array}{r} 51 \\ -9 \\ \hline \end{array}$
15. $\begin{array}{r} 80 \\ -6 \\ \hline \end{array}$

16. $\begin{array}{r} 53 \\ -27 \\ \hline \end{array}$
17. $\begin{array}{r} 25 \\ -4 \\ \hline \end{array}$
18. $\begin{array}{r} 74 \\ -46 \\ \hline \end{array}$
19. $\begin{array}{r} 95 \\ -86 \\ \hline \end{array}$
20. $\begin{array}{r} 47 \\ -19 \\ \hline \end{array}$

Multiply.

21. 4×3
22. 5×6
23. 8×7
24. 2×5
25. 7×4

26. 3×3
27. 9×9
28. 7×9
29. 6×4
30. 5×7

31. $\begin{array}{r} 9 \\ \times 8 \\ \hline \end{array}$
32. $\begin{array}{r} 4 \\ \times 9 \\ \hline \end{array}$
33. $\begin{array}{r} 6 \\ \times 3 \\ \hline \end{array}$
34. $\begin{array}{r} 8 \\ \times 4 \\ \hline \end{array}$
35. $\begin{array}{r} 7 \\ \times 6 \\ \hline \end{array}$

Divide.

36. $45 \div 9$
37. $56 \div 8$
38. $32 \div 8$
39. $49 \div 7$
40. $18 \div 9$

41. $6\overline{)54}$
42. $7\overline{)28}$
43. $3\overline{)15}$
44. $3\overline{)21}$
45. $8\overline{)64}$

46. $9\overline{)72}$
47. $7\overline{)63}$
48. $6\overline{)42}$
49. $5\overline{)35}$
50. $4\overline{)20}$

UNIT 6

The Centimeter Ruler

The length of the screwdriver is between 9 cm and 10 cm.
The length is 9 cm to the nearest centimeter.

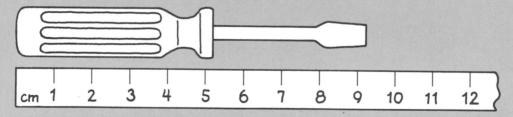

The length of the screw is
halfway between 3 cm and 4 cm.
We choose the greater number.
We say the length is 4 cm
to the nearest centimeter.

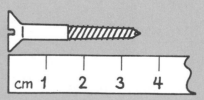

118

Measurement

a Measure the length to the nearest centimeter.

1.

2.

3.

4.

5.

6.

7.

Perimeter

The <u>perimeter</u> of a shape is the distance around it.

Add the lengths of the sides of the door.

1 m
2 m
1 m
+2 m
———
6 m

The perimeter is 6 m.

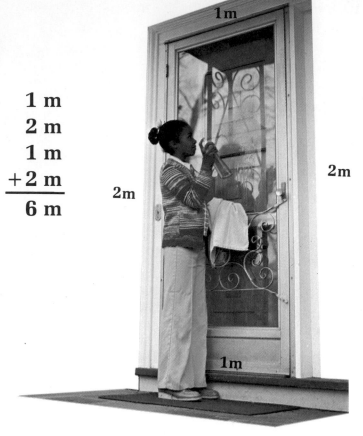

1m

2m

2m

2m

1m

a What is the perimeter?

1.

2 cm

2 cm   2 cm

2 cm

2.

3 cm

1 cm   1 cm

3 cm

3.

2 cm

2 cm

1 cm

3 cm

4.

3 cm

4 cm

3 cm

5.

2 cm   2 cm

2 cm   2 cm

2 cm

6.

1 cm

2 cm

1 cm

1 cm

3 cm

2 cm

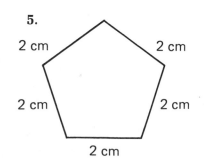

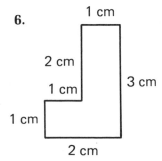

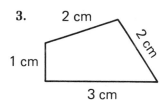

b Measure the sides to the nearest centimeter.
What is the perimeter?

7.

8.

9.

10.

c Solve.

11. What is the perimeter of a square plot 4 m on each side?

12. Meg's garden is 2 m long on each of its four sides.
How many meters of fencing are needed to go around it?

The Inch Ruler

The length of the brush is between 4 inches and 5 inches.
The length is 5 inches to the nearest inch.

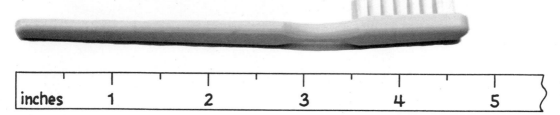

The length of the tube is halfway between 2 inches and
3 inches. We choose the greater number.
We say the length is 3 inches to the nearest inch.

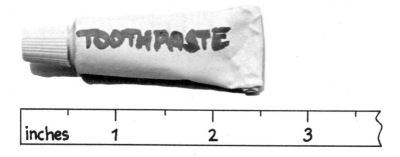

a Measure the length to the nearest inch.

1. _____

2. _____

3. _____

4. _____

5. _____

6. _____

122

b Measure the length to the nearest inch.

7.

8.

9.

10.

11.

c Measure the sides to the nearest inch.
What is the perimeter?

12.

13.

14.

Area

The area of a shape is the number of square units that fit inside it. We may use the unit shown.

 1 square unit

3 rows of 4 square units
Count them all or multiply.

$$3 \times 4 = 12$$

The area of the shape is 12 square units.

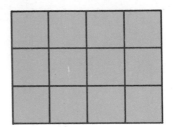

a What is the area?

1.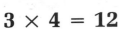

2.

3.

4.

5.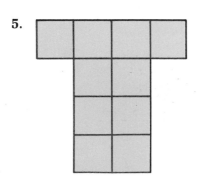

6.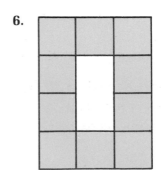

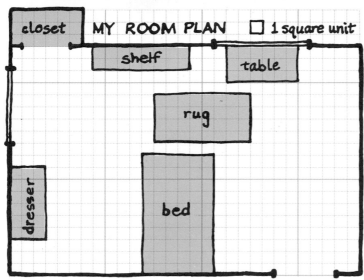

MY ROOM PLAN □ 1 square unit

closet

shelf

table

rug

dresser

bed

b What is the area?

7. rug

8. table top

9. closet floor

10. bed

11. shelf

12. dresser top

The dot game

On squared paper, mark off an area with dots. Take turns with a friend joining any two dots to make the side of a square. If you complete a square on your turn, label it as yours and take another turn.

When the squares are all complete, the player with the greater area wins. Who won this game, Rosa or Sam?

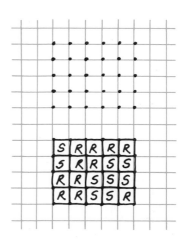

125

Volume

The <u>volume</u> of a box is the number of cubic units that fit inside it. We may use the unit shown.

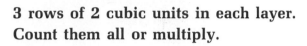
1 cubic unit

3 rows of 2 cubic units in each layer. Count them all or multiply.

one layer ▶ **3 × 2 = 6**

four layers ▶ **4 × 6 = 24**

The volume of the box is 24 cubic units.

a What is the volume?

1.

2.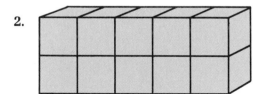

3.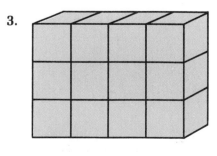

126

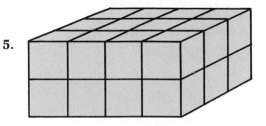 What is the volume?

4.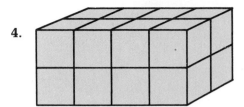

5.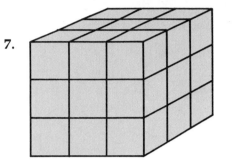

6.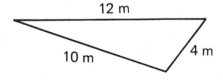

7.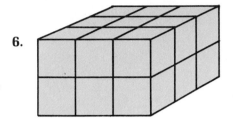

Review A   (pages 118–127)

1. Measure the length to the nearest centimeter.

_____

2. What is the perimeter?

12 m

10 m

4 m

3. Measure the length to the nearest inch.

_____

4. What is the area?

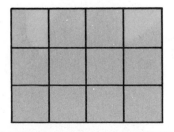

5. What is the volume?

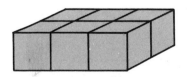

Some Metric Units

This cube measures
1 cm on all edges.
A <u>milliliter</u> (ml) of
liquid would fill this
cube. A liter (ℓ) is 1000 ml.

One of the glasses shown
holds about 250 ml.
Four glasses hold about
1 ℓ of milk.

a Choose the better answer.
Write a or b.

1. a. 4 ml
  b. 4 ℓ

2. a. 200 ml
    b. 20 ℓ

3. a. 5 ml
    b. 125 ml

4. a. 1 ℓ
    b. 10 ℓ

b Write ml or ℓ to name the better unit for .

5. The pen has 1 ▢ of ink left in it.

6. Lola brings 1 ▢ of cola to the party.

7. The pitcher has 75 ▢ of cream in it.

8. A full bathtub has 75 ▢ of water.

9. My tea kettle holds 2 ▢ of water when full.

10. The cocoa mug holds 260 ▢ of cocoa.

11. The canary drank 1 ▢ of water in one gulp.

c Mike mixed the lemonade and grape juice in a bowl.

12. How many milliliters does he have in all?

13. How many liters does he have in all?

> **Party Punch**
> 250 ml lemonade
> 750 ml grape juice
> 1 ℓ ginger ale

Sue added the ginger ale to the lemonade and grape juice.

14. How many milliliters do they have in all?

15. How many liters do they have in all?

Some United States Units

We may measure liquids with a cup.
1 pint (pt) is 2 cups.
1 quart (qt) is 2 pints.
1 gallon (gal) is 4 quarts.

a How many?

1. cups in 1 pint
2. cups in 3 pints
3. cups in 2 pints
4. cups in 1 quart
5. pints in 1 quart
6. pints in 2 quarts
7. pints in 4 quarts
8. pints in 1 gallon
9. quarts in 1 gallon
10. quarts in 3 gallons

b Complete.

	11.	12.	13.	14.
cups	?	?	?	?
pints	4	5	8	9

	15.	16.	17.	18.
pints	4	6	10	12
quarts	?	?	?	?

	19.	20.	21.	22.
quarts	?	?	12	20
gallons	2	8	?	?

	23.	24.	25.	26.
pints	8	16	?	?
gallons	?	?	3	6

c Solve.

27. How many quart jars are needed to hold 2 gallons of stewed tomatoes?

28. A recipe makes 12 pints of strawberry jam. How many quarts is this?

29. How many quarts of punch does this recipe make?

> Cranberry Punch
>
> 6 cups cranberry juice
> 3 cups orange juice
> 1 cup pineapple juice
> 2 cups ginger ale

Time

We use many different units to measure time.

1 minute is 60 seconds.
1 hour is 60 minutes.
1 day is 24 hours.
1 week is 7 days.
1 year is 52 weeks.
1 year is 12 months.

a Complete.

1. There are ___ months in 1 year.
2. There are ___ minutes in 1 hour.
3. There are ___ weeks in 1 year.
4. There are ___ hours in 1 day.
5. There are ___ seconds in 1 minute.
6. There are ___ days in 1 week.
7. There are ___ days in 2 weeks.
8. There are ___ days in 3 weeks.

February

S	M	T	W	T	F	S
				1	2	3
4	5	6	7	8	9	10
11	12	13	14	15	16	17
18	19	20	21	22	23	24
25	26	27	28			

132

b Solve.

9. Vacation begins in 3 weeks. How many days is this?

10. You sleep 9 hours of the day. How many hours are you awake?

11. The baby is 3 months old. How many months to the baby's first birthday?

12. Bill's birthday is January 8. What is the date a week before his birthday?

13. There are 365 days in the year. There are 180 school days. How many days are not school days?

14. School starts in 1 hour. Flora needs 10 minutes to walk to school. How many minutes does she have to get ready?

Review B   (pages 128–133)

Write ml or ℓ to name the best unit for ▓.

1. 2 ▓ of ink in the pen

2. 4 ▓ of punch for the party

3. 2 ▓ of paint for doors

4. 200 ▓ of milk in the glass

How many?

5. cups in 1 pint

6. pints in 1 quart

7. quarts in 1 gallon

8. pints in 1 gallon

9. minutes in 1 hour

10. hours in 1 day

11. months in 1 year

12. weeks in 1 year

Problem Solving   Problem • Plan • Arithmetic • Answer

 Give the answer. | How many days?
How many weeks?

We divide 14 by 7 to solve both problems below,
but the answers to the problems are different.

7 days in a week
14 days of vacation
How many weeks?

| Answer: 2 weeks |

$7 a day to rent a tent
$14 paid
How many days of rent?

| Answer: 2 days |

Write A, B, C, or D to match the problem and answer.

1. 12 ℓ of gasoline in the tank
   6 ℓ used up driving
   How many liters are left?

   A. 6 months
   B. 6 days
   C. 6 ℓ
   D. 6¢

2. 12 days of sun this month
   6 days of rain this month
   How many more days of sun?

3. 12 months in a year
   6 months gone this year
   How many months are left?

4. 12¢ to make a liter of lemonade
   6¢ to make a liter of tea
   How much more to make a liter
   of lemonade?

Unit Test

Measure the length to the nearest centimeter.   (pages 118–119)

1. _____   2. _____

What is the perimeter?   (pages 120–121)

3.

9 m

3 m   3 m

9 m

4.

5 m

3 m

4 m

What is the area?   (pages 124–125)

1 square unit

5.

6.

What is the volume?   (pages 126–127)

1 cubic unit

7.

8.

Write ml or ℓ to name the better unit for ▦.   (pages 128–129)

9. 1 ▦ in a full milk bottle

10. 2 ▦ in an eye dropper

How many?   (pages 132–133)

11. months in 1 year

12. days in 2 weeks

Solve.   (page 134)

13. $7 earned each day
$28 needed
How many days to earn it?

14. 7 days in a week
28 days this month
How many weeks this
month?

Taking Another Look

Pages 118–119

_____

about 3 cm

Measure the length to the nearest centimeter.

1. _____   2. _____

3. _____   4. _____

Pages 120–121

Add the lengths of the sides to find the perimeter.

What is the perimeter?

1.

16 m

12 m   12 m

16 m

2.

7 m

12 m   14 m

Pages 124–125

□ **1 square unit**

Count the number of square units to find the area.

What is the area?

1.

2.

Pages 126–127

  1 cubic unit

Count the number of cubic units to find the volume.

What is the volume?

1.

2.

Pages 128–129

A teaspoon holds about 5 ml of liquid.

Write ml or l to name the better unit for ▨.

1. The ink bottle has 100 ▨ of ink in it.

2. The water jug holds 20 ▨ when full.

3. The milkman brings us 2 ▨ of milk.

4. There are 50 ▨ in the bottle of nose drops.

5. Tim squeezed 30 ▨ of juice from the orange.

6. Carmen washed her hands in 3 ▨ of water.

7. The engine holds 3 ▨ of oil.

8. The recipe asks for 5 ▨ of vanilla.

Pages 132–133

7 days in a week

$$\begin{array}{r} 7 \\ \times 2 \\ \hline 14 \end{array}$$

14 days in 2 weeks

How many?

1. months in 1 year

2. minutes in 1 hour

3. days in 3 weeks

4. weeks in 1 year

5. seconds in 1 minute

6. hours in 1 day

Page 134

1. **Problem**
2. **Plan**
3. **Arithmetic**
4. **Answer**

Write A or B to match the problem and answer.

1. 20 l of water in the boat
   15 l bailed out
   How many liters are left?

    A. 5 boats
    B. 5 l

2. 20 boats in the water
   15 of them racing
   How many not racing?

Something Extra • TEMPERATURE

We tell how hot or cold something is by measuring its
temperature. Temperature may be measured in degrees Celsius.

For zero degrees Celsius we write 0°C.
Water freezes at this temperature.

Write the temperature
from the scale.

1. water freezes

2. water boils

3. a very cold day

4. a very hot day

5. room temperature

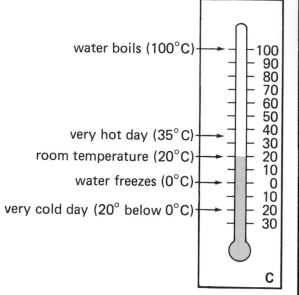

water boils (100°C)

very hot day (35°C)
room temperature (20°C)
water freezes (0°C)
very cold day (20° below 0°C)

C

Write A, B, C, or D to choose the best temperature.

6. a day for skating on the pond   A. 34°C

7. a day for swimming at the beach   B. 190°C

8. an oven ready for baking cookies   C. 19°C

9. a room for sleeping   D. 5° below 0°C

10. Normal body temperature is 37°C.
    Nancy's temperature rose one degree when she was sick.
    What was her temperature then?

11. Ted has a fever. His temperature is 2° above normal.
    What is his temperature?

Reviewing Needed Skills

Write the standard form.

1. 2 tens
2. 4 tens
3. 3 hundreds
4. 8 hundreds
5. 2 thousands
6. 5 thousands
7. 4 tens 7 ones
8. 6 tens 3 ones
9. 2 tens 9 ones
10. 3 tens 5 ones
11. 4 hundreds 2 tens
12. 2 hundreds 8 ones
13. 2 thousand 348
14. 4 thousand 507

Round to the nearest ten.

15. 83
16. 29
17. 35
18. 41
19. 76
20. 212
21. 769
22. 102
23. 298
24. 423

Round to the nearest hundred.

25. 320
26. 459
27. 803
28. 776
29. 934
30. 4189
31. 2041
32. 2061
33. 8431
34. 7676

Multiply.

35.	36.	37.	38.	39.	40.
3 $\times 3$	6 $\times 4$	5 $\times 8$	7 $\times 6$	9 $\times 9$	2 $\times 5$

41.	42.	43.	44.	45.	46.
8 $\times 8$	3 $\times 2$	7 $\times 1$	8 $\times 7$	3 $\times 6$	4 $\times 7$

47.	48.	49.	50.	51.	52.
6 $\times 6$	9 $\times 5$	8 $\times 9$	9 $\times 7$	6 $\times 9$	7 $\times 7$

53.	54.	55.	56.	57.	58.
9 $\times 4$	5 $\times 5$	4 $\times 3$	8 $\times 3$	7 $\times 5$	3 $\times 9$

UNIT 7

Tens, Hundreds, Thousands

4 × 2 is 8.

4 × 2 tens is 8 tens.

4 × 2 hundreds is 8 hundreds.

4 × 2 thousands is 8 thousands.

2	20	200	2000
×4	×4	×4	×4
8	80	800	8000

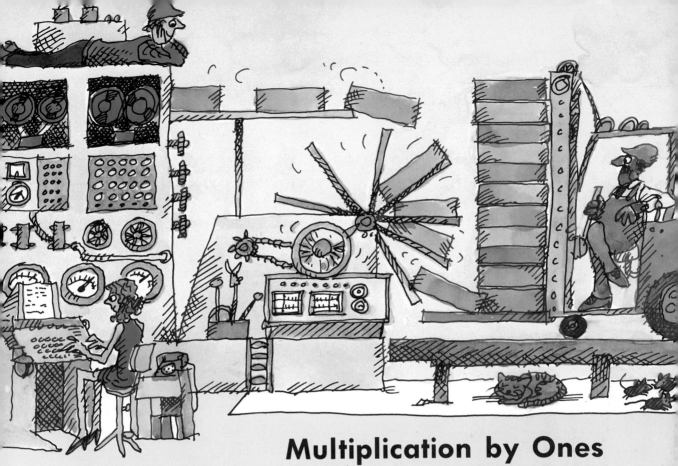

Multiplication by Ones

a Multiply.

1. 10 ×3	**2.** 100 ×3	**3.** 1000 ×3	**4.** 10 ×8	**5.** 100 ×8	**6.** 1000 ×8

7. 20 ×3	**8.** 200 ×3	**9.** 2000 ×3	**10.** 30 ×3	**11.** 300 ×3	**12.** 3000 ×3

13. 40 ×2	**14.** 400 ×2	**15.** 4000 ×2	**16.** 30 ×2	**17.** 300 ×2	**18.** 3000 ×2

19. 1 m is 100 cm.
2 m are ▦ cm.

20. 1 km is 1000 m.
2 km are ▦ m.

21. 1 kg is 1000 g.
4 kg are ▦ g.

22. 1 ℓ is 1000 ml.
6 ℓ are ▦ ml.

Tens, Hundreds, Thousands

Look for a pattern in these examples.

4	40	400	4000
×3	×3	×3	×3
12	120	1200	12,000

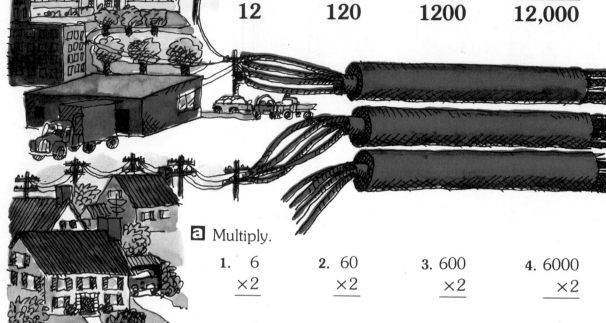

a Multiply.

1. 6 ×2	2. 60 ×2	3. 600 ×2	4. 6000 ×2
5. 8 ×3	6. 80 ×3	7. 800 ×3	8. 8000 ×3
9. 7 ×5	10. 70 ×5	11. 700 ×5	12. 7000 ×5
13. 4 ×8	14. 40 ×8	15. 400 ×8	16. 4000 ×8
17. 5 ×2	18. 50 ×2	19. 500 ×2	20. 5000 ×2
21. 6 ×5	22. 60 ×5	23. 600 ×5	24. 6000 ×5

b Multiply.

25. 50
×5

26. 90
×7

27. 800
×6

28. 900
×5

29. 7000
×7

30. 4000
×5

31. 70
×3

32. 60
×6

33. 200
×9

34. 400
×4

35. 3000
×9

36. 6000
×7

37. 40
×9

38. 50
×8

39. 600
×4

40. 800
×8

41. 5000
×2

42. 9000
×6

c Solve.

43. 20 houses on the street
2 telephones in each
How many telephones in all?

44. 400 numbers on a page
4 pages of phone numbers
How many phone numbers in all?

45. 5000 calls a day
7 days in a week
How many calls in a week?

46. 4000 m of wire on a spool
6 spools
How many meters of wire?

Mr. Bell's invention

The telephone was invented by Alexander Graham Bell.
The centennial of his invention was in 1976.
What does *centennial* mean?
What does *bicentennial* mean?

Two-place Multiplication

**Multiply the
3 ones by 2.**

**Multiply the
4 tens by 2.**

$$\begin{array}{r} 43 \\ \times 2 \\ \hline \end{array}$$ $$\begin{array}{r} 43 \\ \times 2 \\ \hline 6 \end{array}$$

$$\begin{array}{r} 43 \\ \times 2 \\ \hline 86 \end{array}$$

The product of tens and
ones may be hundreds,
tens, and ones.

$$\begin{array}{r} 43 \\ \times 3 \\ \hline 129 \end{array}$$

a Multiply.

1. $\begin{array}{r} 2 \\ \times 3 \\ \hline \end{array}$	2. $\begin{array}{r} 10 \\ \times 3 \\ \hline \end{array}$	3. $\begin{array}{r} 12 \\ \times 3 \\ \hline \end{array}$	4. $\begin{array}{r} 2 \\ \times 4 \\ \hline \end{array}$	5. $\begin{array}{r} 20 \\ \times 4 \\ \hline \end{array}$	6. $\begin{array}{r} 22 \\ \times 4 \\ \hline \end{array}$
7. $\begin{array}{r} 1 \\ \times 3 \\ \hline \end{array}$	8. $\begin{array}{r} 30 \\ \times 3 \\ \hline \end{array}$	9. $\begin{array}{r} 31 \\ \times 3 \\ \hline \end{array}$	10. $\begin{array}{r} 2 \\ \times 2 \\ \hline \end{array}$	11. $\begin{array}{r} 50 \\ \times 2 \\ \hline \end{array}$	12. $\begin{array}{r} 52 \\ \times 2 \\ \hline \end{array}$
13. $\begin{array}{r} 3 \\ \times 3 \\ \hline \end{array}$	14. $\begin{array}{r} 90 \\ \times 3 \\ \hline \end{array}$	15. $\begin{array}{r} 93 \\ \times 3 \\ \hline \end{array}$	16. $\begin{array}{r} 1 \\ \times 9 \\ \hline \end{array}$	17. $\begin{array}{r} 80 \\ \times 9 \\ \hline \end{array}$	18. $\begin{array}{r} 81 \\ \times 9 \\ \hline \end{array}$
19. $\begin{array}{r} 13 \\ \times 3 \\ \hline \end{array}$	20. $\begin{array}{r} 23 \\ \times 3 \\ \hline \end{array}$	21. $\begin{array}{r} 33 \\ \times 3 \\ \hline \end{array}$	22. $\begin{array}{r} 53 \\ \times 3 \\ \hline \end{array}$	23. $\begin{array}{r} 63 \\ \times 3 \\ \hline \end{array}$	24. $\begin{array}{r} 73 \\ \times 3 \\ \hline \end{array}$

b Multiply.

25. 62
    ×2

26. 83
    ×3

27. 71
    ×4

28. 54
    ×2

29. 21
    ×6

30. 44
    ×2

31. 91
    ×5

32. 42
    ×3

33. 51
    ×6

34. 32
    ×4

35. 61
    ×9

36. 73
    ×3

37. 81
    ×8

38. 52
    ×2

39. 92
    ×4

40. 52
    ×3

41. 41
    ×6

42. 81
    ×6

43. 73
    ×2

44. 61
    ×7

45. 53
    ×3

46. 81
    ×5

47. 31
    ×9

48. 82
    ×3

c Solve.

49. The class uses 3 rolls of film on the field trip. There are 12 pictures on each roll. How many pictures do they have of the field trip?

50. The teacher chooses 14 good pictures. Two copies are made of each. How many copies are made in all?

51. The album fits 6 photos on each page. The teacher has filled 21 pages with class photos. How many photos is that in all?

52. Each box holds 43 slides. How many slides do 3 boxes hold?

Two-place Multiplication

Multiply the 9 ones by 4.
Give the 3 tens
to the tens.

Multiply the 2 tens by 4.
Add the 3 tens.

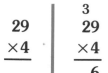

```
    |   3
29  |  29
×4  |  ×4
    |   6
```

```
    3
   29
   ×4
  116
```

a Multiply.

1. 3 ×4	2. 10 ×4	3. 13 ×4	4. 8 ×5	5. 10 ×5	6. 18 ×5
7. 6 ×3	8. 20 ×3	9. 26 ×3	10. 9 ×2	11. 40 ×2	12. 49 ×2
13. 7 ×6	14. 10 ×6	15. 17 ×6	16. 5 ×9	17. 10 ×9	18. 15 ×9
19. 9 ×3	20. 60 ×3	21. 69 ×3	22. 8 ×8	23. 70 ×8	24. 78 ×8

b Multiply.

25.	47 ×3	26.	25 ×4	27.	53 ×6	28.	38 ×5	29.	66 ×2	30.	84 ×7
31.	19 ×8	32.	53 ×4	33.	45 ×6	34.	74 ×7	35.	57 ×2	36.	28 ×5
37.	43 ×6	38.	32 ×9	39.	86 ×3	40.	62 ×6	41.	98 ×7	42.	37 ×5

DAILY PRODUCTION OF THE LO-FI RADIOTRONICS CO.

AM RADIOS

AM-FM RADIOS

POCKET RADIOS

BALL RADIOS

c The picture graph shows the number of radios made in a day. Each picture of a radio stands for 25 radios.

43. How many AM radios are made in a day?

44. How many AM–FM radios are made in a day?

45. How many pocket radios are made in a day?

46. How many ball radios are made in a day?

Estimating Products

About how much do
3 batteries cost?
Round 39 to 40.

$$\begin{array}{r} 40¢ \\ \times 3 \\ \hline \end{array}$$
120¢ or $1.20

$1.20 is an estimate
of the cost.

Exactly how much do
3 batteries cost?

$$\begin{array}{r} 2 \\ 39¢ \\ \times 3 \\ \hline \end{array}$$
117¢ or $1.17

$1.17 is the cost.

a Multiply.

1.	30 ×2	29 ×2	2.	40 ×4	37 ×4	3.	40 ×3	44 ×3
4.	50 ×6	48 ×6	5.	30 ×9	26 ×9	6.	100 ×2	98 ×2
7.	20¢ ×4	19¢ ×4	8.	30¢ ×3	34¢ ×3	9.	60¢ ×7	59¢ ×7
10.	50¢ ×2	49¢ ×2	11.	20¢ ×6	18¢ ×6	12.	100¢ ×3	99¢ ×3

b Estimate the cost. Then figure the exact cost.

13. 2 at 37¢ each
14. 6 at 19¢ each
15. 3 at 54¢ each
16. 5 at 16¢ each
17. 4 at 88¢ each
18. 8 at 49¢ each
19. 2 at 97¢ each
20. 6 at 69¢ each
21. 3 at 55¢ each
22. 4 at $18 each
23. 2 at $36 each
24. 3 at $24 each

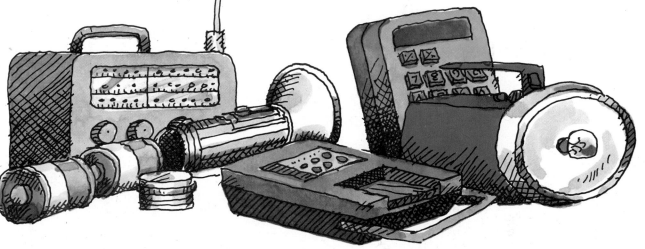

Review A (pages 140–149)

1. 10
    ×2

2. 30
    ×3

3. 200
    ×4

4. 3000
    ×2

5. 70
    ×2

6. 20
    ×5

7. 400
    ×3

8. 8000
    ×6

9. 42
    ×2

10. 13
    ×3

11. 62
    ×4

12. 91
    ×9

13. 23
    ×4

14. 35
    ×3

15. 67
    ×8

16. 49
    ×6

Estimate the cost of 4 batteries.

17. 29¢ each
18. 47¢ each
19. 68¢ each
20. 73¢ each

Three-place Multiplication

Multiply 218 by 4.

Multiply the 8 ones by 4.	Multiply the 1 ten by 4. Add the 3 tens.	Multiply the 2 hundreds by 4.
3 218 ×4 ‾‾‾ 2	3 218 ×4 ‾‾‾ 72	3 218 ×4 ‾‾‾ 872

Multiply 208 by 4.
Do not forget to multiply
the 0 tens by 4. Then add
the 3 tens.

3
208
×4
‾‾‾
832

a Multiply.

1. 23 ×2	2. 100 ×2	3. 123 ×2	4. 34 ×2	5. 600 ×2	6. 634 ×2
7. 23 ×4	8. 100 ×4	9. 123 ×4	10. 17 ×4	11. 200 ×4	12. 217 ×4
13. 28 ×3	14. 500 ×3	15. 528 ×3	16. 18 ×5	17. 600 ×5	18. 618 ×5
19. 300 ×3	20. 301 ×3	21. 306 ×3	22. 700 ×4	23. 702 ×4	24. 708 ×4

b Multiply.

25. 325 ×3	26. 248 ×2	27. 117 ×5
28. 536 ×2	29. 624 ×4	30. 727 ×3
31. 409 ×5	32. 624 ×3	33. 928 ×3
34. 718 ×4	35. 449 ×2	36. 805 ×2
37. 519 ×3	38. 617 ×4	39. 316 ×5
40. 824 ×4	41. 425 ×2	42. 906 ×3
43. 745 ×2	44. 523 ×4	45. 817 ×3

Using estimates

Jenny and Jerry estimate that the answer to this example is <u>about</u> 600. Then they multiply 209 by 3 on their calculator.

$$209 \atop {\times 3}$$

Jenny gets the answer 212.

Jerry gets the answer 870.

They know by their estimate that their answers are not reasonable. What did they do wrong on the calculator?

Three-place Multiplication

Compare these examples.

Example 1	Example 2	Example 3
	3	1 3
2 1 2	2 1 8	2 4 8
× 4	× 4	× 4
8 4 8	8 7 2	9 9 2

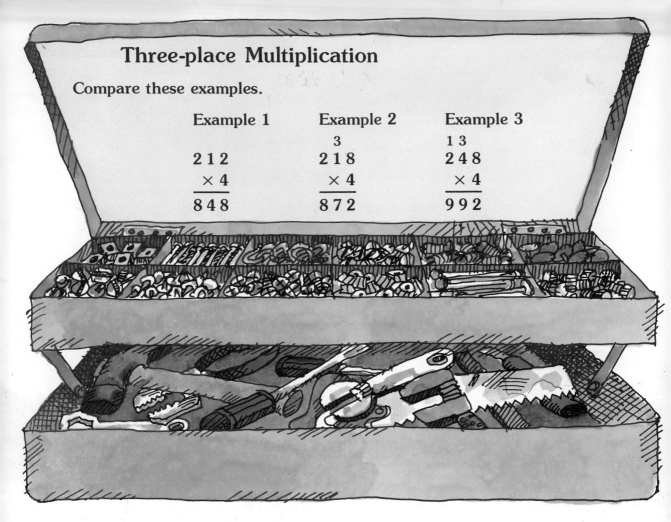

a Multiply.

1. 2   2. 12   3. 212   4. 4   5. 34   6. 234
   ×3   ×3   ×3   ×2   ×2   ×2

7. 6   8. 16   9. 216   10. 5   11. 45   12. 345
   ×4   ×4   ×4   ×2   ×2   ×2

13. 3   14. 63   15. 263   16. 7   17. 27   18. 327
    ×4   ×4   ×4   ×4   ×4   ×4

19. 223   20. 223   21. 223   22. 223   23. 223   24. 223
    ×2   ×3   ×4   ×5   ×6   ×7

b Multiply

25. 194 ×3	26. 137 ×5	27. 246 ×2	28. 375 ×7	29. 484 ×3	30. 285 ×4
31. 223 ×8	32. 494 ×6	33. 153 ×4	34. 429 ×9	35. 348 ×2	36. 176 ×5
37. 462 ×7	38. 218 ×3	39. 256 ×8	40. 263 ×6	41. 374 ×9	42. 449 ×4
43. 707 ×2	44. 516 ×5	45. 335 ×6	46. 436 ×8	47. 358 ×3	48. 186 ×9
49. 409 ×7	50. 238 ×4	51. 429 ×5	52. 517 ×6	53. 368 ×9	54. 604 ×8

c Solve.

55. The Super Speedy Donut Machine needs 6 hole punchers. How many punchers are needed to make 314 machines?

56. The Monster Model Super Speedy is held together by 485 bolts. How many bolts are needed for 5 machines?

57. The Midget Model has 5 rollers in it. How many rollers are in 326 Midget Models?

Four-place Multiplication

We multiply thousands as we did ones, tens, and hundreds.

Example 1

$$4321 \times 2 = 8642$$

Example 2

$$\overset{1}{4327} \times 2 = 8654$$

Example 3

$$\overset{1\ 1}{4367} \times 2 = 8734$$

Example 4

$$\overset{1\ 1\ 1}{4567} \times 2 = 9134$$

a Multiply.

1. 3 ×2	2. 23 ×2	3. 423 ×2	4. 1423 ×2	5. 6423 ×2
6. 7 ×4	7. 17 ×4	8. 217 ×4	9. 2217 ×4	10. 8217 ×4
11. 8 ×3	12. 68 ×3	13. 268 ×3	14. 1268 ×3	15. 9268 ×3
16. 9 ×5	17. 49 ×5	18. 649 ×5	19. 1649 ×5	20. 5649 ×5
21. 3000 ×3	22. 3002 ×3	23. 3007 ×3	24. 3020 ×3	25. 3070 ×3

b Multiply.

26. 3062 ×4	27. 8156 ×5	28. 2963 ×3	29. 3862 ×6	30. 3884 ×7
31. 9306 ×2	32. 4059 ×8	33. 9742 ×5	34. 4825 ×2	35. 2785 ×8
36. 4773 ×6	37. 5317 ×4	38. 1834 ×9	39. 2647 ×7	40. 9158 ×4
41. 6048 ×5	42. 3714 ×2	43. 9760 ×7	44. 4935 ×9	45. 1674 ×8
46. 1764 ×3	47. 1695 ×7	48. 3573 ×5	49. 9850 ×3	50. 5806 ×9
51. 5914 ×6	52. 7046 ×4	53. 6805 ×6	54. 6727 ×9	55. 3863 ×8

c Solve.

56. The press prints 7496 papers in a day.
How many papers are printed in 5 days?

57. About 4250 words are on a page of the newspaper.
About how many words are on 4 pages of the newspaper?

58. Two sheets of paper are used for each copy of <u>Hometown News</u>. How many sheets of paper are used for 2500 copies?

Multiplication with Money

When we multiply dollars and cents by ones, the answer is dollars and cents.

$$
\begin{array}{r}
\overset{1\ \ 1}{\$\,3\,.\,8\,9} \\
\times\ 2 \\
\hline
\$\,7\,.\,7\,8
\end{array}
\qquad
\begin{array}{r}
\overset{2\ \ 1}{\$\,1\,7\,.\,2\,5} \\
\times\ 3 \\
\hline
\$\,5\,1\,.\,7\,5
\end{array}
\qquad
\begin{array}{r}
\overset{3}{\$\ \,.\,6\,9} \\
\times\ 4 \\
\hline
\$\,2\,.\,7\,6
\end{array}
$$

a Multiply.

1. $.25 ×3	2. $1.25 ×3	3. $6.25 ×3	4. $16.25 ×3	5. $36.25 ×3
6. $.49 ×2	7. $3.49 ×2	8. $5.49 ×2	9. $25.49 ×2	10. $50.49 ×2
11. $.50 ×3	12. $2.50 ×3	13. $8.50 ×3	14. $18.50 ×3	15. $27.50 ×3
16. $.05 ×5	17. $1.05 ×5	18. $6.05 ×5	19. $12.05 ×5	20. $65.05 ×5

156

b What is the cost?

21. 2 toasters at $13.88 each

22. 3 fans at $16.67 each

23. 4 mixers at $20.45 each

24. 6 irons at $11.98 each

25. 9 clocks at $10.49 each

26. 5 trays at $14.96 each

c Estimate the cost by rounding to the nearest dollar before you multiply.

27. 7 radios at $27.46 each

28. 4 lamps at $18.77 each

29. 3 timers at $10.39 each

30. 8 fans at $15.63 each

Review B (pages 150–157)

1. 324 ×2	2. 123 ×4	3. 216 ×6	4. 308 ×3
5. 248 ×3	6. 187 ×9	7. 184 ×6	8. 555 ×2
9. 3132 ×3	10. 4329 ×2	11. 3068 ×5	12. 4782 ×9
13. $.87 ×3	14. $4.68 ×2	15. $5.88 ×3	16. $12.25 ×4

Extra practice on p. 323

Problem Solving   Problem • Plan • Arithmetic • Answer

Understand the problem.	What do you know? What do you want to know?

Sometimes we get numbers from a graph to solve a problem.

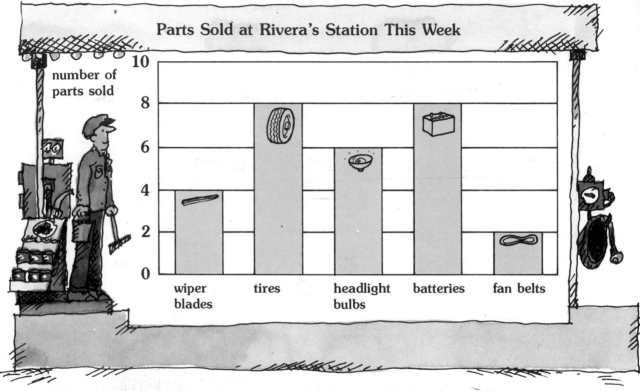

Parts Sold at Rivera's Station This Week

number of parts sold

The graph shows that the station sold 4 wiper blades this week.

1. Fan belts sell for $3.69 each. What was the value of the fan belt sales this week?

2. The price of a headlight bulb is $4.78. What was the value of the headlight bulb sales this week?

3. Tires sell for $34.99 each. Estimate this week's tire sales to the nearest dollar.

4. Batteries cost $40.53 each. Were battery sales about $320 this week?

Unit Test

Multiply. (pages 140–143)

1. 10 ×2	2. 100 ×5	3. 1000 ×4	4. 50 ×3	5. 300 ×3	6. 2000 ×4

Multiply. (pages 144–147)

7. 23 ×3	8. 72 ×4	9. 29 ×2	10. 35 ×3	11. 36 ×8	12. 99 ×9

Estimate the cost of 4 spark plugs. (pages 148–149)

13. 59¢ each   14. 63¢ each   15. 76¢ each   16. 98¢ each

Multiply. (pages 150–153)

17. 132 ×3	18. 224 ×4	19. 209 ×3	20. 134 ×5	21. 468 ×3

Multiply. (pages 154–157)

22. 3132 ×3	23. 5427 ×5	24. 1674 ×6	25. $2.39 ×3	26. $46.57 ×2

Solve. (page 158)

27. This year twice as many used cars were sold as in 1970. How many were sold this year?

28. Next year's sales goal is twice the 1975 sales. What is the goal?

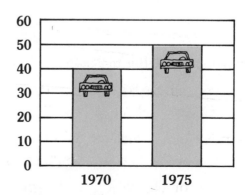

Used Cars Sold at Carlotta's Car Lot

159

Taking Another Look

Pages 140–143

$$\begin{array}{r} 6 \\ \times 4 \\ \hline 24 \end{array} \qquad \begin{array}{r} 60 \\ \times 4 \\ \hline 240 \end{array}$$

$$\begin{array}{r} 600 \\ \times 4 \\ \hline 2400 \end{array} \qquad \begin{array}{r} 6000 \\ \times 4 \\ \hline 24{,}000 \end{array}$$

Multiply.

1. $\begin{array}{r} 3 \\ \times 2 \\ \hline \end{array}$ 2. $\begin{array}{r} 30 \\ \times 2 \\ \hline \end{array}$ 3. $\begin{array}{r} 8 \\ \times 9 \\ \hline \end{array}$ 4. $\begin{array}{r} 8000 \\ \times 9 \\ \hline \end{array}$

5. $\begin{array}{r} 30 \\ \times 3 \\ \hline \end{array}$ 6. $\begin{array}{r} 600 \\ \times 5 \\ \hline \end{array}$ 7. $\begin{array}{r} 40 \\ \times 2 \\ \hline \end{array}$ 8. $\begin{array}{r} 9000 \\ \times 7 \\ \hline \end{array}$

9. $\begin{array}{r} 100 \\ \times 5 \\ \hline \end{array}$ 10. $\begin{array}{r} 4000 \\ \times 8 \\ \hline \end{array}$ 11. $\begin{array}{r} 700 \\ \times 6 \\ \hline \end{array}$ 12. $\begin{array}{r} 60 \\ \times 8 \\ \hline \end{array}$

Pages 144–147

$$\begin{array}{r} 4 \\ 3\,6 \\ \times 7 \\ \hline 2\,5\,2 \end{array}$$

Multiply the 6 ones by 7. Give the 4 tens to the tens.
Multiply the 3 tens by 7. Add the 4 tens.

Multiply.

1. $\begin{array}{r} 10 \\ \times 4 \\ \hline \end{array}$ 2. $\begin{array}{r} 12 \\ \times 4 \\ \hline \end{array}$ 3. $\begin{array}{r} 16 \\ \times 4 \\ \hline \end{array}$ 4. $\begin{array}{r} 36 \\ \times 4 \\ \hline \end{array}$

5. $\begin{array}{r} 13 \\ \times 2 \\ \hline \end{array}$ 6. $\begin{array}{r} 47 \\ \times 6 \\ \hline \end{array}$ 7. $\begin{array}{r} 18 \\ \times 9 \\ \hline \end{array}$ 8. $\begin{array}{r} 61 \\ \times 5 \\ \hline \end{array}$

9. $\begin{array}{r} 22 \\ \times 2 \\ \hline \end{array}$ 10. $\begin{array}{r} 38 \\ \times 4 \\ \hline \end{array}$ 11. $\begin{array}{r} 52 \\ \times 3 \\ \hline \end{array}$ 12. $\begin{array}{r} 39 \\ \times 7 \\ \hline \end{array}$

13. $\begin{array}{r} 58 \\ \times 3 \\ \hline \end{array}$ 14. $\begin{array}{r} 93 \\ \times 6 \\ \hline \end{array}$ 15. $\begin{array}{r} 85 \\ \times 9 \\ \hline \end{array}$ 16. $\begin{array}{r} 64 \\ \times 8 \\ \hline \end{array}$

Pages 148–149

$$\begin{array}{r} 78¢ \\ \times 3 \\ \hline \end{array} \qquad \begin{array}{r} 80¢ \\ \times 3 \\ \hline 240¢ \end{array}$$

Estimate the cost.

1. 2 at 48¢ each   2. 6 at 37¢ each

3. 8 at 79¢ each   4. 5 at 96¢ each

5. 3 at $18 each   6. 4 at $55 each

Pages 150–153

$$\begin{array}{r} 1\;1 \\ 3\;2\;3 \\ \times\;6 \\ \hline 1\;9\;3\;8 \end{array}$$

Multiply.

1. 100 ×4	2. 123 ×4	3. 153 ×4	4. 453 ×4
5. 518 ×3	6. 463 ×4	7. 189 ×5	8. 227 ×2
9. 647 ×8	10. 708 ×5	11. 349 ×2	12. 907 ×9

Pages 154–157

$$\begin{array}{r} 3\;2\;4 \\ 5\;6\;4\;9 \\ \times\;5 \\ \hline 2\;8,2\;4\;5 \end{array}$$

Multiply.

1. 3412 ×2	2. 3418 ×2	3. 3468 ×2	4. 3568 ×2
5. 1638 ×5	6. 2091 ×6	7. 3845 ×6	8. 6278 ×3
9. $6.25 ×4	10. $.68 ×3	11. $36.25 ×7	12. $8.09 ×6

Page 158

1. **Problem**
2. **Plan**
3. **Arithmetic**
4. **Answer**

Solve.

1. What is the total value of my jazz records at $4.59 each?

2. Estimate to the nearest dollar the total value of my folk records at $3.97 each.

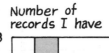
Number of records I have

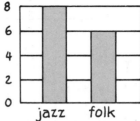

Something Extra • SELLING COOKIES

Anne James
name
4 Apple Way
address

SALES RECORD CHART

PRICE $ 1.25 PER BOX

CUSTOMER	Mint Thins	Orange Cremes	Choco Cremes	Sugar Cookies	Peanut Butter	Total Boxes	Amount Due
Mom	2	1	2	1	2	?	?
Uncle John	1	1				?	?
McHales	1		1	2	2	?	?
Romeros		2		1		?	?
Akawas	1	1		1	1	?	?
Griffins	1	2	1		1	?	?
Albertis			1			?	?
Fines	3	1	2	1		?	?
					TOTAL ▶		?

1. Who is selling cookies?

2. Who is the first customer?

3. How many boxes of cookies does Mom buy?

4. The price of one box is $1.25. How much does Mom pay Anne?

5. What are the missing numbers in the Sales Record Chart for each of the other customers?

6. Uncle John pays for his cookies with a five-dollar bill. What is his change?

7. What kind of cookie is the best seller?

8. What is the total value of the Mint Thins sold by Anne?

Reviewing Needed Skills

Write the standard form.

1. $90 + 6$
2. $50 + 3$
3. $700 + 50 + 4$
4. $300 + 60 + 9$
5. 8 tens
6. 3 tens 2 ones
7. 3 hundreds 6 tens 3 ones
8. 2 hundreds 7 tens 9 ones

Write the digit that is in the tens' place.

9. 74
10. 97
11. 15
12. 21
13. 236
14. 785
15. 670
16. 259
17. 305
18. 516

Add or subtract.

19.	20.	21.	22.	23.	24.
23	19	65	72	47	83
$+\ 6$	$+17$	-43	-66	$+35$	$+68$

25.	26.	27.	28.	29.	30.
92	58	41	77	28	43
$-\ 7$	-18	$+39$	$+66$	$-\ 9$	-27

31.	32.	33.	34.	35.	36.
84	59	64	37	91	98
$+16$	$+34$	-58	$-\ 8$	$+\ 9$	$+\ 3$

Multiply or divide.

37. 8×7
38. 4×6
39. 3×9
40. 8×8
41. 5×5
42. 8×4
43. 9×9
44. 9×5
45. $9\overline{)72}$
46. $4\overline{)36}$
47. $6\overline{)42}$
48. $3\overline{)15}$
49. $2\overline{)16}$
50. $7\overline{)49}$
51. $6\overline{)30}$
52. $3\overline{)21}$

53.	54.	55.	56.
20	42	38	29
$\times 3$	$\times 4$	$\times 2$	$\times 5$

UNIT 8

Division with Remainders

15 tent pegs. How many groups of six?

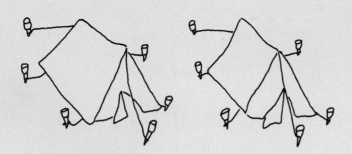

2 sixes

$2 \times 6 = 12$

3 extra pegs

$12 + 3 = 15$

Division

a Answer the question.

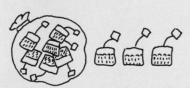

1. How many twos in 9 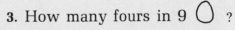 ?
2. How many extra 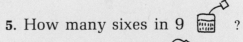 ?

3. How many fours in 9 ?
4. How many extra ◯ ?

5. How many sixes in 9 🧂 ?
6. How many extra 🧂 ?

7. How many fives in 11 CANDY ?
8. How many extra CANDY ?

165

Division with Remainders

How many sixes in 15?

To divide 15 by 6,
we subtract as many
sixes as we can.

Subtract 2 × 6.

$$\begin{array}{r} 2 \\ 6{\overline{\smash{)}\,15}} \\ -12 \\ \hline 3 \end{array}$$ Remainder

The quotient is 2. The remainder is 3. We may write 2 R3.

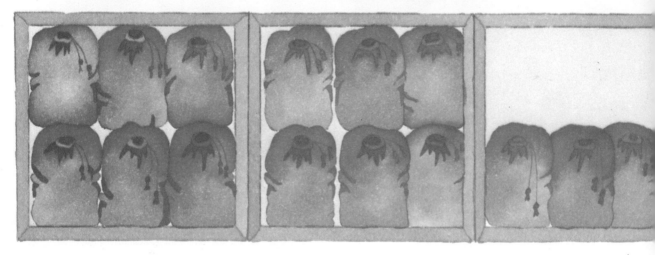

a Divide.

1. $\begin{array}{r} 6{\overline{\smash{)}\,7}} \\ -6 \\ \hline 1 \end{array}$

2. $\begin{array}{r} 6{\overline{\smash{)}\,8}} \\ -6 \\ \hline 2 \end{array}$

3. $\begin{array}{r} 6{\overline{\smash{)}\,9}} \\ -6 \\ \hline 3 \end{array}$

4. $\begin{array}{r} 6{\overline{\smash{)}\,10}} \\ -6 \\ \hline 4 \end{array}$

5. $\begin{array}{r} 6{\overline{\smash{)}\,11}} \\ -6 \\ \hline 5 \end{array}$

6. $\begin{array}{r} 6{\overline{\smash{)}\,13}} \\ -12 \\ \hline \end{array}$

7. $\begin{array}{r} 6{\overline{\smash{)}\,14}} \\ -12 \\ \hline \end{array}$

8. $\begin{array}{r} 6{\overline{\smash{)}\,15}} \\ -12 \\ \hline \end{array}$

9. $\begin{array}{r} 6{\overline{\smash{)}\,16}} \\ -12 \\ \hline \end{array}$

10. $\begin{array}{r} 6{\overline{\smash{)}\,17}} \\ -12 \\ \hline \end{array}$

11. $\begin{array}{r} 2 \\ 3{\overline{\smash{)}\,8}} \\ - \\ \hline \end{array}$

12. $\begin{array}{r} 3 \\ 4{\overline{\smash{)}\,14}} \\ - \\ \hline \end{array}$

13. $\begin{array}{r} 7 \\ 3{\overline{\smash{)}\,22}} \\ - \\ \hline \end{array}$

14. $\begin{array}{r} 4 \\ 8{\overline{\smash{)}\,39}} \\ - \\ \hline \end{array}$

15. $\begin{array}{r} 9 \\ 9{\overline{\smash{)}\,88}} \\ - \\ \hline \end{array}$

b Divide.

16. $4 \overline{)19}$ 17. $3 \overline{)16}$ 18. $6 \overline{)55}$ 19. $5 \overline{)43}$ 20. $7 \overline{)24}$ 21. $2 \overline{)19}$

22. $2 \overline{)13}$ 23. $5 \overline{)27}$ 24. $7 \overline{)45}$ 25. $7 \overline{)33}$ 26. $9 \overline{)50}$ 27. $9 \overline{)75}$

28. $3 \overline{)29}$ 29. $5 \overline{)13}$ 30. $6 \overline{)27}$ 31. $4 \overline{)33}$ 32. $8 \overline{)54}$ 33. $8 \overline{)21}$

34. $4 \overline{)22}$ 35. $6 \overline{)37}$ 36. $9 \overline{)38}$ 37. $8 \overline{)63}$ 38. $3 \overline{)19}$ 39. $2 \overline{)15}$

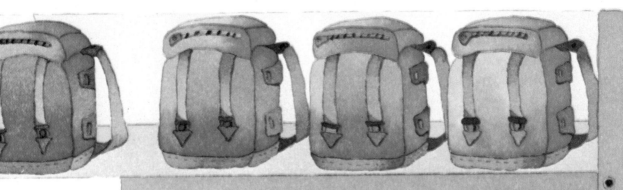

c Solve.

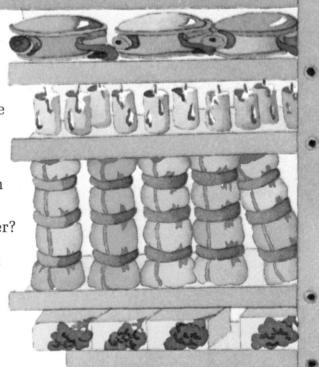

40. How many $3 canteens can we buy with $25? How much money is left?

41. How many 8¢ candles can we get with 75¢? What is our change?

42. How many 9 g servings are in an 84 g pack of grape drink? How many grams are left over?

43. How many $7 foam pads can we get with $36? How much money is left?

44. How many $5 stuff bags can we get for the price of a $21 backpack? How much money left?

Tens as Quotients

3 twos are in 6.

$$\begin{array}{r} 3 \\ 2\overline{)\ 6} \\ -6 \\ \hline 0 \end{array}$$

The quotient is 3.
The remainder is 0.

30 twos are in 60.

$$\begin{array}{r} 30 \\ 2\overline{)\ 60} \\ -60 \\ \hline 0 \end{array}$$

The quotient is 30.
The remainder is 0.

a Divide.

1. $\begin{array}{r} 2\overline{)\ 8} \\ -8 \\ \hline 0 \end{array}$

2. $\begin{array}{r} 2\overline{)\ 80} \\ -80 \\ \hline 0 \end{array}$

3. $\begin{array}{r} 2\overline{)\ 4} \\ -4 \\ \hline 0 \end{array}$

4. $\begin{array}{r} 2\overline{)\ 40} \\ -40 \\ \hline 0 \end{array}$

5. $\begin{array}{r} 2\overline{)\ 16} \\ -16 \\ \hline 0 \end{array}$

6. $\begin{array}{r} 2\overline{)\ 160} \\ -160 \\ \hline 0 \end{array}$

7. $\begin{array}{r} 5\overline{)\ 25} \\ -25 \\ \hline 0 \end{array}$

8. $\begin{array}{r} 5\overline{)\ 250} \\ -250 \\ \hline 0 \end{array}$

9. $3\overline{)6}$

10. $3\overline{)60}$

11. $7\overline{)21}$

12. $7\overline{)210}$

168

b Divide.

13. $3\overline{)90}$ 14. $8\overline{)240}$

15. $2\overline{)140}$ 16. $4\overline{)40}$

17. $3\overline{)150}$ 18. $2\overline{)180}$

19. $4\overline{)280}$ 20. $2\overline{)60}$

21. $6\overline{)240}$ 22. $9\overline{)360}$

23. $5\overline{)350}$ 24. $8\overline{)80}$

25. $3\overline{)270}$ 26. $9\overline{)450}$

27. $6\overline{)60}$ 28. $7\overline{)210}$

29. $2\overline{)120}$ 30. $9\overline{)540}$

c Round to the nearest ten dollars to solve.

31. A ski rack costs $39. Two sisters share the cost equally. About how much does each pay?

32. Eight skiers share the cost of $156 worth of supplies. About how much does each pay?

33. Mike is saving to buy a $19 sweater. About how much will he need to save each week to buy it in 2 weeks?

34. A family of 4 rents skis for $38 in all. About how much is the rental cost per person?

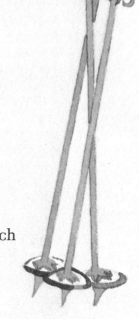

Two-stage Division

We divide 68 by 2 in two stages.

First we divide the tens.   **Then we divide the ones.**

Divide 6 by 2.
Subtract 3 × 2.

$$
\begin{array}{r}
3 \\
2\overline{)\,68} \\
-6 \\
\hline
0
\end{array}
$$

Divide 8 by 2.
Subtract 4 × 2.

$$
\begin{array}{r}
34 \\
2\overline{)\,68} \\
-6\!\downarrow \\
\hline
08 \\
-8 \\
\hline
0
\end{array}
$$

The quotient is 34.

a Divide.

1.
$$
\begin{array}{r}
1\; \\
2\overline{)\,22} \\
-2 \\
\hline
02 \\
-2 \\
\hline
0
\end{array}
$$

2.
$$
\begin{array}{r}
1\; \\
2\overline{)\,24} \\
-2 \\
\hline
04 \\
-4 \\
\hline
0
\end{array}
$$

3.
$$
\begin{array}{r}
1\; \\
2\overline{)\,26} \\
-2 \\
\hline
06 \\
-6 \\
\hline
0
\end{array}
$$

4.
$$
\begin{array}{r}
1\; \\
2\overline{)\,28} \\
-2 \\
\hline
08 \\
-8 \\
\hline
0
\end{array}
$$

5.
$$
\begin{array}{r}
2\; \\
2\overline{)\,42} \\
-4 \\
\hline
02 \\
-2 \\
\hline
0
\end{array}
$$

6.
$$
\begin{array}{r}
2\; \\
2\overline{)\,44} \\
-4 \\
\hline
04 \\
-4 \\
\hline
0
\end{array}
$$

7.
$$
\begin{array}{r}
3\; \\
2\overline{)\,46} \\
-4 \\
\hline
06 \\
-6 \\
\hline
0
\end{array}
$$

8.
$$
\begin{array}{r}
2\overline{)\,48} \\
-4 \\
\hline
08 \\
-8 \\
\hline
0
\end{array}
$$

9.
$$
\begin{array}{r}
2\overline{)\,82} \\
-8 \\
\hline
02 \\
-2 \\
\hline
0
\end{array}
$$

10.
$$
\begin{array}{r}
2\overline{)\,84} \\
-8 \\
\hline
04 \\
-4 \\
\hline
0
\end{array}
$$

11. $2\overline{)\,86}$

12. $2\overline{)\,88}$

13. $3\overline{)\,93}$

14. $3\overline{)\,96}$

15. $3\overline{)\,99}$

b Divide.

16. $3\overline{)69}$　　17. $2\overline{)64}$　　18. $8\overline{)88}$　　19. $4\overline{)84}$　　20. $2\overline{)62}$　　21. $3\overline{)36}$

22. $4\overline{)48}$　　23. $3\overline{)66}$　　24. $2\overline{)68}$　　25. $5\overline{)55}$　　26. $2\overline{)86}$　　27. $4\overline{)88}$

28. $9\overline{)99}$　　29. $3\overline{)39}$　　30. $2\overline{)82}$　　31. $3\overline{)63}$　　32. $6\overline{)66}$　　33. $2\overline{)66}$

c Solve.

34. 24 marshmallows
    2 for each person
    How many people having two?

35. 36 people canoeing
    3 people in each canoe
    How many canoes?

36. 88 km to paddle
    8 km each day
    How many days to paddle?

37. 48 tent pegs
    4 pegs in each tent
    How many tents?

To divide or not to divide

The campers have 24 clothespins. What is the greatest
number of towels they can hang on a line if each towel
needs 2 clothespins to hold it up?

Draw a picture to help you answer.

Two-stage Division

We divide 78 by 2 in two stages.

First we divide the tens.

Divide 7 by 2.   2)$\overline{78}$ 3

Subtract 3 × 2.

$$\begin{array}{r} 3 \\ 2\overline{)\,78} \\ -6 \\ \hline 1 \end{array}$$

▶

Then we divide the ones.

$$\begin{array}{r} 39 \\ 2\overline{)\,78} \\ -6\downarrow \\ \hline 18 \\ -18 \\ \hline 0 \end{array}$$

Divide 18 by 2.

Subtract 9 × 2.

The quotient is 39.

a Divide.

1. $\begin{array}{r} 1\blacksquare \\ 2\overline{)\,30} \\ -2 \\ \hline 10 \\ -10 \\ \hline 0 \end{array}$

2. $\begin{array}{r} 1\blacksquare \\ 2\overline{)\,32} \\ -2 \\ \hline 12 \\ -12 \\ \hline 0 \end{array}$

3. $\begin{array}{r} 1\blacksquare \\ 2\overline{)\,34} \\ -2 \\ \hline 14 \\ -14 \\ \hline 0 \end{array}$

4. $\begin{array}{r} 1\blacksquare \\ 2\overline{)\,36} \\ -2 \\ \hline 16 \\ -16 \\ \hline 0 \end{array}$

5. $\begin{array}{r} 1\blacksquare \\ 2\overline{)\,38} \\ -2 \\ \hline 18 \\ -18 \\ \hline 0 \end{array}$

6. $\begin{array}{r} 1\blacksquare \\ 3\overline{)\,42} \\ -3 \\ \hline 12 \\ -12 \\ \hline 0 \end{array}$

7. $\begin{array}{r} \blacksquare5 \\ 3\overline{)\,45} \\ -3 \\ \hline 15 \\ -15 \\ \hline 0 \end{array}$

8. $\begin{array}{r} \blacksquare\blacksquare \\ 3\overline{)\,48} \\ -3 \\ \hline 18 \\ -18 \\ \hline 0 \end{array}$

9. $\begin{array}{r} \blacksquare\blacksquare \\ 3\overline{)\,51} \\ -3 \\ \hline 21 \\ -21 \\ \hline 0 \end{array}$

10. $\begin{array}{r} \blacksquare\blacksquare \\ 3\overline{)\,54} \\ -3 \\ \hline 24 \\ -24 \\ \hline 0 \end{array}$

11. $4\overline{)\,60}$

12. $4\overline{)\,64}$

13. $4\overline{)\,68}$

14. $4\overline{)\,72}$

15. $4\overline{)\,76}$

b Divide.

16. $4\overline{)52}$ 17. $3\overline{)75}$ 18. $2\overline{)54}$ 19. $5\overline{)65}$ 20. $4\overline{)96}$ 21. $6\overline{)84}$

22. $3\overline{)72}$ 23. $6\overline{)96}$ 24. $4\overline{)56}$ 25. $5\overline{)60}$ 26. $7\overline{)84}$ 27. $2\overline{)56}$

28. $5\overline{)85}$ 29. $7\overline{)91}$ 30. $2\overline{)98}$ 31. $4\overline{)92}$ 32. $8\overline{)96}$ 33. $5\overline{)80}$

34. $6\overline{)90}$ 35. $2\overline{)52}$ 36. $7\overline{)98}$ 37. $5\overline{)90}$ 38. $2\overline{)76}$ 39. $6\overline{)78}$

40. $3\overline{)78}$ 41. $3\overline{)57}$ 42. $5\overline{)70}$

43. $6\overline{)72}$ 44. $5\overline{)95}$ 45. $5\overline{)75}$

Review A   (pages 164–173)

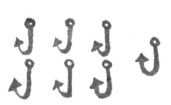

1. How many twos in 7 ?
2. How many extra ?
3. How many sixes in 7 ?
4. How many extra ?

5. $2\overline{)5}$ 6. $6\overline{)14}$ 7. $5\overline{)29}$ 8. $8\overline{)50}$

9. $2\overline{)40}$ 10. $3\overline{)90}$ 11. $2\overline{)160}$ 12. $5\overline{)150}$

13. $2\overline{)48}$ 14. $3\overline{)96}$ 15. $9\overline{)99}$ 16. $4\overline{)48}$

17. $2\overline{)36}$ 18. $3\overline{)54}$ 19. $6\overline{)96}$ 20. $5\overline{)70}$

Extra practice on p. 324

Division with Remainders

We divide 58 by 3 in two stages.

Divide 5 by 3. $3\overline{)58}$ with quotient 1
Subtract 1 × 3. -3
                      2

→

                    $3\overline{)58}$ with quotient 19
                     -3
Divide 28 by 3. 28
Subtract 9 × 3. -27
                        1

The quotient is 19. The remainder is 1.
We may write 19 R1.

a Divide.

1. $6\overline{)73}$ 2. $6\overline{)74}$ 3. $6\overline{)75}$ 4. $6\overline{)76}$ 5. $6\overline{)77}$
   -6 -6 -6 -6 -6
   13 14 15 16 17
   -12 -12 -12 -12 -12

6. $6\overline{)79}$ 7. $6\overline{)80}$ 8. $6\overline{)81}$ 9. $6\overline{)82}$ 10. $6\overline{)83}$

11. $2\overline{)25}$ 12. $2\overline{)35}$ 13. $2\overline{)45}$ 14. $2\overline{)55}$ 15. $2\overline{)65}$

16. $4\overline{)97}$ 17. $5\overline{)97}$ 18. $6\overline{)97}$ 19. $7\overline{)97}$ 20. $8\overline{)97}$

174

b Divide.

21. $2\overline{)97}$ 22. $3\overline{)43}$ 23. $8\overline{)89}$ 24. $5\overline{)72}$ 25. $6\overline{)85}$ 26. $4\overline{)53}$

27. $2\overline{)49}$ 28. $3\overline{)58}$ 29. $5\overline{)81}$ 30. $7\overline{)85}$ 31. $7\overline{)92}$ 32. $3\overline{)47}$

33. $7\overline{)99}$ 34. $4\overline{)69}$ 35. $8\overline{)92}$ 36. $5\overline{)73}$ 37. $4\overline{)85}$ 38. $3\overline{)67}$

39. $4\overline{)95}$ 40. $6\overline{)87}$ 41. $5\overline{)78}$ 42. $8\overline{)91}$ 43. $7\overline{)98}$ 44. $6\overline{)76}$

c Solve.

45. How many groups of 4 in 49 campers? How many extra campers?

46. How many pairs of socks in 25 socks all the same? How many extra socks?

47. How many teams of 7 in 95 campers? How many not on a team?

48. How many pairs of swimmers in 35 swimmers? How many extra?

Two-stage Division

We divide 126 by 3 in two stages.

Divide 12 by 3.
Subtract 4 × 3.

$$\begin{array}{r} 4 \\ 3)\overline{126} \\ -12 \\ \hline 0 \end{array}$$

➤

$$\begin{array}{r} 42 \\ 3)\overline{126} \\ -12 \\ \hline 06 \\ -6 \\ \hline 0 \end{array}$$

Divide 6 by 3.
Subtract 2 × 3.

The quotient is 42.

a Divide.

1. $\begin{array}{r} 6 \\ 2)\overline{124} \\ -12 \\ \hline 04 \\ -4 \\ \hline 0 \end{array}$
2. $\begin{array}{r} 6 \\ 2)\overline{126} \\ -12 \\ \hline 06 \\ -6 \\ \hline 0 \end{array}$
3. $\begin{array}{r} 4 \\ 2)\overline{128} \\ -12 \\ \hline 08 \\ -8 \\ \hline 0 \end{array}$
4. $\begin{array}{r} 4 \\ 2)\overline{148} \\ -14 \\ \hline 08 \\ -8 \\ \hline 0 \end{array}$
5. $\begin{array}{r} \\ 2)\overline{168} \\ -16 \\ \hline 08 \\ -8 \\ \hline 0 \end{array}$

6. $3)\overline{213}$
7. $3)\overline{216}$
8. $3)\overline{219}$
9. $3)\overline{249}$
10. $3)\overline{279}$

11. $5)\overline{155}$
12. $5)\overline{205}$
13. $5)\overline{255}$
14. $5)\overline{305}$
15. $5)\overline{355}$

16. $4)\overline{124}$
17. $4)\overline{128}$
18. $4)\overline{164}$
19. $4)\overline{168}$
20. $4)\overline{204}$

176

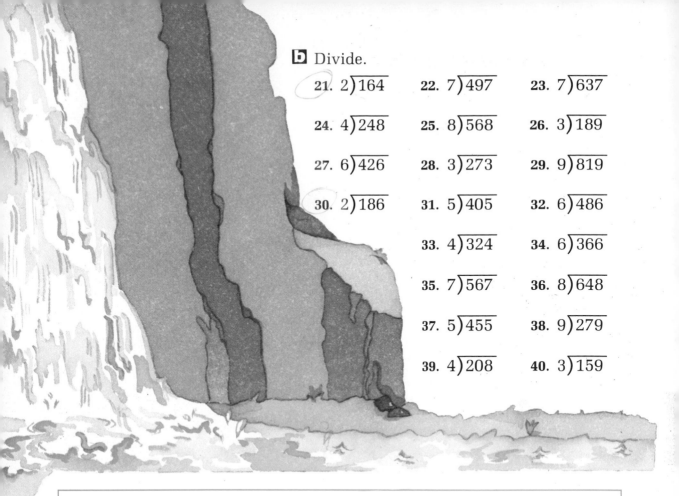

b Divide.

21. $2\overline{)164}$ 22. $7\overline{)497}$ 23. $7\overline{)637}$

24. $4\overline{)248}$ 25. $8\overline{)568}$ 26. $3\overline{)189}$

27. $6\overline{)426}$ 28. $3\overline{)273}$ 29. $9\overline{)819}$

30. $2\overline{)186}$ 31. $5\overline{)405}$ 32. $6\overline{)486}$

             33. $4\overline{)324}$ 34. $6\overline{)366}$

             35. $7\overline{)567}$ 36. $8\overline{)648}$

             37. $5\overline{)455}$ 38. $9\overline{)279}$

             39. $4\overline{)208}$ 40. $3\overline{)159}$

Let's compare

The waterfall is 18 m wide.
The tree is 2 m wide.

Compare widths by subtraction.
18 − 2 = 16
The waterfall is 16 m wider.

Compare widths by division.
18 ÷ 2 = 9
The waterfall is 9 times as
wide as the tree.

The waterfall is 105 m high.
The tree is 5 m high. Compare
their heights in two ways.

177

Two-stage Division

We divide 135 by 3 in two stages.

Divide 13 by 3.
Subtract 4 × 3.

$$
\begin{array}{r}
4 \\
3\overline{)\,135} \\
-12 \\
\hline
1
\end{array}
$$

▶

$$
\begin{array}{r}
45 \\
3\overline{)\,135} \\
-12\!\downarrow \\
\hline
15 \\
\end{array}
$$

Divide 15 by 3.
Subtract 5 × 3.

$$
\begin{array}{r}
15 \\
-15 \\
\hline
0
\end{array}
$$

The quotient is 45.

We can travel 135 km in 3 days if we travel 45 km each day.

GILA BEND
135 km

a Divide.

1.
$$
\begin{array}{r}
5 \\
3\overline{)\,165} \\
-15 \\
\hline
15 \\
-15 \\
\hline
0
\end{array}
$$

2.
$$
\begin{array}{r}
5 \\
3\overline{)\,168} \\
-15 \\
\hline
18 \\
-18 \\
\hline
0
\end{array}
$$

3.
$$
\begin{array}{r}
7 \\
3\overline{)\,171} \\
-15 \\
\hline
21 \\
-21 \\
\hline
0
\end{array}
$$

4.
$$
\begin{array}{r}
8 \\
3\overline{)\,174} \\
-15 \\
\hline
24 \\
-24 \\
\hline
0
\end{array}
$$

5.
$$
\begin{array}{r}
3\overline{)\,177} \\
-15 \\
\hline
27 \\
-27 \\
\hline
0
\end{array}
$$

6. $6\overline{)\,210}$

7. $6\overline{)\,216}$

8. $6\overline{)\,222}$

9. $6\overline{)\,228}$

10. $6\overline{)\,234}$

11. $7\overline{)\,371}$

12. $7\overline{)\,378}$

13. $7\overline{)\,385}$

14. $7\overline{)\,392}$

15. $7\overline{)\,399}$

178

b Divide.

16. $9\overline{)468}$ 17. $5\overline{)440}$ 18. $8\overline{)736}$ 19. $4\overline{)352}$ 20. $5\overline{)225}$

21. $4\overline{)176}$ 22. $8\overline{)576}$ 23. $5\overline{)435}$ 24. $3\overline{)291}$ 25. $7\overline{)455}$

26. $2\overline{)154}$ 27. $7\overline{)364}$ 28. $6\overline{)552}$ 29. $6\overline{)498}$ 30. $4\overline{)252}$

31. $3\overline{)282}$ 32. $4\overline{)196}$ 33. $2\overline{)138}$ 34. $6\overline{)204}$ 35. $7\overline{)329}$

36. $3\overline{)174}$ 37. $3\overline{)147}$ 38. $9\overline{)828}$ 39. $8\overline{)232}$ 40. $5\overline{)420}$

Patterns in remainders

$$2\overline{)2} \quad \begin{array}{r} 1 \\ -2 \\ \hline 0 \end{array}$$

$$2\overline{)3} \quad \begin{array}{r} 1 \\ -2 \\ \hline 1 \end{array}$$

$$2\overline{)4} \quad \begin{array}{r} 2 \\ -4 \\ \hline 0 \end{array}$$

$$2\overline{)5} \quad \begin{array}{r} 2 \\ -4 \\ \hline 1 \end{array}$$

1. List the remainders for the examples above. What is the greatest remainder?

2. What is the greatest remainder when any number is divided by 2?

3. List the remainders when you divide 3, 4, 5, 6, 7, and 8 by 3. What is the greatest remainder?

4. What is the greatest remainder when any number is divided by 4?

Division with Remainders

We divide 137 by 3 in two stages.

Divide 13 by 3.   3) 137
Subtract 4 × 3.   − 12
                       1

4
3) 137
− 12

Divide 17 by 3.   17
Subtract 5 × 3.   − 15
                       2

45
3) 137
− 12

The quotient is 45. The remainder is 2.
We may write 45 R2.

a Divide.

1. 6)167   2. 6)166   3. 6)165   4. 6)164   5. 6)163

6. 8)497   7. 8)498   8. 8)499   9. 8)500   10. 8)501

11. 7)447   12. 7)446   13. 7)445   14. 7)444   15. 7)443

16. 9)253   17. 9)254   18. 9)255   19. 9)256   20. 9)257

b Divide.

21. 4)253 22. 5)462 23. 7)537 24. 2)155 25. 6)592

26. 5)174 27. 8)731 28. 3)136 29. 4)290 30. 3)292

31. 9)357 32. 8)234 33. 2)197 34. 6)434 35. 3)131

36. 4)375 37. 5)426 38. 6)373 39. 8)753 40. 7)654

Review B   (pages 174–181)

1. 3)53   2. 5)64   3. 2)97   4. 3)85

5. 2)168   6. 3)159   7. 5)455   8. 6)246

9. 2)178   10. 4)192   11. 6)354   12. 3)291

13. 3)173   14. 5)277   15. 9)883   16. 6)279

Extra practice on p. 325

Problem Solving   Problem • Plan • Arithmetic • Answer

	Understand the problem.	What do you know? What do you want to know?

Some problems do not give you all the facts you need.

The Roberto family takes a 2-hour walk every day to get in shape. How many hours of walking is that in a week?

To solve this problem, you need to know that a week has 7 days. Some facts like this are in the Table of Measures on page 336.

1. We shall be on vacation for 21 days. How many weeks is that?

2. We must call the campground 24 hours before we arrive. How many days is this?

3. We make 3 dozen cookies to bring on our trip. How many cookies is that in all?

4. Which is a longer vacation, 2 weeks or 10 days?

5. The trip takes an hour. We have traveled for 45 minutes. How many minutes do we have left to travel?

6. I spend 3 months of the year in the country and the rest in the city. How many months am I in the city?

Unit Test

Divide.   (pages 164–167)

1. $3\overline{)26}$ 2. $7\overline{)52}$ 3. $4\overline{)33}$ 4. $9\overline{)76}$ 5. $8\overline{)69}$

Divide.   (pages 168–169)

6. $4\overline{)80}$ 7. $7\overline{)350}$ 8. $9\overline{)540}$ 9. $6\overline{)360}$

Divide.   (pages 170–173)

10. $3\overline{)69}$ 11. $4\overline{)84}$ 12. $2\overline{)56}$ 13. $6\overline{)84}$ 14. $5\overline{)75}$

Divide.   (pages 174–175)

15. $4\overline{)57}$ 16. $6\overline{)83}$ 17. $5\overline{)91}$ 18. $3\overline{)74}$

Divide.   (pages 176–179)

19. $2\overline{)148}$ 20. $4\overline{)244}$ 21. $3\overline{)168}$ 22. $5\overline{)270}$ 23. $6\overline{)396}$

Divide.   (pages 180–181)

24. $4\overline{)154}$ 25. $8\overline{)172}$ 26. $5\overline{)369}$ 27. $6\overline{)475}$ 28. $7\overline{)646}$

Solve.   (page 182)

29. We had 14 sunny days of vacation.
How many sunny weeks is that?

30. The family spends 3 hours each day at the beach.
How many minutes is that?

Taking Another Look

Pages 164–167

3 fours are in 14.

Subtract
3 × 4.
Remainder

$$\begin{array}{r} 3 \\ 4\overline{)\ 14} \\ -12 \\ \hline 2 \end{array}$$

Divide.

1. $5\overline{)6}$ 2. $5\overline{)7}$ 3. $5\overline{)8}$ 4. $5\overline{)9}$

5. $4\overline{)14}$ 6. $3\overline{)8}$ 7. $8\overline{)43}$ 8. $9\overline{)78}$

9. $6\overline{)39}$ 10. $7\overline{)57}$ 11. $2\overline{)11}$ 12. $5\overline{)28}$

13. $4\overline{)38}$ 14. $6\overline{)27}$ 15. $3\overline{)19}$ 16. $8\overline{)69}$

Pages 168–169

20 fours are in 80.

$$\begin{array}{r} 20 \\ 4\overline{)\ 80} \\ -80 \\ \hline 0 \end{array}$$

Divide.

1. $3\overline{)6}$ 2. $3\overline{)60}$ 3. $5\overline{)20}$ 4. $5\overline{)200}$

5. $7\overline{)280}$ 6. $8\overline{)320}$ 7. $2\overline{)60}$ 8. $9\overline{)360}$

9. $6\overline{)240}$ 10. $4\overline{)160}$ 11. $5\overline{)350}$ 12. $3\overline{)120}$

13. $9\overline{)630}$ 14. $7\overline{)490}$ 15. $8\overline{)640}$ 16. $6\overline{)480}$

Pages 170–173

Divide in two stages.

Divide 5
by 3.
Divide 24
by 3.

$$\begin{array}{r} 18 \\ 3\overline{)\ 54} \\ -3 \\ \hline 24 \\ -24 \\ \hline 0 \end{array}$$

Divide.

1. $3\overline{)63}$ 2. $3\overline{)66}$ 3. $3\overline{)72}$ 4. $3\overline{)75}$

5. $7\overline{)77}$ 6. $4\overline{)84}$ 7. $2\overline{)62}$ 8. $4\overline{)48}$

9. $3\overline{)96}$ 10. $5\overline{)55}$ 11. $2\overline{)86}$ 12. $3\overline{)69}$

13. $2\overline{)54}$ 14. $3\overline{)81}$ 15. $5\overline{)85}$ 16. $4\overline{)96}$

17. $3\overline{)48}$ 18. $6\overline{)72}$ 19. $8\overline{)96}$ 20. $2\overline{)36}$

21. $7\overline{)98}$ 22. $5\overline{)70}$ 23. $4\overline{)64}$ 24. $6\overline{)84}$

Divide in two stages.

Divide 8
by 6.
Divide 21
by 6.

$$\begin{array}{r} 13 \\ 6\overline{)\ 81} \\ -6\downarrow \\ \hline 21 \\ -18 \\ \hline 3 \end{array}$$

Divide.

1. $5\overline{)76}$ 2. $5\overline{)77}$ 3. $5\overline{)78}$ 4. $5\overline{)79}$

5. $4\overline{)63}$ 6. $6\overline{)79}$ 7. $3\overline{)55}$ 8. $2\overline{)77}$

9. $8\overline{)98}$ 10. $4\overline{)73}$ 11. $5\overline{)88}$ 12. $3\overline{)41}$

13. $2\overline{)59}$ 14. $5\overline{)64}$ 15. $4\overline{)95}$ 16. $3\overline{)77}$

Divide in two stages when the quotient is tens and ones.

Divide.

1. $3\overline{)156}$ 2. $3\overline{)159}$ 3. $3\overline{)162}$ 4. $3\overline{)165}$

5. $2\overline{)188}$ 6. $6\overline{)486}$ 7. $5\overline{)455}$ 8. $4\overline{)248}$

9. $3\overline{)297}$ 10. $6\overline{)372}$ 11. $8\overline{)424}$ 12. $7\overline{)595}$

Divide in two stages when the quotient is tens and ones.

Divide.

1. $7\overline{)162}$ 2. $7\overline{)163}$ 3. $7\overline{)164}$ 4. $7\overline{)165}$

5. $4\overline{)257}$ 6. $3\overline{)286}$ 7. $5\overline{)339}$ 8. $6\overline{)591}$

9. $2\overline{)193}$ 10. $8\overline{)730}$ 11. $9\overline{)847}$ 12. $4\overline{)211}$

---

1. **Problem**
2. **Plan**
3. **Arithmetic**
4. **Answer**

Solve.

1. Linda swam every day for 182 days while on the swim team. How many weeks is that?

2. Jim rides his bike for 2 hours each day. How many hours a week does he ride his bike?

Something Extra • AVERAGES

Tina's record shows the time it took her to walk to school. Figure her <u>average</u> time like this:

1. Add the five numbers.

   $10 + 8 + 11 + 7 + 9 = 45$

2. Divide the sum by 5.

   $45 \div 5 = 9$

The average is 9 minutes.

Tina's Record	
Mon.	. . . 10 minutes
Tues.	. . . 8 minutes
Wed.	. . . 11 minutes
Thurs.	. . . 7 minutes
Fri.	. . . 9 minutes

Figure the average of these times.

1. 15 minutes	2. 26 minutes	3. 5 hours
18 minutes	32 minutes	8 hours
12 minutes	19 minutes	2 hours
16 minutes	23 minutes	4 hours
14 minutes	20 minutes	6 hours

4. How many points did Jim score in all?

5. How many scores are listed?

6. Figure Jim's average score by dividing the sum of his scores by 4.

7. Give a rule for figuring the average of a list of 6 scores.

Jim's Scores
8 points
12 points
10 points
14 points

Figure the average of these scores.

8. 10	9. 11	10. 115	11. 20	12. 99
8	20	101	24	80
9	14	98	16	100
13	22	85	12	95
	13	91	19	78
			23	88

Reviewing Needed Skills

Write < or > for ▓.

1. 20 ▓ 30   2. 55 ▓ 45   3. 7 ▓ 9

4. 76 ▓ 67   5. 10 ▓ 8   6. 63 ▓ 59

7. 48 ▓ 51   8. 101 ▓ 98   9. 19 ▓ 22

10. 204 ▓ 240 11. 510 ▓ 496 12. 808 ▓ 880

13. 763 ▓ 764 14. 914 ▓ 841 15. 423 ▓ 342

16. 799 ▓ 907 17. 211 ▓ 199 18. 505 ▓ 550

Multiply.

19. 8 ×9
20. 6 ×3
21. 7 ×9
22. 6 ×5
23. 4 ×3
24. 5 ×7

25. 7 ×8
26. 8 ×8
27. 6 ×7
28. 4 ×6
29. 9 ×9
30. 4 ×5

31. 8 ×4
32. 7 ×3
33. 4 ×4
34. 2 ×5
35. 6 ×8
36. 9 ×5

37. 6 ×6
38. 9 ×0
39. 3 ×8
40. 4 ×9
41. 5 ×5
42. 0 ×6

Divide.

43. 7)49   44. 3)9   45. 2)14   46. 9)18   47. 3)21   48. 9)81

49. 6)54   50. 7)56   51. 8)32   52. 4)28   53. 5)25   54. 6)42

55. 9)37   56. 7)62   57. 3)19   58. 6)27   59. 4)34   60. 5)34

61. 8)59   62. 5)42   63. 7)65   64. 3)22   65. 9)49   66. 4)19

67. 6)43   68. 4)30   69. 8)75   70. 9)26   71. 5)38   72. 7)48

187

UNIT 9

Fractions

There are four parts of the same size. Each part is a <u>fourth</u>.

One fourth is shaded.
$\frac{1}{4}$ is shaded.

Three fourths are not shaded.
$\frac{3}{4}$ are not shaded.

$\frac{1}{4}$ and $\frac{3}{4}$ are <u>fractions</u>.

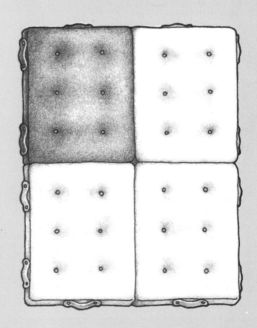

Fractions and Decimals

a Write the fraction for the shaded part.

1.

2.

3.

4.

5.

6.

7.

8.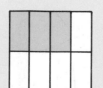

9.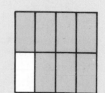

Fractions

4 of the 6 boxes are checked.

$\frac{4}{6}$ of the boxes are checked.

$\frac{4}{6}$ ◀ numerator
 ◀ denominator

We read the fraction as *four sixths*.

Fitness Test	
✓	dash
✓	distance jog
✓	softball throw
✓	sit-ups
	pull-ups
	broad jump

a Complete.

1. ▓ of the 6 students are running.　　2. $\frac{▓}{6}$ are running.

3. ▓ of the 5 students have a ball.　　4. $\frac{▓}{5}$ have a ball.

5. 3 of the ▓ students are up.　　6. $\frac{3}{▓}$ are up.

7. 2 of the ▓ students are jumping.　　8. $\frac{2}{▓}$ are jumping.

190

b Write the fraction for the
boxes checked.

9. ☑ ☑ ☐

10. ☑ ☑ ☑ ☐

11. ☑ ☑ ☐ ☐ ☐

12. ☑ ☑ ☑ ☑ ☐ ☐

13. ☑ ☐ ☐

14. ☑ ☐ ☐ ☐

15. ☑ ☐

16. ☐ ☐ ☑ ☑

17. ☑ ☑ ☑ ☑ ☐

18. ☑ ☑ ☑ ☐ ☐

19. ☐ ☐ ☐ ☐ ☐ ☑

20. ☑ ☐ ☐ ☐ ☑ ☐

c Write the fraction.

21. 2 of the 6 fitness tests will be done today.

22. 2 of the 4 classes are taking the tests.

23. 4 of the 10 students are jogging.

24. 6 of the 10 students completed the dash in good time.

25. 75 out of 100 students pass the tests.

Write A, B, C, or D to match the fractions.

26. the fraction with numerator 4   A. $\frac{3}{4}$

27. one half   B. $\frac{1}{3}$

28. three fourths   C. $\frac{4}{5}$

29. the fraction with denominator 3   D. $\frac{1}{2}$

Equal Fractions

$\frac{1}{2}$ of the pool is for racing.

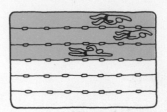

$\frac{3}{6}$ of the pool is for racing.

$$\frac{1}{2} = \frac{3}{6}$$

$\frac{1}{2}$ and $\frac{3}{6}$ are <u>equal</u> <u>fractions</u>.

a Complete.

1. $\frac{1}{2} = \frac{\blacksquare}{4}$

2. $\frac{1}{2} = \frac{\blacksquare}{8}$

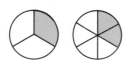

3. $\frac{1}{3} = \frac{\blacksquare}{6}$

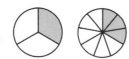

4. $\frac{1}{3} = \frac{\blacksquare}{9}$

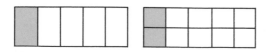

5. $\frac{1}{5} = \frac{\blacksquare}{10}$

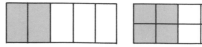

6. $\frac{2}{5} = \frac{\blacksquare}{10}$

192

b Complete.

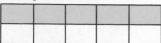

7. $\frac{1}{2} = \frac{\square}{10}$

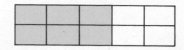

8. $\frac{3}{5} = \frac{\square}{10}$

9. $\frac{2}{4} = \frac{\square}{8}$

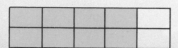

10. $\frac{4}{5} = \frac{\square}{10}$

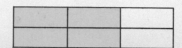

11. $\frac{2}{3} = \frac{\square}{6}$

12. $\frac{3}{4} = \frac{\square}{8}$

Words in math

One *fifth* is $\frac{1}{5}$.
A fifth is a fraction.

I am *fifth* in line.
Fifth is a place in order.

Write *Fraction* or *Order* for the underlined word.

1. Linda won the <u>third</u> swimming race.

2. Linda's team won a <u>third</u> of the races.

3. I have lived here one <u>fourth</u> of my life.

4. My house is the <u>fourth</u> from the corner.

5. Mr. Chan is the <u>sixth</u> teacher in the lunch line.

6. A <u>sixth</u> of the people choose soup for lunch.

Equal Fractions

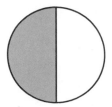 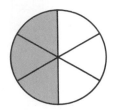

1 part is shaded. $3 \times 1 = 3$ 3 parts are shaded.
2 parts in all $3 \times 2 = 6$ 6 parts in all

$$\frac{1}{2} = \frac{3 \times 1}{3 \times 2} = \frac{3}{6}$$

Multiply the numerator and the denominator of a fraction by the same number. The answer is an equal fraction.

a Complete.

1. $\frac{1}{2} = \frac{2 \times 1}{2 \times 2} = \frac{\blacksquare}{4}$

2. $\frac{1}{2} = \frac{3 \times 1}{3 \times 2} = \frac{\blacksquare}{6}$

3. $\frac{1}{2} = \frac{\blacksquare}{8}$

4. $\frac{1}{3} = \frac{2 \times 1}{2 \times 3} = \frac{\blacksquare}{6}$

5. $\frac{1}{3} = \frac{3 \times 1}{3 \times 3} = \frac{3}{\blacksquare}$

6. $\frac{1}{3} = \frac{4}{\blacksquare}$

7. $\frac{1}{4} = \frac{2 \times 1}{2 \times 4} = \frac{\blacksquare}{8}$

8. $\frac{2}{4} = \frac{2 \times 2}{2 \times 4} = \frac{\blacksquare}{8}$

9. $\frac{3}{4} = \frac{\blacksquare}{8}$

10. $\frac{1}{5} = \frac{2 \times 1}{2 \times 5} = \frac{\blacksquare}{10}$

11. $\frac{2}{5} = \frac{2 \times 2}{2 \times 5} = \frac{4}{\blacksquare}$

12. $\frac{3}{5} = \frac{\blacksquare}{10}$

b Multiply numerator and denominator by 3 to complete.

13. $\frac{1}{2} = \frac{\blacksquare}{6}$ 14. $\frac{1}{3} = \frac{3}{9}$ 15. $\frac{2}{3} = \frac{\blacksquare}{9}$

16. $\frac{1}{4} = \frac{\blacksquare}{12}$ 17. $\frac{1}{5} = \frac{\blacksquare}{15}$ 18. $\frac{2}{4} = \frac{\blacksquare}{12}$

Multiply numerator and denominator by 4 to complete.

19. $\frac{1}{5} = \frac{\blacksquare}{20}$ 20. $\frac{1}{3} = \frac{\blacksquare}{12}$ 21. $\frac{2}{3} = \frac{\blacksquare}{12}$

22. $\frac{2}{4} = \frac{\blacksquare}{16}$ 23. $\frac{2}{5} = \frac{\blacksquare}{20}$ 24. $\frac{1}{4} = \frac{\blacksquare}{16}$

c Complete.

25. $\frac{1}{2} = \frac{\blacksquare}{10}$ 26. $\frac{1}{3} = \frac{\blacksquare}{6}$ 27. $\frac{1}{6} = \frac{\blacksquare}{12}$

28. $\frac{3}{6} = \frac{\blacksquare}{12}$ 29. $\frac{2}{3} = \frac{\blacksquare}{6}$ 30. $\frac{1}{2} = \frac{\blacksquare}{4}$

31. $\frac{1}{4} = \frac{\blacksquare}{8}$ 32. $\frac{1}{5} = \frac{\blacksquare}{10}$ 33. $\frac{1}{8} = \frac{\blacksquare}{16}$

34. $\frac{2}{4} = \frac{\blacksquare}{8}$ 35. $\frac{1}{2} = \frac{\blacksquare}{12}$ 36. $\frac{4}{5} = \frac{\blacksquare}{10}$

37. $\frac{1}{6} = \frac{\blacksquare}{30}$ 38. $\frac{3}{4} = \frac{\blacksquare}{12}$ 39. $\frac{1}{5} = \frac{\blacksquare}{25}$

Write A, B, C, or D to match equal fractions.

40. $\frac{1}{2}$ A. $\frac{4}{6}$

41. $\frac{2}{3}$ B. $\frac{6}{8}$

42. $\frac{1}{5}$ C. $\frac{2}{4}$

43. $\frac{3}{4}$ D. $\frac{2}{10}$

Equal Fractions

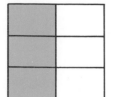 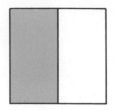

3 parts are shaded. $3 \div 3 = 1$ 1 part is shaded.
6 parts in all $6 \div 3 = 2$ 2 parts in all

$$\frac{3}{6} = \frac{3 \div 3}{6 \div 3} = \frac{1}{2}$$

Divide the numerator and the denominator of a fraction by the same number. The answer is an equal fraction.

a Complete.

1. $\dfrac{2}{4} = \dfrac{2 \div 2}{4 \div 2} = \dfrac{\blacksquare}{2}$

2. $\dfrac{3}{6} = \dfrac{3 \div 3}{6 \div 3} = \dfrac{\blacksquare}{2}$

3. $\dfrac{4}{8} = \dfrac{\blacksquare}{2}$

4. $\dfrac{2}{6} = \dfrac{2 \div 2}{6 \div 2} = \dfrac{\blacksquare}{3}$

5. $\dfrac{3}{9} = \dfrac{3 \div 3}{9 \div 3} = \dfrac{1}{\blacksquare}$

6. $\dfrac{4}{12} = \dfrac{\blacksquare}{3}$

7. $\dfrac{2}{8} = \dfrac{2 \div 2}{8 \div 2} = \dfrac{\blacksquare}{4}$

8. $\dfrac{4}{8} = \dfrac{4 \div 2}{8 \div 2} = \dfrac{2}{\blacksquare}$

9. $\dfrac{6}{8} = \dfrac{\blacksquare}{4}$

10. $\dfrac{2}{10} = \dfrac{2 \div 2}{10 \div 2} = \dfrac{\blacksquare}{5}$

11. $\dfrac{4}{10} = \dfrac{4 \div 2}{10 \div 2} = \dfrac{2}{\blacksquare}$

12. $\dfrac{6}{10} = \dfrac{\blacksquare}{5}$

13. $\dfrac{6}{12} = \dfrac{6 \div 2}{12 \div 2} = \dfrac{\blacksquare}{6}$

14. $\dfrac{6}{12} = \dfrac{6 \div 3}{12 \div 3} = \dfrac{\blacksquare}{4}$

15. $\dfrac{6}{12} = \dfrac{\blacksquare}{2}$

b Divide numerator and denominator by 3 to complete.

16. $\dfrac{3}{6} = \dfrac{\blacksquare}{2}$
17. $\dfrac{3}{9} = \dfrac{\blacksquare}{3}$
18. $\dfrac{6}{9} = \dfrac{\blacksquare}{3}$
19. $\dfrac{3}{12} = \dfrac{\blacksquare}{4}$

Divide numerator and denominator by 4 to complete.

20. $\dfrac{4}{20} = \dfrac{\blacksquare}{5}$
21. $\dfrac{8}{20} = \dfrac{\blacksquare}{5}$
22. $\dfrac{8}{12} = \dfrac{\blacksquare}{3}$
23. $\dfrac{4}{16} = \dfrac{\blacksquare}{4}$

c Complete.

24. $\dfrac{5}{10} = \dfrac{\blacksquare}{2}$
25. $\dfrac{4}{6} = \dfrac{\blacksquare}{3}$
26. $\dfrac{8}{16} = \dfrac{\blacksquare}{2}$
27. $\dfrac{2}{10} = \dfrac{\blacksquare}{5}$

28. $\dfrac{10}{15} = \dfrac{\blacksquare}{3}$
29. $\dfrac{6}{12} = \dfrac{\blacksquare}{6}$
30. $\dfrac{9}{15} = \dfrac{\blacksquare}{5}$
31. $\dfrac{10}{16} = \dfrac{\blacksquare}{8}$

Review A   (pages 188–197)

Write the fraction for the shaded part.

1.
2.
3.
4.

Write the fraction.

5. 2 of the 6 boxes

6. 1 of the 2 lemons

7. 3 of the 4 brands

8. 2 of the 3 stores

9.
10.
11.
12.

$\dfrac{1}{2} = \dfrac{\blacksquare}{4}$
$\dfrac{1}{2} = \dfrac{\blacksquare}{6}$
$\dfrac{1}{3} = \dfrac{\blacksquare}{6}$
$\dfrac{2}{3} = \dfrac{\blacksquare}{6}$

13. $\dfrac{1}{4} = \dfrac{\blacksquare}{8}$
14. $\dfrac{3}{4} = \dfrac{\blacksquare}{8}$
15. $\dfrac{1}{2} = \dfrac{\blacksquare}{10}$
16. $\dfrac{1}{5} = \dfrac{\blacksquare}{10}$

17. $\dfrac{2}{4} = \dfrac{\blacksquare}{2}$
18. $\dfrac{3}{6} = \dfrac{\blacksquare}{2}$
19. $\dfrac{6}{8} = \dfrac{\blacksquare}{4}$
20. $\dfrac{4}{6} = \dfrac{\blacksquare}{3}$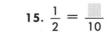

Fractions in Order

$\frac{1}{6}$ $\qquad$ $\frac{2}{6}$ $\qquad$ $\frac{3}{6}$ $\qquad$ $\frac{4}{6}$ $\qquad$ $\frac{5}{6}$

These fractions are in order from least to greatest.
The denominators are all the same. We compare numerators.

2 is less than 5. $\qquad\qquad$ 5 is greater than 2.

$\qquad$ 2 < 5 $\qquad\qquad\qquad\qquad$ 5 > 2

$\qquad$ $\frac{2}{6} < \frac{5}{6}$ $\qquad\qquad\qquad\qquad$ $\frac{5}{6} > \frac{2}{6}$

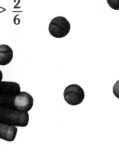

a Write < or > for ▨.

  $\qquad$ $\qquad$ $\qquad$

1. $\frac{1}{6}$ ▨ $\frac{5}{6}$ $\qquad$ 2. $\frac{3}{6}$ ▨ $\frac{1}{6}$ $\qquad$ 3. $\frac{3}{6}$ ▨ $\frac{5}{6}$ $\qquad$ 4. $\frac{4}{6}$ ▨ $\frac{2}{6}$

5. 4 ▨ 3 $\qquad$ 6. 2 ▨ 7 $\qquad$ 7. 1 ▨ 3 $\qquad$ 8. 2 ▨ 1

$\frac{4}{5}$ ▨ $\frac{3}{5}$ $\qquad$ $\frac{2}{8}$ ▨ $\frac{7}{8}$ $\qquad$ $\frac{1}{5}$ ▨ $\frac{3}{5}$ $\qquad$ $\frac{2}{3}$ ▨ $\frac{1}{3}$

9. 3 ▨ 2 $\qquad$ 10. 4 ▨ 2 $\qquad$ 11. 3 ▨ 5 $\qquad$ 12. 1 ▨ 2

$\frac{3}{4}$ ▨ $\frac{2}{4}$ $\qquad$ $\frac{4}{5}$ ▨ $\frac{2}{5}$ $\qquad$ $\frac{3}{8}$ ▨ $\frac{5}{8}$ $\qquad$ $\frac{1}{7}$ ▨ $\frac{2}{7}$

b Write < or > for ▦.

13. $\frac{3}{4}$ ▦ $\frac{1}{4}$ 14. $\frac{3}{8}$ ▦ $\frac{7}{8}$

15. $\frac{2}{6}$ ▦ $\frac{4}{6}$ 16. $\frac{4}{8}$ ▦ $\frac{1}{8}$

17. $\frac{2}{5}$ ▦ $\frac{4}{5}$ 18. $\frac{5}{10}$ ▦ $\frac{8}{10}$

19. $\frac{3}{5}$ ▦ $\frac{1}{5}$ 20. $\frac{1}{4}$ ▦ $\frac{2}{4}$

21. $\frac{5}{6}$ ▦ $\frac{2}{6}$ 22. $\frac{5}{8}$ ▦ $\frac{2}{8}$

23. $\frac{9}{10}$ ▦ $\frac{7}{10}$ 24. $\frac{5}{8}$ ▦ $\frac{6}{8}$

c List the fractions in order from least to greatest.

25. $\frac{3}{8}$ $\frac{1}{8}$ $\frac{5}{8}$ 26. $\frac{4}{5}$ $\frac{2}{5}$ $\frac{1}{5}$

27. $\frac{2}{6}$ $\frac{5}{6}$ $\frac{3}{6}$ 28. $\frac{3}{10}$ $\frac{6}{10}$ $\frac{5}{10}$

29. $\frac{7}{8}$ $\frac{2}{8}$ $\frac{5}{8}$ 30. $\frac{4}{10}$ $\frac{6}{10}$ $\frac{1}{10}$

31. $\frac{7}{9}$ $\frac{4}{9}$ $\frac{1}{9}$ 32. $\frac{5}{10}$ $\frac{2}{10}$ $\frac{9}{10}$

Shooting baskets

Some friends take an equal number of turns to shoot baskets.
Pedro makes $\frac{1}{2}$ of his shots. Jane makes $\frac{1}{3}$ of her shots.
Who makes more baskets?

Think of $\frac{1}{2}$ as $\frac{3}{6}$. Think of $\frac{1}{3}$ as $\frac{2}{6}$.
$\frac{3}{6} > \frac{2}{6}$ so $\frac{1}{2} > \frac{1}{3}$. Pedro makes more baskets.
Millie makes $\frac{6}{12}$ of her shots. Does she beat Pedro?

199

Part of a Number

$\frac{1}{3}$ of the 6 students are tall.

2 of the 6 students are tall.

$$3\overline{)6}^{\,2} \quad \blacktriangleright \quad \frac{1}{3} \text{ of 6 is } 2.$$

a Write the number.

● ● ●
○ ○ ○

1. $\frac{1}{2}$ of 6

● ○ ○
● ○ ○

2. $\frac{1}{3}$ of 6

● ○ ○
○ ○ ○

3. $\frac{1}{6}$ of 6

▲ ▲ ▲ ▲
△ △ △ △

4. $\frac{1}{2}$ of 8

▲ △ △ △
▲ △ △ △

5. $\frac{1}{4}$ of 8

▲ △ △ △
△ △ △ △

6. $\frac{1}{8}$ of 8

7. $2\overline{)12}$

8. $\frac{1}{2}$ of 12

9. $3\overline{)12}$

10. $\frac{1}{3}$ of 12

11. $4\overline{)12}$

12. $\frac{1}{4}$ of 12

13. $6\overline{)12}$

14. $\frac{1}{6}$ of 12

15. $3\overline{)9}$

16. $\frac{1}{3}$ of 9

17. $9\overline{)9}$

18. $\frac{1}{9}$ of 9

b Write the number.

19. $\frac{1}{2}$ of 10   20. $\frac{1}{3}$ of 6   21. $\frac{1}{5}$ of 10   22. $\frac{1}{5}$ of 5

23. $\frac{1}{6}$ of 12   24. $\frac{1}{3}$ of 15   25. $\frac{1}{4}$ of 16   26. $\frac{1}{10}$ of 10

27. $\frac{1}{5}$ of 20   28. $\frac{1}{8}$ of 16   29. $\frac{1}{12}$ of 12   30. $\frac{1}{2}$ of 14

31. $\frac{1}{2}$ of 16   32. $\frac{1}{4}$ of 4   33. $\frac{1}{4}$ of 20   34. $\frac{1}{5}$ of 15

35. $\frac{1}{2}$ of 4   36. $\frac{1}{3}$ of 24   37. $\frac{1}{4}$ of 24   38. $\frac{1}{9}$ of 18

39. $\frac{1}{5}$ of 25   40. $\frac{1}{2}$ of 18   41. $\frac{1}{6}$ of 36   42. $\frac{1}{4}$ of 36

43. $\frac{1}{8}$ of 24   44. $\frac{1}{3}$ of 18   45. $\frac{1}{3}$ of 21   46. $\frac{1}{2}$ of 20

c Solve.

47. Half of the 24 students have been measured. How many is that?

48. $\frac{1}{6}$ of the 24 students are tall. How many is that?

49. $\frac{1}{8}$ of the 24 students can wear last year's coats. How many students is that?

50. A third of the 24 students need bigger sneakers. How many students is that?

51. A fourth of the 24 students need taller desks. How many students is that?

Part of a Number

$\frac{1}{3}$ of 12 is 4.

$\frac{2}{3}$ of 12 is 2 × 4.

$\frac{2}{3}$ of 12 is 8.

a Write the number.

● ○ ○   ● ○ ○ ○

1. $\frac{1}{3}$ of 3   2. $\frac{2}{3}$ of 3   3. $\frac{1}{4}$ of 4   4. $\frac{3}{4}$ of 4

● ○ ○   ● ○ ○ ○
● ○ ○   ● ○ ○ ○

5. $\frac{1}{3}$ of 6   6. $\frac{2}{3}$ of 6   7. $\frac{1}{4}$ of 8   8. $\frac{3}{4}$ of 8

9. $\frac{1}{4}$ of 12   10. $\frac{2}{4}$ of 12   11. $\frac{1}{5}$ of 5   12. $\frac{2}{5}$ of 5

13. $\frac{1}{5}$ of 10   14. $\frac{3}{5}$ of 10   15. $\frac{1}{6}$ of 6   16. $\frac{5}{6}$ of 6

17. $\frac{1}{6}$ of 12   18. $\frac{2}{6}$ of 12   19. $\frac{1}{3}$ of 15   20. $\frac{2}{3}$ of 15

b Write the number.

21. $\frac{2}{3}$ of 9

22. $\frac{3}{4}$ of 12

23. $\frac{3}{5}$ of 5

24. $\frac{2}{6}$ of 6

25. $\frac{2}{4}$ of 8

26. $\frac{2}{5}$ of 15

27. $\frac{2}{3}$ of 12

28. $\frac{2}{5}$ of 25

29. $\frac{3}{4}$ of 16

30. $\frac{4}{6}$ of 6

31. $\frac{4}{5}$ of 10

32. $\frac{3}{8}$ of 16

33. $\frac{3}{5}$ of 15

34. $\frac{2}{5}$ of 10

35. $\frac{5}{6}$ of 12

36. $\frac{4}{5}$ of 15

37. $\frac{2}{3}$ of 18

38. $\frac{3}{4}$ of 20

39. $\frac{3}{5}$ of 20

40. $\frac{3}{8}$ of 8

41. $\frac{3}{4}$ of 24

42. $\frac{3}{8}$ of 24

43. $\frac{2}{5}$ of 30

44. $\frac{2}{3}$ of 30

c Solve.

45. $\frac{3}{5}$ of the 5 glasses have milk. How many is that?

46. $\frac{2}{3}$ of the 6 apples are red. How many are red?

47. The salad has 5 vegetables in it. $\frac{2}{5}$ of them are leaves. How many are leaves?

48. Erik grows 7 kinds of plants. $\frac{2}{7}$ of them have roots to eat. How many kinds have roots to eat?

49. Mia uses $\frac{2}{3}$ of a dozen eggs. How many eggs is that?

Tenths

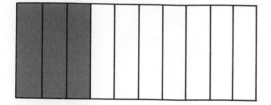

10 parts of the same size
$\frac{3}{10}$ are shaded.

0.3 is the decimal for $\frac{3}{10}$.

We read 0.3 as *3 tenths*
or *zero point three*.
The point is a <u>decimal point</u>.

a Write the decimal for the shaded part.

1.

2.

3.

4.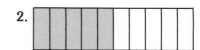

5.

6.

b Write the decimal.

7. five tenths   8. two tenths   9. one tenth   10. six tenths

11. $\frac{7}{10}$ 12. $\frac{3}{10}$ 13. $\frac{9}{10}$ 14. $\frac{4}{10}$

15. 9 out of 10 students like recess.

16. 2 of the 10 teachers have playground duty.

17. 5 of the 10 students are on the blue team.

18. 1 of the 10 teachers ran in the Olympic Games.

19. 3 of the 10 friends meet at the playground after school.

c Write < or > for ▨.

20. $\frac{1}{10} < \frac{2}{10}$ 21. $\frac{6}{10} > \frac{3}{10}$

    0.1 ▨ 0.2   0.6 ▨ 0.3

22. $\frac{2}{10} < \frac{7}{10}$ 23. $\frac{9}{10} > \frac{8}{10}$

    0.2 ▨ 0.7   0.9 ▨ 0.8

24. $\frac{5}{10} < \frac{7}{10}$ 25. $\frac{4}{10} > \frac{1}{10}$

    0.5 ▨ 0.7   0.4 ▨ 0.1

Hundredths

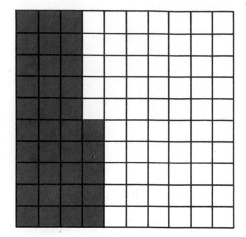

100 parts of the same size

$\frac{35}{100}$ are shaded.

0.35 is the decimal for $\frac{35}{100}$.

We read 0.35 as *35 hundredths* or *zero point three five.*

$$\frac{35}{100} = 0.35 \qquad \frac{30}{100} = 0.30 \qquad \frac{5}{100} = 0.05$$

a Write the decimal.

1. 45 hundredths   2. 40 hundredths   3. 5 hundredths

4. 69 hundredths   5. 60 hundredths   6. 9 hundredths

7. 32 hundredths   8. 30 hundredths   9. 2 hundredths

10. $\frac{26}{100}$ 11. $\frac{20}{100}$ 12. $\frac{6}{100}$ 13. $\frac{72}{100}$ 14. $\frac{70}{100}$ 15. $\frac{2}{100}$

16. $\frac{33}{100}$ 17. $\frac{30}{100}$ 18. $\frac{3}{100}$ 19. $\frac{11}{100}$ 20. $\frac{10}{100}$ 21. $\frac{1}{100}$

22. $\frac{42}{100}$ 23. $\frac{52}{100}$ 24. $\frac{62}{100}$ 25. $\frac{37}{100}$ 26. $\frac{38}{100}$ 27. $\frac{39}{100}$

28. $\frac{40}{100}$ 29. $\frac{50}{100}$ 30. $\frac{60}{100}$ 31. $\frac{7}{100}$ 32. $\frac{8}{100}$ 33. $\frac{9}{100}$

b Write the decimal.

34. 35 of the 100 lockers are for our homeroom.

35. 10 of the 100 lockers are not in use.

36. 8 of the 100 lockers need to be fixed.

37. 55 of the 100 lockers have sneakers in them.

38. 29 of the 100 lockers have been cleaned out.

39. 3 of the 100 lockers store balls and bats.

Review B (pages 198–207)

Write < or > for ▧.

1. $\dfrac{1}{3}$ ▧ $\dfrac{2}{3}$

2. $\dfrac{3}{5}$ ▧ $\dfrac{2}{5}$

3. $\dfrac{2}{4}$ ▧ $\dfrac{1}{4}$

4. $\dfrac{3}{6}$ ▧ $\dfrac{5}{6}$

Write the number.

5. $\dfrac{1}{2}$ of 4

6. $\dfrac{1}{3}$ of 12

7. $\dfrac{1}{5}$ of 5

8. $\dfrac{1}{8}$ of 16

9. $\dfrac{2}{3}$ of 6

10. $\dfrac{5}{6}$ of 6

11. $\dfrac{3}{4}$ of 8

12. $\dfrac{2}{5}$ of 10

Write the decimal.

13. one tenth

14. six tenths

15. $\dfrac{4}{10}$

16. $\dfrac{9}{10}$

17. 35 hundredths

18. 80 hundredths

19. $\dfrac{25}{100}$

20. $\dfrac{9}{100}$

Problem Solving   Problem •Plan •Arithmetic •Answer

1	Understand the problem.	What do you know? • What do you want to know?

Sometimes we get numbers from a table to solve a problem. Three homerooms held running races. The table shows the results.

Room	Blue ribbons won	Red ribbons won	Green ribbons won
201	3	0	3
203	1	4	1
204	2	2	2

1. How many blue ribbons were won in all?

2. What fraction of the blue ribbons did Room 201 win?

3. What fraction of the blue ribbons did Room 203 win?

4. What fraction of the blue ribbons did Room 204 win?

5. How many red ribbons were won in all?

6. What fraction of the red ribbons did Room 203 win?

7. How many green ribbons were won in all?

8. Which room won $\frac{1}{6}$ of the green ribbons?

9. Which room won $\frac{2}{6}$ of the green ribbons?

10. Which room won $\frac{3}{6}$ of the green ribbons?

11. Which room won half of the 6 green ribbons?

12. Which room won a third of the 6 green ribbons?

13. Did any room win half of all 18 ribbons?

14. Did any room win a third of all 18 ribbons?

Unit Test

Write the fraction.   (pages 188–191)

1. 3 of the 5 basketballs need air.

2. 7 of the 8 mats are new.

3. 2 of the 3 games have been played.

4. 1 of the 4 teams wins every game.

Complete.   (pages 192–197)

5. $\frac{1}{2} = \frac{\blacksquare}{4}$
6. $\frac{2}{3} = \frac{\blacksquare}{9}$
7. $\frac{1}{4} = \frac{\blacksquare}{8}$
8. $\frac{3}{8} = \frac{\blacksquare}{16}$

9. $\frac{6}{8} = \frac{\blacksquare}{4}$
10. $\frac{2}{6} = \frac{\blacksquare}{3}$
11. $\frac{8}{10} = \frac{\blacksquare}{5}$
12. $\frac{6}{9} = \frac{\blacksquare}{3}$

Write < or > for $\blacksquare$.   (pages 198–199)

13. $\frac{5}{6} \ \blacksquare \ \frac{4}{6}$
14. $\frac{1}{5} \ \blacksquare \ \frac{3}{5}$
15. $\frac{6}{8} \ \blacksquare \ \frac{7}{8}$
16. $\frac{8}{10} \ \blacksquare \ \frac{6}{10}$

Write the number.   (pages 200–203)

17. $\frac{1}{5}$ of 10
18. $\frac{1}{3}$ of 6
19. $\frac{1}{4}$ of 8
20. $\frac{1}{5}$ of 5

21. $\frac{2}{3}$ of 9
22. $\frac{2}{5}$ of 10
23. $\frac{3}{4}$ of 16
24. $\frac{2}{4}$ of 12

Write the decimal.   (pages 204–207)

25. six tenths

26. nine tenths

27. 52 hundredths

28. 3 hundredths

Solve.   (page 208)

29. What fraction of the 6 games played did the team win?

30. Did the team lose half of the 6 games played?

Games won	Games lost
3	3

Taking Another Look

Pages 188–191

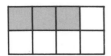

$\frac{3}{8}$ of the box

is shaded.

Write the fraction for the shaded part.

1.

2.

3.

4.

5.

6.

7.

8.

Pages 192–197

$$\frac{2}{3} = \frac{3 \times 2}{3 \times 3} = \frac{6}{9}$$

$$\frac{6}{9} = \frac{6 \div 3}{9 \div 3} = \frac{2}{3}$$

Complete.

1. $\frac{1}{2} = \frac{\blacksquare}{4}$

2. $\frac{2}{4} = \frac{\blacksquare}{8}$

3. $\frac{4}{8} = \frac{\blacksquare}{16}$

4. $\frac{2}{10} = \frac{\blacksquare}{5}$

5. $\frac{4}{10} = \frac{\blacksquare}{5}$

6. $\frac{6}{10} = \frac{\blacksquare}{5}$

7. $\frac{2}{3} = \frac{\blacksquare}{9}$

8. $\frac{1}{5} = \frac{\blacksquare}{10}$

9. $\frac{1}{2} = \frac{\blacksquare}{12}$

10. $\frac{5}{6} = \frac{\blacksquare}{12}$

11. $\frac{1}{3} = \frac{\blacksquare}{9}$

12. $\frac{2}{3} = \frac{\blacksquare}{6}$

13. $\frac{7}{14} = \frac{\blacksquare}{2}$

14. $\frac{9}{12} = \frac{\blacksquare}{4}$

15. $\frac{8}{10} = \frac{\blacksquare}{5}$

16. $\frac{4}{12} = \frac{\blacksquare}{3}$

17. $\frac{4}{6} = \frac{\blacksquare}{3}$

18. $\frac{3}{12} = \frac{\blacksquare}{4}$

$5 < 7$

$\dfrac{5}{8} < \dfrac{7}{8}$

Write $<$ or $>$ for ▨.

1. 4 ▨ 2

2. $\dfrac{4}{5}$ ▨ $\dfrac{2}{5}$

3. $\dfrac{4}{10}$ ▨ $\dfrac{2}{10}$

4. $\dfrac{3}{8}$ ▨ $\dfrac{1}{8}$

5. $\dfrac{4}{6}$ ▨ $\dfrac{2}{6}$

6. $\dfrac{7}{10}$ ▨ $\dfrac{9}{10}$

7. $\dfrac{2}{9}$ ▨ $\dfrac{3}{9}$

8. $\dfrac{2}{3}$ ▨ $\dfrac{1}{3}$

9. $\dfrac{7}{8}$ ▨ $\dfrac{6}{8}$

$$4\overline{)12}\;\;^{3}$$

⬇

$\dfrac{1}{4}$ of 12 is 3.

$\dfrac{3}{4}$ of 12 is 3 × 3.

$\dfrac{3}{4}$ of 12 is 9.

Write the number.

1. $5\overline{)10}$

2. $\dfrac{1}{5}$ of 10

3. $\dfrac{3}{5}$ of 10

4. $\dfrac{1}{3}$ of 12

5. $\dfrac{1}{6}$ of 18

6. $\dfrac{1}{2}$ of 6

7. $\dfrac{1}{3}$ of 9

8. $\dfrac{1}{5}$ of 5

9. $\dfrac{1}{6}$ of 12

10. $\dfrac{3}{4}$ of 8

11. $\dfrac{2}{3}$ of 12

12. $\dfrac{2}{5}$ of 10

---

two tenths

$\dfrac{2}{10} = 0.2$

36 hundredths

$\dfrac{36}{100} = 0.36$

Write the decimal.

1. four tenths

2. 25 hundredths

3. nine tenths

4. 72 hundredths

5. $\dfrac{3}{10}$

6. $\dfrac{47}{100}$

7. $\dfrac{80}{100}$

8. $\dfrac{7}{100}$

---

1. **Problem**
2. **Plan**
3. **Arithmetic**
4. **Answer**

Solve.

1. What fraction of the 12 votes are for Meg?

2. Does Lee have $\dfrac{1}{3}$ of the 12 votes?

Votes for Meg	Votes for Lee
8	4

Something Extra • CIRCLE GRAPHS

Twelve friends name the ice cream flavors they like best. We may use a circle graph to show their favorites.

Favorite Flavors

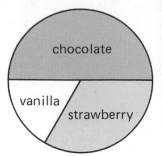

$\frac{1}{2}$ of the circle is for chocolate.

$\frac{1}{2}$ of the 12 friends like chocolate best.

$\frac{1}{2}$ of 12 = 6

6 friends like chocolate best.

1. $\frac{1}{3}$ of the circle is for strawberry.

   How many of the 12 friends like strawberry best?

2. $\frac{1}{6}$ of the circle is for vanilla.

   How many of the 12 friends like vanilla best?

This circle graph shows the supper favorites of the four O'Briens.

The O'Briens' Supper Favorites

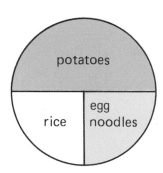

3. What part of the circle is for potatoes?

4. How many of the 4 O'Briens like potatoes best?

5. What part of the circle is for rice?

6. How many of the 4 O'Briens like rice best?

7. What part of the circle is for egg noodles?

8. How many of the 4 O'Briens like egg noodles best?

Reviewing Needed Skills

Add.

1. $\begin{array}{r}46\\+52\\\hline\end{array}$	2. $\begin{array}{r}34\\+23\\\hline\end{array}$	3. $\begin{array}{r}57\\+39\\\hline\end{array}$	4. $\begin{array}{r}19\\+65\\\hline\end{array}$	5. $\begin{array}{r}58\\+67\\\hline\end{array}$
6. $\begin{array}{r}532\\+295\\\hline\end{array}$	7. $\begin{array}{r}465\\+487\\\hline\end{array}$	8. $\begin{array}{r}9051\\+1899\\\hline\end{array}$	9. $\begin{array}{r}7825\\+5493\\\hline\end{array}$	10. $\begin{array}{r}8137\\+5409\\\hline\end{array}$
11. $\begin{array}{r}138\\+920\\\hline\end{array}$	12. $\begin{array}{r}364\\+1560\\\hline\end{array}$	13. $\begin{array}{r}948\\+2390\\\hline\end{array}$	14. $\begin{array}{r}256\\+840\\\hline\end{array}$	15. $\begin{array}{r}204\\+6090\\\hline\end{array}$
16. $\begin{array}{r}586\\+7340\\\hline\end{array}$	17. $\begin{array}{r}198\\+1980\\\hline\end{array}$	18. $\begin{array}{r}86\\+7740\\\hline\end{array}$	19. $\begin{array}{r}421\\+9730\\\hline\end{array}$	20. $\begin{array}{r}385\\+2790\\\hline\end{array}$

Multiply.

21. $\begin{array}{r}8\\\times9\\\hline\end{array}$	22. $\begin{array}{r}6\\\times7\\\hline\end{array}$	23. $\begin{array}{r}9\\\times9\\\hline\end{array}$	24. $\begin{array}{r}8\\\times3\\\hline\end{array}$	25. $\begin{array}{r}7\\\times4\\\hline\end{array}$
26. $\begin{array}{r}23\\\times2\\\hline\end{array}$	27. $\begin{array}{r}41\\\times2\\\hline\end{array}$	28. $\begin{array}{r}67\\\times3\\\hline\end{array}$	29. $\begin{array}{r}34\\\times8\\\hline\end{array}$	30. $\begin{array}{r}58\\\times9\\\hline\end{array}$
31. $\begin{array}{r}217\\\times5\\\hline\end{array}$	32. $\begin{array}{r}908\\\times4\\\hline\end{array}$	33. $\begin{array}{r}674\\\times9\\\hline\end{array}$	34. $\begin{array}{r}829\\\times7\\\hline\end{array}$	35. $\begin{array}{r}746\\\times6\\\hline\end{array}$
36. $\begin{array}{r}532\\\times9\\\hline\end{array}$	37. $\begin{array}{r}894\\\times3\\\hline\end{array}$	38. $\begin{array}{r}609\\\times8\\\hline\end{array}$	39. $\begin{array}{r}1586\\\times7\\\hline\end{array}$	40. $\begin{array}{r}2947\\\times3\\\hline\end{array}$
41. $\begin{array}{r}8209\\\times5\\\hline\end{array}$	42. $\begin{array}{r}4318\\\times7\\\hline\end{array}$	43. $\begin{array}{r}5469\\\times4\\\hline\end{array}$	44. $\begin{array}{r}7009\\\times8\\\hline\end{array}$	45. $\begin{array}{r}3387\\\times6\\\hline\end{array}$
46. $\begin{array}{r}\$1.98\\\times3\\\hline\end{array}$	47. $\begin{array}{r}\$5.73\\\times8\\\hline\end{array}$	48. $\begin{array}{r}\$23.59\\\times6\\\hline\end{array}$	49. $\begin{array}{r}\$89.21\\\times7\\\hline\end{array}$	50. $\begin{array}{r}\$68.59\\\times4\\\hline\end{array}$

UNIT 10

Multiplication by Ones

Three quarters are used for the wash.

	Multiply the 5 ones by 3.	Multiply the 2 tens by 3. Add the 1 ten.
25 ×3	1 25 ×3 —— 5	1 25 ×3 —— 75

3 × 25¢ is 75¢.

Multiplication

a Multiply.

1. 21 ×2	2. 21 ×3	3. 21 ×4	4. 21 ×5	5. 21 ×6	6. 21 ×7
7. 31 ×2	8. 32 ×2	9. 33 ×2	10. 34 ×2	11. 35 ×2	12. 36 ×2
13. 26 ×2	14. 36 ×2	15. 46 ×2	16. 56 ×2	17. 66 ×2	18. 76 ×2
19. 44 ×4	20. 55 ×5	21. 66 ×6	22. 77 ×7	23. 88 ×8	24. 99 ×9

Multiplication by Ones

Three TV sets were sold today. Multiply 245 by 3.

Multiply the 5 ones by 3.	Multiply the 4 tens by 3. Add the 1 ten.	Multiply the 2 hundreds by 3. Add the 1 hundred.
$\begin{array}{r} 1 \\ 2\,4\,5 \\ \times\ 3 \\ \hline 5 \end{array}$	$\begin{array}{r} 1\ 1 \\ 2\,4\,5 \\ \times\ 3 \\ \hline 3\,5 \end{array}$	$\begin{array}{r} 1\ 1 \\ 2\,4\,5 \\ \times\ 3 \\ \hline 7\,3\,5 \end{array}$

$3 \times \$245$ is $\$735$.

We Also do REPAIRS! Inquire within.

$245.^{00}$

a Multiply.

1. 23 ×3	2. 100 ×3	3. 123 ×3	4. 2123 ×3	5. 5123 ×3
6. 36 ×4	7. 200 ×4	8. 236 ×4	9. 1236 ×4	10. 7236 ×4
11. 323 ×3	12. 1323 ×3	13. 1324 ×3	14. 1364 ×3	15. 5364 ×3

b Multiply.

16. 421
    ×2

17. 316
    ×3

18. 348
    ×4

19. 2311
    ×3

20. 3109
    ×8

21. 231
    ×6

22. 465
    ×5

23. 313
    ×2

24. 2143
    ×5

25. 9185
    ×4

26. 306
    ×7

27. 989
    ×9

28. 542
    ×7

29. 702
    ×4

30. 480
    ×9

31. 2506
    ×8

32. 329
    ×8

33. 4444
    ×3

c Solve.

34. The new shop had 125 repair calls the year it opened. This year it had 3 times as many repair calls. How many is that?

35. On the day of the sale, 5 television sets are sold at $189 each. What is the total value of the sets sold?

36. There are 256 families in the area with 2 radios each. How many radios is that in all?

37. The hotel gets a bill for 8 television sets. Each set is $219. What is the total amount of the bill?

Multiplication by Tens

There are 10 dozen rolls.
How many rolls in all?
10 twelves = 12 tens
10 × 12   = 120

$$\begin{array}{r} 12 \\ \times 10 \\ \hline 120 \end{array}$$

Compare these examples.

12	12	12	12	12	12
×1	×10	×2	×20	×8	×80
12	120	24	240	96	960

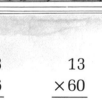

a Multiply.

1.
$$\begin{array}{r} 13 \\ \times 1 \\ \hline \end{array} \qquad \begin{array}{r} 13 \\ \times 10 \\ \hline \end{array}$$
2.
$$\begin{array}{r} 13 \\ \times 2 \\ \hline \end{array} \qquad \begin{array}{r} 13 \\ \times 20 \\ \hline \end{array}$$
3.
$$\begin{array}{r} 13 \\ \times 6 \\ \hline \end{array} \qquad \begin{array}{r} 13 \\ \times 60 \\ \hline \end{array}$$

4.
$$\begin{array}{r} 23 \\ \times 1 \\ \hline \end{array} \qquad \begin{array}{r} 23 \\ \times 10 \\ \hline \end{array}$$
5.
$$\begin{array}{r} 23 \\ \times 3 \\ \hline \end{array} \qquad \begin{array}{r} 23 \\ \times 30 \\ \hline \end{array}$$
6.
$$\begin{array}{r} 23 \\ \times 9 \\ \hline \end{array} \qquad \begin{array}{r} 23 \\ \times 90 \\ \hline \end{array}$$

7.
$$\begin{array}{r} 54 \\ \times 1 \\ \hline \end{array} \qquad \begin{array}{r} 54 \\ \times 10 \\ \hline \end{array}$$
8.
$$\begin{array}{r} 54 \\ \times 2 \\ \hline \end{array} \qquad \begin{array}{r} 54 \\ \times 20 \\ \hline \end{array}$$
9.
$$\begin{array}{r} 54 \\ \times 5 \\ \hline \end{array} \qquad \begin{array}{r} 54 \\ \times 50 \\ \hline \end{array}$$

10.
$$\begin{array}{r} 83 \\ \times 1 \\ \hline \end{array} \qquad \begin{array}{r} 83 \\ \times 10 \\ \hline \end{array}$$
11.
$$\begin{array}{r} 83 \\ \times 3 \\ \hline \end{array} \qquad \begin{array}{r} 83 \\ \times 30 \\ \hline \end{array}$$
12.
$$\begin{array}{r} 83 \\ \times 8 \\ \hline \end{array} \qquad \begin{array}{r} 83 \\ \times 80 \\ \hline \end{array}$$

b Multiply.

13. 16 ×10	**14.** 34 ×20	**15.** 21 ×70	**16.** 14 ×60	**17.** 89 ×10	**18.** 52 ×50
19. 43 ×30	**20.** 72 ×10	**21.** 88 ×20	**22.** 23 ×80	**23.** 10 ×10	**24.** 61 ×30
25. 34 ×10	**26.** 78 ×20	**27.** 65 ×10	**28.** 52 ×40	**29.** 46 ×30	**30.** 21 ×90
31. 92 ×10	**32.** 37 ×20	**33.** 41 ×70	**34.** 83 ×50	**35.** 25 ×40	**36.** 50 ×20

c **37.** How many eggs are in 20 dozen eggs?

38. What is the value of 10 quarters in cents?

39. What is the value of 20 dimes in cents?

40. Each box has 32 cans. How many cans are in 10 boxes?

41. How many hours are in 10 days?

42. How many months are in 10 years?

Multiplication by Ones and Tens

To multiply 24 by 16, we may think of 16 as 1 ten 6 ones.

Multiply 24 by 6.	Multiply 24 by 10.	Add 144 and 240.
24	24	24
×16	×16	×16
———	———	———
144	144	144
	240	240
	———	———
		384

The product of 24 and 16 is 384.

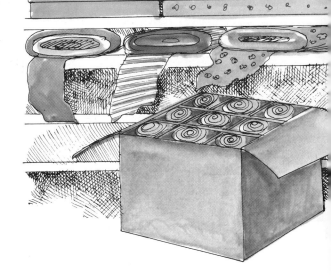

a Multiply.

1.   34
       ×12
       ———
        68
       340
       ▦▦▦

2.   34
       ×13
       ———
       ▦▦▦
       340
       ———
       442

3.   34
       ×14
       ———
       136
       ▦▦▦
       ———
       476

4.   56
       ×17
       ———
       ▦▦▦
       ▦▦▦
       ———
       952

5.   56
       ×18
       ———
       ▦▦▦
       560
       ———
       ▦▦▦

6.   56
       ×19
       ———
       504
       ▦▦▦
       ———
       ▦▦▦

7. 32
     ×3

8. 32
     ×10

9. 32
     ×13

10. 21
      ×4

11. 21
      ×10

12. 21
      ×14

13. 63
      ×2

14. 63
      ×10

15. 63
      ×12

16. 81
      ×5

17. 81
      ×10

18. 81
      ×15

19. 27
      ×3

20. 27
      ×10

21. 27
      ×13

22. 18
      ×8

23. 18
      ×10

24. 18
      ×18

b Multiply.

25. 42 ×12	26. 24 ×13	27. 44 ×14
28. 51 ×16	29. 37 ×18	30. 62 ×11
31. 97 ×12	32. 13 ×13	33. 25 ×17
34. 53 ×19	35. 19 ×16	36. 63 ×15
37. 37 ×14	38. 98 ×13	39. 86 ×16

c Solve.

40. 24 beads in a package
12 packages
How many beads?

41. 36 loops for a potholder
15 potholders
How many loops needed?

Shortcut to eleven

11	12	13
×11	×11	×11
11	12	13
110	120	130
121	132	143

Look at the products. Can you find a shortcut in multiplication by 11?

Use a shortcut to multiply.

1. 11 × 14   2. 11 × 15   3. 11 × 23

4. 11 × 32   5. 11 × 61   6. 11 × 54

Multiplication by Ones and Tens

To multiply 24 by 36, we may think of 36 as 3 tens 6 ones.

Multiply 24 by 6.

```
   24
 × 36
 ────
  144
```

Multiply 24 by 30.

```
   24
 × 36
 ────
  144
  720
```

Add 144 and 720.

```
   24
 × 36
 ────
  144
  720
 ────
  864
```

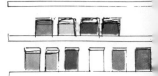

The product of 24 and 36 is 864.

ⓐ Multiply.

1. 42	2. 42	3. 42	4. 42	5. 42	6. 42
×21	×23	×25	×31	×33	×35
42	▓▓▓▓	210	▓▓	▓▓▓	210
840	840	▓▓▓	▓▓▓▓▓	1260	▓▓▓▓
▓▓▓▓	966	1050	1302	▓▓▓▓	▓▓▓▓

7. 23	8. 23	9. 23	10. 31	11. 31	12. 31
× 2	×30	×32	× 3	×20	×23

13. 24	14. 24	15. 24	16. 48	17. 48	18. 48
× 3	×20	×23	× 3	×40	×43

222

b Multiply.

19. 39 ×23	20. 56 ×47	21. 68 ×28	22. 49 ×41	23. 27 ×52	24. 79 ×45
25. 57 ×68	26. 95 ×31	27. 48 ×73	28. 39 ×24	29. 63 ×53	30. 26 ×36
31. 72 ×25	32. 73 ×28	33. 38 ×27	34. 69 ×47	35. 43 ×25	36. 39 ×21
37. 47 ×98	38. 33 ×77	39. 52 ×72	40. 12 ×88	41. 59 ×48	42. 99 ×99
43. 16 ×32	44. 26 ×24	45. 81 ×29	46. 55 ×55	47. 24 ×23	48. 36 ×63

Review A (pages 214–223)

1. 22 ×4	2. 43 ×3	3. 16 ×6	4. 98 ×8
5. 231 ×4	6. 429 ×7	7. 4143 ×2	8. 1479 ×6
9. 18 ×10	10. 69 ×10	11. 23 ×30	12. 46 ×40
13. 24 ×12	14. 91 ×13	15. 18 ×15	16. 83 ×16
17. 31 ×33	18. 58 ×47	19. 26 ×52	20. 87 ×45

Extra practice on p. 328

Three-place Multiplication

Compare these examples.

132	132		132	132		132	132
×1	×10		×2	×20		×6	×60
132	1320		264	2640		792	7920

a Multiply.

1. 213   213   **2.** 213   213   **3.** 213   213
    ×1   ×10   ×3   ×30   ×6   ×60

4. 326   326   **5.** 326   326   **6.** 326   326
    ×1   ×10   ×2   ×20   ×8   ×80

7. 435   435   **8.** 435   435   **9.** 435   435
    ×1   ×10   ×3   ×30   ×7   ×70

10. 648   648   **11.** 648   648   **12.** 648   648
     ×1   ×10   ×4   ×40   ×9   ×90

b Multiply.

13. 638 ×10	14. 249 ×30	15. 162 ×80	16. 795 ×20	17. 524 ×30	18. 387 ×40
19. 193 ×90	20. 465 ×40	21. 766 ×50	22. 817 ×60	23. 653 ×70	24. 296 ×80
25. 938 ×20	26. 389 ×50	27. 544 ×30	28. 914 ×80	29. 326 ×60	30. 493 ×40

 Solve.

31. On Monday 198 hamburgers were sold. Ten times as many were sold on Saturday. How many were sold on Saturday?

32. The store sold 125 cherry pies. It sold 10 times as many apple pies. How many apple pies were sold?

33. There are 225 napkins in a box. How many napkins are in 20 boxes?

34. About 450 pickles are needed each day. About how many are needed for 30 days?

225

Three-place Multiplication

To multiply 124 by 16, we may think of 16 as 1 ten 6 ones.

Multiply 124 by 6.	Multiply 124 by 10.	Add 744 and 1240.
124	124	124
×16	×16	×16
744	744	744
	1240	1240
		1984

The product of 124 and 16 is 1984.

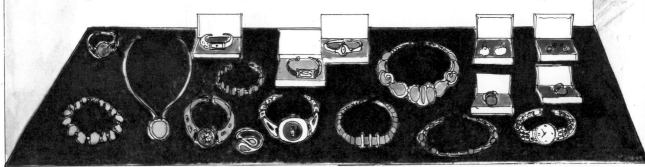

a Multiply.

1. 153	2. 153	3. 153	4. 153	5. 153	6. 153
×13	×14	×15	×16	×17	×18
459	▦	765	▦	▦	1224
1530	1530	▦	▦	1530	▦
▦	2142	2295	2448	▦	▦

7. 132	8. 132	9. 132	10. 247	11. 247	12. 247
×2	×10	×12	×3	×10	×13

13. 482	14. 482	15. 482	16. 319	17. 319	18. 319
×3	×10	×13	×5	×10	×15

19. 265	20. 265	21. 265	22. 528	23. 528	24. 528
×6	×10	×16	×2	×10	×12

b Multiply.

25. 179
    ×12

26. 352
    ×14

27. 816
    ×16

28. 558
    ×13

29. 493
    ×18

30. 288
    ×17

31. 743
    ×16

32. 919
    ×12

33. 256
    ×15

34. 327
    ×19

35. 664
    ×13

36. 195
    ×18

37. 472
    ×14

38. 727
    ×17

39. 347
    ×16

c Solve.

40. The store earns $455 fixing watches and 15 times as much
    selling watches. How much is earned selling watches?

41. The factory packs 12 silver charms in each box and ships
    out 156 boxes. How many charms in all are shipped out?

42. About 350 jewelers are in a big city. About how many
    are in 16 big cities?

Time to Multiply

Which is longer?

1. 1 hour or 3000 seconds?   2. 1 hour or 4000 seconds?

3. 1 day or 2000 minutes?   4. 1 day or 1400 minutes?

5. 10 years or 500 weeks?   6. 10 years or 5000 days?

Three-place Multiplication

To multiply 124 by 36, we may think of 36 as 3 tens 6 ones.

Multiply 124 by 6.

```
  124
×  36
─────
  744
```

Multiply 124 by 30.

```
  124
×  36
─────
  744
 3720
```

Add 744 and 3720.

```
  124
×  36
─────
  744
 3720
─────
 4464
```

The product of 124 and 36 is 4464.

 Multiply.

1.
```
  173
×  24
─────
  692
 3460
─────
```

2.
```
  173
×  25
─────
  ▓▓▓▓
 3460
─────
 4325
```

3.
```
  173
×  26
─────
 1038
 ▓▓▓▓
─────
 4498
```

4.
```
  173
×  37
─────
 ▓▓▓▓
 ▓▓▓▓
─────
 6401
```

5.
```
  173
×  38
─────
 ▓▓▓▓
 5190
─────
 ▓▓▓▓
```

6.
```
  173
×  39
─────
 1557
 ▓▓▓▓
─────
 ▓▓▓▓
```

7.
```
 132
×  3
```

8.
```
 132
× 20
```

9.
```
 132
× 23
```

10.
```
 247
×  6
```

11.
```
 247
× 30
```

12.
```
 247
× 36
```

13.
```
 482
×  8
```

14.
```
 482
× 50
```

15.
```
 482
× 58
```

16.
```
 319
×  9
```

17.
```
 319
× 40
```

18.
```
 319
× 49
```

19.
```
 265
×  7
```

20.
```
 265
× 30
```

21.
```
 265
× 37
```

22.
```
 528
×  5
```

23.
```
 528
× 60
```

24.
```
 528
× 65
```

b Multiply.

25. 217 ×23	26. 452 ×36	27. 393 ×52	28. 624 ×27	29. 811 ×39	30. 573 ×45
31. 663 ×52	32. 149 ×83	33. 256 ×46	34. 165 ×92	35. 493 ×62	36. 719 ×34
37. 327 ×72	38. 508 ×64	39. 836 ×24	40. 781 ×46	41. 637 ×25	42. 348 ×66
43. 514 ×48	44. 276 ×53	45. 194 ×34	46. 358 ×27	47. 716 ×52	48. 605 ×92

c Solve.

49. 124 papers are delivered each week. How many are delivered in 52 weeks?

50. 108 comic strips are drawn for each week. How many are drawn for 52 weeks?

51. 250 people use the corner newsstand. 45 times as many use the subway newsstand. How many people is that?

52. Children's magazine sales total $260. News sales total 55 times as much. How much is that?

Multiplication with Money

We may multiply dollars and cents by ones and tens.
Do not forget the dollar sign and point in the answer.

$$\begin{array}{r} \$\ 2.89 \\ \times 10 \\ \hline \$28.90 \end{array} \qquad \begin{array}{r} \$\ 1.24 \\ \times 20 \\ \hline \$24.80 \end{array} \qquad \begin{array}{r} \$\ 3.12 \\ \times 32 \\ \hline 6\,24 \\ 93\,60 \\ \hline \$99.84 \end{array}$$

a Multiply.

1. $1.56 × 10

2. $2.98 × 10

3. $6.55 × 10

4. $9.99 × 10

5. $2.50 × 10

6. $2.13 × 30

7. $1.58 × 20

8. $3.27 × 50

9. $7.69 × 60

10. $2.50 × 40

11. $4.23 × 11

12. $4.23 × 22

13. $4.23 × 33

14. $4.23 × 44

15. $4.23 × 55

b Multiply.

16. $3.76	17. $2.59	18. $4.32	19. $5.67	20. $8.78
×10	×30	×22	×40	×12

21. $6.95	22. $3.38	23. $7.13	24. $4.82	25. $9.32
×32	×45	×25	×51	×35

c Solve.

26. A baseball coach buys 13 caps at $2.98 each for her team. How much does she pay in all?

27. A buyer for a clothing store orders 75 shirts at $3.49 each. What is the cost of the order?

28. The store sells a dozen jeans for $7.95 each. What is the total amount of the sale?

29. There are 23 pairs of sneakers in stock to sell for $8.99 each. What is the value of the stock of sneakers?

Review B   (pages 224–231)

1. 543	2. 243	3. 187	4. 635
×10	×20	×40	×70

5. 132	6. 246	7. 358	8. 618
×12	×14	×13	×19

9. 123	10. 246	11. 412	12. 385
×36	×23	×62	×25

13. $3.24	14. $4.23	15. $5.98	16. $2.79
×10	×30	×12	×32

Problem Solving   Problem • Plan • Arithmetic • Answer

| 4 | Give the answer. | How much do ten cost? | $200? $2.00? |

Ask yourself whether your answer to a problem makes sense.

One pen costs $.20. How much do 10 pens cost?
$200 or $2.00?

Common sense tells you that $2.00
is a more likely answer than $200.

Write a, b, or c to choose the most likely answer.

1. Ken earns $.25 a day feeding a friend's cat.
   How much does he earn in 10 days?
   a. $.25   b. $2.50   c. $25

2. Lola scores 36 points, 112 points, and 9 points.
   What is her total score?
   a. 1372   b. 481   c. 157

3. Marco and Susan spend 1 dollar, 19 cents, and 35 cents.
   How much do they spend in all?
   a. $.55   b. $.64   c. $1.54

4. The shop sold 30 cups of hot chocolate at 35¢ each.
   What was the total value of the sales?
   a. $10.50   b. $1.05   c. 65¢

5. I had $10.50. I spent $1.88. How much do I have left?
   a. $.38   b. $8.62   c. $12.38

Unit Test

Multiply. (pages 214–217)

1. 34	**2.** 98	**3.** 212	**4.** 576	**5.** 4093
×2	×7	×3	×8	×9

Multiply. (pages 218–219)

6. 24	**7.** 58	**8.** 73	**9.** 45	**10.** 67
×20	×30	×60	×10	×50

Multiply. (pages 220–223)

11. 43	**12.** 56	**13.** 74	**14.** 39	**15.** 87
×12	×18	×36	×42	×68

Multiply. (pages 224–225)

16. 472	**17.** 658	**18.** 926	**19.** 532
×10	×30	×80	×70

Multiply. (pages 226–229)

20. 492	**21.** 657	**22.** 538	**23.** 918	**24.** 769
×13	×16	×24	×45	×56

Multiply. (pages 230–231)

25. $3.68	**26.** $9.27	**27.** $4.56	**28.** $7.89
×20	×60	×32	×48

Write a, b, or c to choose the most likely answer.   (page 232)

29. Candy bars cost $.15 each. How much do 20 cost?
   a. $.30   **b.** $3.00   **c.** $30.00

30. The shop sells bike horns for $2.19 each. What is the total value of 5 horns?
   a. $1095   **b.** $109.50   **c.** $10.95

Taking Another Look

Pages 214–217

$$\begin{array}{r} 2\ 1\ 4 \\ 8\ 3\ 2\ 6 \\ \times\ 7 \\ \hline 5\ 8{,}2\ 8\ 2 \end{array}$$

Multiply.

1. $\begin{array}{r}28\\ \times 4\\ \hline\end{array}$	2. $\begin{array}{r}100\\ \times 4\\ \hline\end{array}$	3. $\begin{array}{r}128\\ \times 4\\ \hline\end{array}$	4. $\begin{array}{r}3128\\ \times 4\\ \hline\end{array}$
5. $\begin{array}{r}32\\ \times 2\\ \hline\end{array}$	6. $\begin{array}{r}84\\ \times 6\\ \hline\end{array}$	7. $\begin{array}{r}353\\ \times 5\\ \hline\end{array}$	8. $\begin{array}{r}296\\ \times 4\\ \hline\end{array}$
9. $\begin{array}{r}817\\ \times 8\\ \hline\end{array}$	10. $\begin{array}{r}924\\ \times 7\\ \hline\end{array}$	11. $\begin{array}{r}3062\\ \times 5\\ \hline\end{array}$	12. $\begin{array}{r}6837\\ \times 3\\ \hline\end{array}$

Pages 218–219

$$\begin{array}{r} 87 \\ \times 5 \\ \hline 435 \end{array} \qquad \begin{array}{r} 87 \\ \times 50 \\ \hline 4350 \end{array}$$

Multiply.

1. $\begin{array}{r}49\\ \times 1\\ \hline\end{array}$	2. $\begin{array}{r}49\\ \times 10\\ \hline\end{array}$	3. $\begin{array}{r}26\\ \times 2\\ \hline\end{array}$	4. $\begin{array}{r}26\\ \times 20\\ \hline\end{array}$
5. $\begin{array}{r}53\\ \times 20\\ \hline\end{array}$	6. $\begin{array}{r}65\\ \times 70\\ \hline\end{array}$	7. $\begin{array}{r}48\\ \times 40\\ \hline\end{array}$	8. $\begin{array}{r}92\\ \times 60\\ \hline\end{array}$
9. $\begin{array}{r}39\\ \times 10\\ \hline\end{array}$	10. $\begin{array}{r}76\\ \times 30\\ \hline\end{array}$	11. $\begin{array}{r}18\\ \times 90\\ \hline\end{array}$	12. $\begin{array}{r}24\\ \times 80\\ \hline\end{array}$

Pages 220–223

$$\begin{array}{r} 96 \\ \times 54 \\ \hline 384 \\ 4800 \\ \hline 5184 \end{array}$$

Multiply.

1. $\begin{array}{r}56\\ \times 3\\ \hline\end{array}$	2. $\begin{array}{r}56\\ \times 13\\ \hline\end{array}$	3. $\begin{array}{r}56\\ \times 23\\ \hline\end{array}$	4. $\begin{array}{r}56\\ \times 63\\ \hline\end{array}$
5. $\begin{array}{r}86\\ \times 18\\ \hline\end{array}$	6. $\begin{array}{r}34\\ \times 13\\ \hline\end{array}$	7. $\begin{array}{r}12\\ \times 45\\ \hline\end{array}$	8. $\begin{array}{r}27\\ \times 68\\ \hline\end{array}$
9. $\begin{array}{r}61\\ \times 58\\ \hline\end{array}$	10. $\begin{array}{r}77\\ \times 33\\ \hline\end{array}$	11. $\begin{array}{r}94\\ \times 82\\ \hline\end{array}$	12. $\begin{array}{r}43\\ \times 29\\ \hline\end{array}$

Pages 224–225

$$247$$
$$\times 3$$
$$741$$

$$247$$
$$\times 30$$
$$7410$$

Multiply.

1. 385
   $\times 4$

2. 385
   $\times 40$

3. 963
   $\times 2$

4. 963
   $\times 20$

5. 826
   $\times 50$

6. 419
   $\times 60$

7. 257
   $\times 90$

8. 738
   $\times 70$

Pages 226–229

$$958$$
$$\times 63$$
$$2874$$
$$57480$$
$$60{,}354$$

Multiply.

1. 426
   $\times 6$

2. 426
   $\times 16$

3. 426
   $\times 36$

4. 426
   $\times 56$

5. 518
   $\times 19$

6. 862
   $\times 27$

7. 773
   $\times 54$

8. 681
   $\times 76$

Pages 230–231

$$\$7.83$$
$$\times 46$$
$$4698$$
$$31320$$
$$\$360.18$$

Multiply.

1. $\$2.49$
   $\times 10$

2. $\$2.49$
   $\times 17$

3. $\$3.65$
   $\times 50$

4. $\$3.65$
   $\times 59$

5. $\$6.17$
   $\times 80$

6. $\$9.23$
   $\times 36$

7. $\$8.77$
   $\times 62$

8. $\$4.39$
   $\times 74$

Page 232

1. **Problem**
2. **Plan**
3. **Arithmetic**
4. **Answer**

Write a, b, or c to choose the most likely answer.

1. A movie ticket costs $2.75. How much do 6 cost?
   a. $16.50   b. $1.65   c. $165.00

2. A plumber charges $12.00 an hour for his work. What does he charge for 8 hours of work?
   a. $9.60   b. $960.00   c. $96.00

Something Extra • TRAIN TIMETABLES

This list will help you with the timetable and the questions.

Lv.—Leave
Arr.—Arrive
A.M.—Between midnight and noon
P.M.—Between noon and midnight
Daily—Every day
Ex.—Except
&—And
Weekday—Monday through Friday

Linden to River City Train Timetable

Lv. Linden	Arr. River City	
6:45 A.M.	7:15 A.M.	Daily Ex. Sat. & Sun.
7:30 A.M.	8:10 A.M.	Daily Ex. Sat. & Sun.
7:33 A.M.	8:07 A.M.	Sat. Only
8:12 A.M.	8:44 A.M.	Daily Ex. Sat. & Sun.
8:54 A.M.	9:20 A.M.	Daily Ex. Sat. & Sun.
9:23 A.M.	9:50 A.M.	Daily Ex. Sun.
9:58 A.M.	10:25 A.M.	Daily Ex. Sat. & Sun.
11:34 A.M.	12:02 P.M.	Daily
3:13 P.M.	3:40 P.M.	Daily Ex. Sat. & Sun.
5:52 P.M.	6:20 P.M.	Daily Ex. Sun.
6:48 P.M.	7:15 P.M.	Sun. Only

SEE BULLETIN BOARD AT STATION
FOR HOLIDAY SCHEDULE

How many trains in the timetable run at these times?

1. on a weekday morning
2. on Saturday
3. on a weekday afternoon
4. on Sunday

5. Which train could you take from Linden to see the 1:30 P.M. movie in River City on Sunday?

6. What is the latest train you can take from Linden to arrive in River City by 2:00 P.M. on a weekday?

7. Do all of the daily trains take the same amount of time to go from Linden to River City?

8. How long does it take the 7:30 train to go from Linden to River City?

9. How long does it take the 8:54 train to go from Linden to River City?

10. Which train do you think makes more stops between Linden and River City, the 7:30 train or the 8:54 train?

11. Clare rides the 8:12 train to River City every weekday. How many minutes in all does she ride the 8:12 train in a week?

12. Does Clare ride the 8:12 more than 2 hours each week?

Reviewing Needed Skills

Subtract.

1. 70 −30	2. 69 −35	3. 20 −15	4. 68 −23	5. 91 −73	6. 46 −28
7. 463 −142	8. 987 −465	9. 820 −568	10. 763 −491	11. 592 −263	12. 200 −155
13. 326 −187	14. 548 −362	15. 917 − 49	16. 258 − 79	17. 434 − 86	18. 404 − 86

Multiply.

19. 32 ×2	20. 13 ×3	21. 40 ×7	22. 91 ×6	23. 36 ×4	24. 90 ×8
25. 69 ×4	26. 78 ×5	27. 53 ×8	28. 23 ×9	29. 80 ×6	30. 31 ×4
31. 19 ×5	32. 70 ×9	33. 97 ×8	34. 84 ×7	35. 56 ×5	36. 62 ×9
37. 48 ×3	38. 61 ×5	39. 77 ×7	40. 25 ×4	41. 33 ×6	42. 90 ×9

Divide.

43. $8\overline{)56}$	44. $9\overline{)81}$	45. $7\overline{)49}$	46. $3\overline{)27}$	47. $4\overline{)20}$
48. $6\overline{)39}$	49. $5\overline{)48}$	50. $2\overline{)17}$	51. $9\overline{)65}$	52. $8\overline{)49}$
53. $7\overline{)427}$	54. $9\overline{)657}$	55. $4\overline{)216}$	56. $8\overline{)568}$	57. $3\overline{)261}$
58. $6\overline{)391}$	59. $4\overline{)218}$	60. $9\overline{)735}$	61. $5\overline{)432}$	62. $7\overline{)382}$

UNIT 11

Two-place Quotients

We divide 268 by 3 in two stages.

Divide 26 by 3.
Subtract 8 × 3.

$$
\begin{array}{r}
8 \\
3\overline{)\,268} \\
-24 \\
\hline
2
\end{array}
$$

➡

$$
\begin{array}{r}
89 \\
3\overline{)\,268} \\
-24\downarrow \\
\hline
28 \\
-27 \\
\hline
1
\end{array}
$$

Divide 28 by 3.
Subtract 9 × 3.

The quotient is 89. The remainder is 1.

Division

a Divide.

1. 5)85   2. 5)86   3. 5)87   4. 5)88   5. 5)89

6. 8)96   7. 8)97   8. 8)98   9. 8)99   10. 8)100

11. 8)128   12. 8)129   13. 8)130   14. 8)131   15. 8)132

16. 4)256   17. 4)257   18. 4)258   19. 4)259   20. 4)260

21. 9)396   22. 9)397   23. 9)398   24. 9)399   25. 9)400

26. 7)287   27. 7)288   28. 7)289   29. 7)290   30. 7)291

31. 6)114   32. 6)115   33. 6)116   34. 6)117   35. 6)118

Three-place Quotients

We divide 369 by 3 in three stages.

Divide the hundreds.

Divide 3 by 3.
Subtract 1 × 3.

$$
\begin{array}{r}
1 \\
3{\overline{)\,369}} \\
-3 \\
\hline
0
\end{array}
$$

Divide the tens.

Divide 6 by 3.
Subtract 2 × 3.

$$
\begin{array}{r}
12 \\
3{\overline{)\,369}} \\
-3 \\
\hline
06 \\
-6 \\
\hline
0
\end{array}
$$

Divide the ones.

Divide 9 by 3.
Subtract 3 × 3.

$$
\begin{array}{r}
123 \\
3{\overline{)\,369}} \\
-3 \\
\hline
06 \\
-6 \\
\hline
09 \\
-9 \\
\hline
0
\end{array}
$$

The quotient is 123.

a Divide.

1.
$$
\begin{array}{r}
11 \\
2{\overline{)\,422}} \\
-4 \\
\hline
02 \\
-2 \\
\hline
02 \\
-2 \\
\hline
0
\end{array}
$$

2.
$$
\begin{array}{r}
2\ 2 \\
2{\overline{)\,424}} \\
-4 \\
\hline
02 \\
-2 \\
\hline
04 \\
-4 \\
\hline
0
\end{array}
$$

3.
$$
\begin{array}{r}
21 \\
2{\overline{)\,426}} \\
-4 \\
\hline
02 \\
-2 \\
\hline
06 \\
-6 \\
\hline
0
\end{array}
$$

4.
$$
\begin{array}{r}
3 \\
2{\overline{)\,446}} \\
-4 \\
\hline
04 \\
-4 \\
\hline
06 \\
-6 \\
\hline
0
\end{array}
$$

5.
$$
\begin{array}{r}
 \\
2{\overline{)\,466}} \\
-4 \\
\hline
06 \\
-6 \\
\hline
06 \\
-6 \\
\hline
0
\end{array}
$$

6. $3{\overline{)\,300}}$

7. $3{\overline{)\,336}}$

8. $3{\overline{)\,366}}$

9. $3{\overline{)\,396}}$

10. $3{\overline{)\,399}}$

11. $4{\overline{)\,800}}$

12. $4{\overline{)\,844}}$

13. $4{\overline{)\,848}}$

14. $4{\overline{)\,884}}$

15. $4{\overline{)\,888}}$

b Divide.

16. $2\overline{)264}$ 17. $3\overline{)966}$

18. $4\overline{)488}$ 19. $2\overline{)468}$

20. $3\overline{)639}$ 21. $2\overline{)824}$

22. $2\overline{)682}$ 23. $3\overline{)936}$

24. $3\overline{)666}$ 25. $7\overline{)777}$

c Solve.

26. Rent for a 2-family unit is $486. How much per family?

27. 3 sun panels heat a unit. How many units do 336 sun panels heat?

Hurry and take your time

There once was a student from Spinnet
Who did 1 to 10 in a minute
And when she was done,
She did 10 to 1
Before she had time to begin it.

Write just the answer. Time yourself.

1. $2\overline{)200}$ 2. $2\overline{)220}$ 3. $2\overline{)202}$ 4. $2\overline{)222}$ 5. $5\overline{)505}$

6. $7\overline{)770}$ 7. $4\overline{)400}$ 8. $9\overline{)999}$ 9. $6\overline{)606}$ 10. $8\overline{)880}$

Write the answers for 10 to 1. Can you beat your own time?

Three-place Quotients

We divide 375 by 3 in three stages.

Divide 3 by 3.
Subtract 1 × 3.

$$\begin{array}{r} 1 \\ 3\overline{)\ 375} \\ -3 \\ \hline 0 \end{array}$$

▶ Divide 7 by 3.
Subtract 2 × 3.

$$\begin{array}{r} 12 \\ 3\overline{)\ 375} \\ -3\downarrow \\ \hline 07 \\ -6 \\ \hline 1 \end{array}$$

▶ Divide 15 by 3.
Subtract 5 × 3.

$$\begin{array}{r} 125 \\ 3\overline{)\ 375} \\ -3 \\ \hline 07 \\ -6\downarrow \\ \hline 15 \\ -15 \\ \hline 0 \end{array}$$

The quotient is 125.

a Divide.

1. $5\overline{)500}$ 2. $5\overline{)75}$ 3. $5\overline{)575}$

4. $4\overline{)400}$ 5. $4\overline{)56}$ 6. $4\overline{)456}$

7. $6\overline{)600}$ 8. $6\overline{)96}$ 9. $6\overline{)696}$

10. $4\overline{)64}$ 11. $4\overline{)640}$ 12. $4\overline{)644}$

13. $3\overline{)54}$ 14. $3\overline{)540}$ 15. $3\overline{)546}$

16. $5\overline{)555}$ 17. $5\overline{)655}$

18. $5\overline{)755}$ 19. $5\overline{)855}$

20. $7\overline{)777}$ 21. $7\overline{)784}$

22. $7\overline{)791}$ 23. $7\overline{)798}$

24. $3\overline{)342}$ 25. $3\overline{)423}$

26. $3\overline{)372}$ 27. $5\overline{)580}$ 28. $4\overline{)892}$ 29. $5\overline{)595}$ 30. $4\overline{)928}$

31. $3\overline{)723}$ 32. $6\overline{)672}$ 33. $2\overline{)364}$ 34. $8\overline{)968}$ 35. $5\overline{)805}$

36. $4\overline{)768}$ 37. $5\overline{)900}$ 38. $7\overline{)847}$ 39. $6\overline{)786}$ 40. $2\overline{)298}$

41. $6\overline{)906}$ 42. $7\overline{)917}$ 43. $6\overline{)846}$ 44. $2\overline{)566}$ 45. $7\overline{)987}$

c Solve.

46. 560 timetables stacked
    5 stacks
    How many in a stack?

47. 230 km of rail to build
    2 weeks to build it
    How many kilometers per week?

48. $345 trip costs
    3 friends sharing costs
    How much each?

49. 456 people to seat
    4 to a seat
    How many seats?

50. 456 travelers
    $\frac{1}{2}$ of them students
    How many students?

51. 456 tickets to punch
    3 conductors
    How many tickets each?

Three-place Quotients

We divide 471 by 3 in three stages.

Divide 4 by 3. $3\overline{)471}$ with 1 above
Subtract 1 × 3. -3
                   1 ▶ Divide 17 by 3. $3\overline{)471}$ with 15 above
                          Subtract 5 × 3. -3
                                            17
                                            -15
                                            2 ▶ Divide 21 by 3. $3\overline{)471}$ with 157 above
                                                   Subtract 7 × 3. -3
                                                                     17
                                                                     -15
                                                                     21
                                                                     -21
                                                                     0

The quotient is 157.

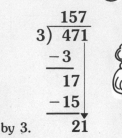

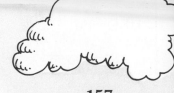

 Divide.

1. $3\overline{)432}$ → $\blacksquare 44$
    -3
    13
    -12
    12
    -12
    0

2. $3\overline{)435}$ → $1\blacksquare 5$
    -3
    13
    -12
    15
    -15
    0

3. $3\overline{)438}$ → $14\blacksquare$
    -3
    13
    -12
    18
    -18
    0

4. $3\overline{)441}$ → $\blacksquare\blacksquare 7$
    -3
    14
    -12
    21
    -21
    0

5. $3\overline{)444}$ → $\blacksquare\blacksquare\blacksquare$
    -3
    14
    -12
    24
    -24
    0

6. $5\overline{)675}$
7. $5\overline{)680}$
8. $5\overline{)685}$
9. $5\overline{)690}$
10. $5\overline{)695}$

11. $4\overline{)612}$
12. $4\overline{)616}$
13. $4\overline{)620}$
14. $4\overline{)624}$
15. $4\overline{)628}$

16. $3\overline{)822}$
17. $3\overline{)825}$
18. $3\overline{)828}$
19. $3\overline{)831}$
20. $3\overline{)834}$

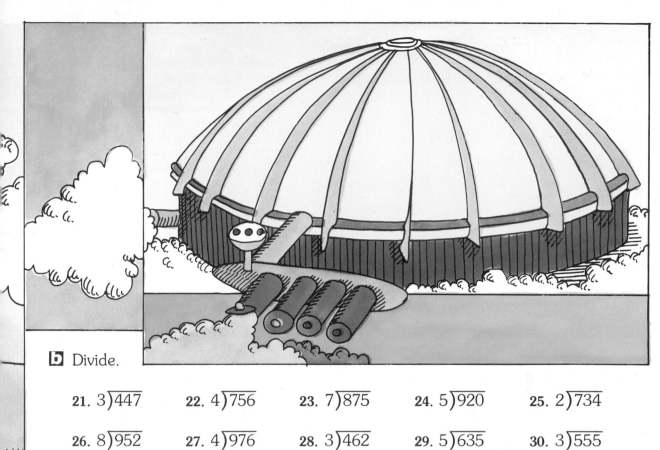

b Divide.

21. 3)447 22. 4)756 23. 7)875 24. 5)920 25. 2)734

26. 8)952 27. 4)976 28. 3)462 29. 5)635 30. 3)555

31. 5)815 32. 4)780 33. 7)924 34. 2)998 35. 6)924

36. 7)896 37. 2)576 38. 5)770 39. 4)912 40. 8)984

What's missing?

Complete the number.

```
        123              212              123              321              121
1. 3)36▨         2. 4)8 8          3. 2) 46         4. 3) 6          5. 4)4▨▨
```

```
        423              222              122              342              313
6. 2)▨▨6         7. 3)▨▨▨          8. 4)▨▨▨          9. 2)▨▨▨         10. 3)▨▨▨
```

```
        128              328              364              488              286
11. 2)▨56        12. 2)6▨6         13. 2)7▨8         14. 2)9▨6        15. 3)▨58
```

245

Three-place Quotients

We divide 571 by 4 in three stages.

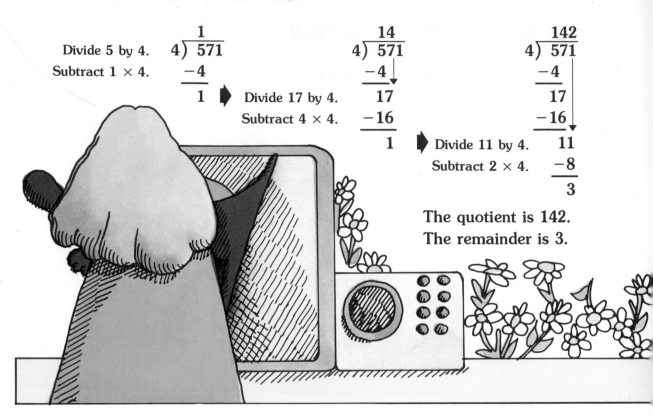

Divide 5 by 4.
Subtract 1 × 4.

$$4{\overline{\smash{)}\,571}} \quad \begin{array}{r} 1 \\ -4 \\ \hline 1 \end{array}$$

Divide 17 by 4.
Subtract 4 × 4.

$$4{\overline{\smash{)}\,571}} \quad \begin{array}{r} 14 \\ -4\downarrow \\ \hline 17 \\ -16 \\ \hline 1 \end{array}$$

Divide 11 by 4.
Subtract 2 × 4.

$$4{\overline{\smash{)}\,571}} \quad \begin{array}{r} 142 \\ -4 \\ \hline 17 \\ -16\downarrow \\ \hline 11 \\ -8 \\ \hline 3 \end{array}$$

The quotient is 142.
The remainder is 3.

a Divide.

1. $4{\overline{\smash{)}\,465}}$ quotient ▮16
   -4 ; 06 ; -4 ; 25 ; -24 ; ▮

2. $4{\overline{\smash{)}\,565}}$ quotient 1▮1
   -4 ; 16 ; -16 ; 05 ; -4 ; ▮

3. $4{\overline{\smash{)}\,665}}$ quotient 16▮
   -4 ; 26 ; -24 ; 25 ; -24 ; ▮

4. $4{\overline{\smash{)}\,765}}$ quotient ▮▮▮
   -4 ; 36 ; -36 ; 05 ; -4 ; ▮

5. $4{\overline{\smash{)}\,865}}$ quotient ▮▮▮
   -8 ; 06 ; -4 ; 25 ; -24 ; ▮

6. $6{\overline{\smash{)}\,669}}$

7. $6{\overline{\smash{)}\,689}}$

8. $6{\overline{\smash{)}\,789}}$

9. $6{\overline{\smash{)}\,889}}$

10. $6{\overline{\smash{)}\,989}}$

11. $4{\overline{\smash{)}\,489}}$

12. $4{\overline{\smash{)}\,499}}$

13. $4{\overline{\smash{)}\,599}}$

14. $4{\overline{\smash{)}\,699}}$

15. $4{\overline{\smash{)}\,799}}$

b Divide.

16. 8)958   17. 2)323   18. 6)827   19. 3)494   20. 4)729

21. 3)344   22. 7)919   23. 5)587   24. 8)893   25. 5)958

26. 6)743   27. 8)993   28. 2)875   29. 7)783   30. 6)967

31. 7)921   32. 3)401   33. 2)369

34. 3)524   35. 4)871   36. 2)999

37. 5)766   38. 6)915

39. 4)929   40. 7)874

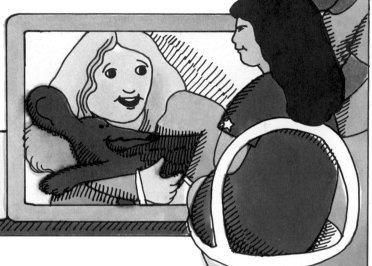

Review A (pages 238–247)

1. 5)76   2. 7)91   3. 3)283   4. 6)306

5. 3)963   6. 2)864   7. 4)888   8. 3)363

9. 4)472   10. 3)576   11. 2)658   12. 5)750

13. 3)522   14. 7)966   15. 2)376   16. 6)924

17. 8)890   18. 3)517   19. 6)823   20. 4)971

Extra practice on p. 330

Zero in the Quotient

We divide 314 by 3 in three stages.

Divide 3 by 3.
Subtract 1 × 3.

$$\begin{array}{r} 1 \\ 3\overline{)\ 314} \\ -3 \\ \hline 0 \end{array}$$
➡
Divide 1 by 3.
Subtract 0 × 3.

$$\begin{array}{r} 10 \\ 3\overline{)\ 314} \\ -3 \downarrow \\ \hline 01 \\ -0 \\ \hline 1 \end{array}$$
➡
Divide 14 by 3.
Subtract 4 × 3.

$$\begin{array}{r} 104 \\ 3\overline{)\ 314} \\ -3 \\ \hline 01 \\ -0 \downarrow \\ \hline 14 \\ -12 \\ \hline 2 \end{array}$$

In the second stage we write 0 in the quotient because
no threes can be subtracted.

SEAWEED NATIONAL PARK
DO NOT FEED THE FISH

a Divide.

1. $\begin{array}{r} ▮0 \\ 6\overline{)\ 61} \\ -6 \\ \hline 01 \\ -0 \\ \hline ▮ \end{array}$
2. $\begin{array}{r} ▮0 \\ 6\overline{)\ 62} \\ -6 \\ \hline 02 \\ -▮ \\ \hline 2 \end{array}$
3. $\begin{array}{r} 1▮ \\ 6\overline{)\ 63} \\ -6 \\ \hline 03 \\ -0 \\ \hline ▮ \end{array}$
4. $\begin{array}{r} 1▮ \\ 6\overline{)\ 64} \\ -6 \\ \hline 04 \\ -▮ \\ \hline 4 \end{array}$
5. $\begin{array}{r} ▮▮ \\ 6\overline{)\ 65} \\ -6 \\ \hline 05 \\ -0 \\ \hline 5 \end{array}$

6. $\begin{array}{r} 10▮ \\ 6\overline{)606} \end{array}$
7. $\begin{array}{r} 10▮ \\ 6\overline{)612} \end{array}$
8. $\begin{array}{r} 1▮3 \\ 6\overline{)618} \end{array}$
9. $\begin{array}{r} 1▮▮ \\ 6\overline{)624} \end{array}$
10. $\begin{array}{r} ▮▮▮ \\ 6\overline{)630} \end{array}$

11. $3\overline{)306}$
12. $3\overline{)305}$
13. $3\overline{)304}$
14. $3\overline{)303}$
15. $3\overline{)302}$

16. $9\overline{)981}$
17. $9\overline{)971}$
18. $9\overline{)961}$
19. $9\overline{)951}$
20. $9\overline{)941}$

b Divide.

21. 2)‾4‾1‾   22. 4)‾8‾3‾

23. 7)‾7‾6‾   24. 3)‾9‾2‾

25. 5)‾5‾4‾0‾   26. 3)‾6‾0‾6‾

27. 8)‾8‾7‾3‾   28. 2)‾8‾1‾7‾

29. 4)‾8‾0‾4‾   30. 5)‾3‾5‾0‾

31. 7)‾4‾9‾6‾   32. 3)‾9‾2‾7‾

33. 2)‾1‾2‾1‾   34. 2)‾8‾0‾2‾

35. 6)‾6‾4‾2‾   36. 9)‾1‾8‾1‾

37. 3)‾7‾2‾0‾   38. 2)‾2‾1‾4‾

39. 7)‾1‾4‾0‾   40. 5)‾6‾0‾0‾

Is nothing missing?

The example shown is wrong.
Someone forgot to write 0 in the
quotient in the second stage.

```
      14
3)  314
   -3
   ___
    014
   -12
   ___
     2
```

Correct each example.

1. $\dfrac{36}{3)918}$ 2. $\dfrac{24}{2)408}$ 3. $\dfrac{21}{4)824}$ 4. $\dfrac{26}{3)780}$ 5. $\dfrac{3}{5)150}$

Division by Tens

To estimate the quotient when dividing 85 by 40, we may divide 8 by 4.

Compare these examples.

$$\begin{array}{r} 2 \\ 4\overline{)8} \\ -8 \\ \hline 0 \end{array} \qquad \begin{array}{r} 2 \\ 40\overline{)80} \\ -80 \\ \hline 0 \end{array} \qquad \begin{array}{r} 2 \\ 40\overline{)85} \\ -80 \\ \hline 5 \end{array}$$

When we divide 85 by 40, the quotient is 2 and the remainder is 5.

a Divide.

1. $2\overline{)8}$ 2. $20\overline{)80}$ 3. $20\overline{)83}$

4. $2\overline{)6}$ 5. $20\overline{)60}$ 6. $20\overline{)65}$

7. $3\overline{)6}$ 8. $30\overline{)60}$ 9. $30\overline{)67}$

10. $3\overline{)12}$ 11. $30\overline{)120}$ 12. $30\overline{)126}$

13. $5\overline{)25}$ 14. $50\overline{)250}$ 15. $50\overline{)259}$

16. $9\overline{)81}$ 17. $90\overline{)810}$ 18. $90\overline{)812}$

19. $2\overline{)7}$ 20. $20\overline{)70}$ 21. $20\overline{)73}$

22. $3\overline{)8}$ 23. $30\overline{)80}$ 24. $30\overline{)84}$

25. $3\overline{)14}$ 26. $30\overline{)140}$ 27. $30\overline{)142}$

28. $5\overline{)28}$ 29. $50\overline{)280}$ 30. $50\overline{)283}$

b Divide.

31. $30\overline{)90}$ 32. $20\overline{)40}$ 33. $50\overline{)150}$ 34. $60\overline{)240}$ 35. $30\overline{)210}$

36. $20\overline{)43}$ 37. $30\overline{)154}$ 38. $30\overline{)92}$ 39. $40\overline{)81}$ 40. $20\overline{)165}$

41. $90\overline{)186}$ 42. $20\overline{)87}$ 43. $30\overline{)63}$ 44. $20\overline{)181}$ 45. $70\overline{)425}$

46. $20\overline{)75}$ 47. $30\overline{)51}$ 48. $20\overline{)134}$ 49. $20\overline{)32}$ 50. $60\overline{)375}$

51. $40\overline{)96}$ 52. $30\overline{)162}$ 53. $60\overline{)83}$ 54. $40\overline{)250}$ 55. $50\overline{)67}$

56. $30\overline{)59}$ 57. $60\overline{)423}$ 58. $50\overline{)320}$ 59. $10\overline{)78}$ 60. $90\overline{)730}$

c Solve.

61. The lab ship tests 60 samples from the ocean floor in 30 weeks. How many samples is that per week?

62. Sea farmers work in teams of 20. How many teams can be formed from 88 workers? How many extra workers?

63. 100 fish herders are grouped into 20 teams of equal size. How many fish herders are on each team?

64. 320 students are taking ocean studies. There are 40 students in each class. How many classes are there?

65. 30 undersea domes form a colony. How many colonies can be formed from 125 new domes? How many extra domes?

Division by Tens and Ones

To divide 85 by 37, we may think of rounding 37 *up* to 40. We may then divide 8 by 4 to estimate the quotient.

Estimate the quotient as 2.
Subtract 2 × 37.

$$\begin{array}{r} 2 \\ 37\overline{)85} \\ -74 \\ \hline 11 \end{array}$$

The quotient is 2. The remainder is 11.

a Divide.

1. $30\overline{)62}$ $26\overline{)62}$ 2. $20\overline{)44}$ $18\overline{)44}$ 3. $40\overline{)82}$ $36\overline{)82}$

4. $30\overline{)75}$ $28\overline{)75}$ 5. $50\overline{)72}$ $43\overline{)72}$ 6. $20\overline{)37}$ $19\overline{)37}$

7. $40\overline{)71}$ $39\overline{)71}$ 8. $60\overline{)93}$ $52\overline{)93}$ 9. $30\overline{)66}$ $24\overline{)66}$

10. $20\overline{)163}$ $19\overline{)163}$ 11. $40\overline{)251}$ $36\overline{)251}$ 12. $50\overline{)181}$ $48\overline{)181}$

b Divide.

13. $28\overline{)76}$ 14. $17\overline{)84}$ 15. $32\overline{)89}$ 16. $59\overline{)97}$ 17. $43\overline{)82}$

18. $38\overline{)99}$ 19. $44\overline{)65}$ 20. $26\overline{)71}$ 21. $19\overline{)94}$ 22. $37\overline{)73}$

23. $52\overline{)252}$ 24. $36\overline{)143}$ 25. $47\overline{)152}$ 26. $28\overline{)211}$ 27. $61\overline{)111}$

c Choose the best answer.

28. The glacier moved a big boulder 18 km and a small one
    42 km. How many times as far was the small one moved?

    a. about 4 times　　　b. about 2 times　　　c. about 20 times

29. In the last 65 years the island lost 150 cm of beach to
    the sea. How many centimeters is that per year?

    a. about 6 cm　　　b. about 4 cm　　　c. about 2 cm

30. The volcano built up a cone 65 m high in 19 days.
    How many meters is that per day?

    a. about 3 m　　　b. about 6 m　　　c. about 45 m

More or less?

A student divided 68 by 32
and wrote the answer 1 R36.
The correct answer is 2 R4.
The work was not complete.

$$\begin{array}{r} 1 \\ 32\overline{)\,68} \\ -32 \\ \hline 36 \end{array}$$ ◀ Another 32
can be
subtracted.

Write Yes if the work is complete.
If it is not complete, write the correct answer.

1. $\begin{array}{r} 1 \\ 35\overline{)\,68} \\ -35 \\ \hline 33 \end{array}$　　2. $\begin{array}{r} 4 \\ 12\overline{)\,80} \\ -48 \\ \hline 32 \end{array}$　　3. $\begin{array}{r} 3 \\ 27\overline{)\,92} \\ -81 \\ \hline 11 \end{array}$　　4. $\begin{array}{r} 3 \\ 18\overline{)\,75} \\ -54 \\ \hline 21 \end{array}$　　5. $\begin{array}{r} 2 \\ 32\overline{)\,98} \\ -64 \\ \hline 34 \end{array}$

Two-place Quotients

Compare these examples.

Divide 850 by 40 in two stages. Divide by 4 to estimate the quotient.

```
      21
40) 850
   -80↓
    50
   -40
    10
```

The quotient is 21.
The remainder is 10.

To divide 850 by 37, think of rounding 37 up to 40. Then divide by 4 to estimate.

```
      22
37) 850
   -74↓
   110
   -74
    36
```

The quotient is 22.
The remainder is 36.

a Divide.

```
        ▮4              ▮6              2▮              2▮              ▮▮
1. 30) 740     2. 28) 740     3. 40) 950     4. 39) 950     5. 39) 958
   -60             -56             -80             -78             -78
   140             180             150             170             178
  -120            -168            -120            -156            -156
    20              12              30              14              22
```

6. 20) 530   7. 19) 530   8. 50) 820   9. 47) 820   10. 47) 826

11. 30) 680   12. 28) 680   13. 40) 510   14. 38) 510   15. 38) 519

16. 20) 830   17. 19) 830   18. 60) 750   19. 59) 750   20. 59) 756

254

b Divide.

21. $37 \overline{)490}$ 22. $59 \overline{)743}$ 23. $18 \overline{)210}$ 24. $45 \overline{)802}$ 25. $28 \overline{)603}$

26. $19 \overline{)522}$ 27. $38 \overline{)712}$ 28. $54 \overline{)640}$ 29. $27 \overline{)615}$ 30. $66 \overline{)826}$

31. $76 \overline{)853}$ 32. $68 \overline{)721}$ 33. $79 \overline{)914}$ 34. $44 \overline{)517}$ 35. $36 \overline{)646}$

36. $88 \overline{)910}$ 37. $47 \overline{)889}$ 38. $53 \overline{)616}$ 39. $29 \overline{)572}$ 40. $83 \overline{)967}$

41. $59 \overline{)815}$ 42. $48 \overline{)815}$ 43. $32 \overline{)400}$ 44. $72 \overline{)811}$ 45. $39 \overline{)523}$

Review B (pages 248–255)

1. $3 \overline{)62}$ 2. $4 \overline{)408}$ 3. $6 \overline{)617}$ 4. $4 \overline{)123}$

5. $30 \overline{)90}$ 6. $40 \overline{)160}$ 7. $30 \overline{)122}$ 8. $50 \overline{)262}$

9. $25 \overline{)64}$ 10. $18 \overline{)32}$ 11. $47 \overline{)81}$ 12. $56 \overline{)143}$

13. $30 \overline{)710}$ 14. $83 \overline{)977}$ 15. $46 \overline{)821}$ 16. $17 \overline{)407}$

Problem Solving   Problem • Plan • Arithmetic • Answer

2	Make a plan.	What do you do to solve the problem?

There are 787 people in a space colony. A ship
brings 278 new people and returns 195 to earth.
How many people are in the colony now?

To solve this problem, we plan two steps in arithmetic.

Add 787 and 278.

Subtract 195 from the sum.

The answer is 870 people.

$$\begin{array}{r} 787 \\ +\ 278 \\ \hline 1065 \end{array} \qquad \begin{array}{r} 1065 \\ -\ 195 \\ \hline 870 \end{array}$$

1. Two cargo ships arrive each weekday, one on Saturday, and
   none on Sunday. How many cargo ships is that in a week?

2. This cargo is 25 washers worth $365 each and an air car
   worth $2500. What is the value of this cargo?

3. A Telcall to Earth costs $6.50 for the first 3 minutes
   and $1.50 for each minute after that. What is the cost
   of a 5-minute Telcall to Earth?

4. There are 278 new people. If 100 are children and half
   of the rest are farmers, how many are farmers?

5. 200 people work 8 hours a day to run the farm.
   How many work hours do all 200 put in together in a week?

6. Frozen dairy drink comes in a can which holds 350 ml.
   If 3 cans of water are mixed with a can of dairy
   drink, how many milliliters are there in all?

7. A tenth of the 600 barrels of mine ore are for the colony.
   The rest go to Earth. How many barrels go to Earth?

256

Unit Test

Divide.   (pages 238–239)

1. $6\overline{)98}$ 2. $3\overline{)172}$ 3. $8\overline{)692}$ 4. $4\overline{)275}$ 5. $9\overline{)781}$

Divide.   (pages 240–243)

6. $2\overline{)464}$ 7. $3\overline{)639}$ 8. $6\overline{)684}$ 9. $4\overline{)928}$ 10. $7\overline{)847}$

Divide.   (pages 244–247)

11. $5\overline{)965}$ 12. $6\overline{)876}$ 13. $3\overline{)748}$ 14. $2\overline{)913}$ 15. $7\overline{)865}$

Divide.   (pages 248–249)

16. $4\overline{)83}$ 17. $6\overline{)64}$ 18. $3\overline{)925}$ 19. $2\overline{)413}$ 20. $7\overline{)748}$

Divide.   (pages 250–253)

21. $30\overline{)120}$ 22. $40\overline{)186}$ 23. $28\overline{)73}$ 24. $19\overline{)149}$

Divide.   (pages 254–255)

25. $18\overline{)445}$ 26. $37\overline{)542}$ 27. $53\overline{)895}$ 28. $28\overline{)491}$

Solve.   (page 256)

29. A company has 18 bosses and 288 other workers.
One third are working on a building.
How many are working on the building?

30. The building will have 4 sides and 32 floors. Every
floor will have 28 windows on each side.
How many windows is that in all?

Taking Another Look

Pages 238–239

```
      64
4) 258
  −24
    18
   −16
     2
```

Divide.

1. 6)96
2. 6)99
3. 6)101
4. 3)164
5. 7)598
6. 4)351
7. 5)482
8. 9)747
9. 6)537
10. 8)732
11. 3)218
12. 7)325

Pages 240–243

```
     243
3) 729
  −6
    12
   −12
     09
    − 9
      0
```

Divide.

1. 4)484
2. 4)464
3. 4)564
4. 5)565
5. 7)917
6. 3)984
7. 6)846
8. 2)304
9. 8)896
10. 4)684
11. 3)459
12. 7)784
13. 5)855
14. 6)672
15. 2)566

Pages 244–247

```
     139
6) 836
  −6
    23
   −18
     56
    −54
      2
```

Divide.

1. 7)861
2. 7)863
3. 7)865
4. 4)936
5. 5)768
6. 3)501
7. 8)920
8. 6)794
9. 2)576
10. 3)449
11. 7)924
12. 4)622
13. 7)896
14. 2)352
15. 5)816

Pages 248–249

Right:
$$2\overline{)416}$$
with quotient 208

Wrong:
$$2\overline{)416}$$
with quotient 28

Divide.

1. $3\overline{)306}$ 2. $3\overline{)312}$ 3. $3\overline{)314}$

4. $4\overline{)432}$ 5. $2\overline{)613}$ 6. $8\overline{)856}$

7. $3\overline{)906}$ 8. $7\overline{)744}$ 9. $6\overline{)602}$

Pages 250–253

$$24\overline{)91}$$
quotient 3
-72
19

Divide.

1. $30\overline{)90}$ 2. $30\overline{)94}$ 3. $28\overline{)94}$

4. $20\overline{)70}$ 5. $40\overline{)280}$ 6. $60\overline{)367}$

7. $36\overline{)89}$ 8. $58\overline{)111}$ 9. $36\overline{)241}$

Pages 254–255

$$38\overline{)925}$$
quotient 24
-76
165
-152
13

Divide.

1. $20\overline{)630}$ 2. $19\overline{)630}$ 3. $19\overline{)634}$

4. $48\overline{)690}$ 5. $62\overline{)900}$ 6. $34\overline{)509}$

7. $53\overline{)838}$ 8. $19\overline{)263}$ 9. $28\overline{)491}$

10. $68\overline{)964}$ 11. $28\overline{)612}$ 12. $47\overline{)798}$

Page 256

1. **Problem**
2. **Plan**
3. **Arithmetic**
4. **Answer**

Solve.

1. Each of 6 groups collected 14 bags of trash.
   57 of the bags hold bottles and cans. The other
   bags hold paper. How many bags hold paper?

2. 284 new trees are planted. 68 of them are maples.
   Half of the rest are pines. How many are pines?

259

Something Extra • FACTORS

$2 \times 6 = 12$ $3 \times 4 = 12$ $1 \times 12 = 12$

2 and 6 are called <u>factors</u> of the product 12.
1, 2, 3, 4, 6, and 12 are all factors of 12.

Write the other factor to complete.

1. $1 \times \boxed{} = 3$ 2. $2 \times \boxed{} = 8$ 3. $3 \times \boxed{} = 9$ 4. $5 \times \boxed{} = 10$

5. $2 \times \boxed{} = 4$ 6. $5 \times \boxed{} = 15$ 7. $3 \times \boxed{} = 6$ 8. $4 \times \boxed{} = 16$

9. $6 \times \boxed{} = 42$ 10. $9 \times \boxed{} = 72$ 11. $1 \times \boxed{} = 10$ 12. $7 \times \boxed{} = 56$

We may test for factors by division. If 2 divides 24
without a remainder, 2 is a factor of 24.

$$
\begin{array}{r}
12 \\
2\overline{)\,24} \\
-2 \\
\hline
04 \\
-\ 4 \\
\hline
0
\end{array}
$$

2 is a factor of 24.
The quotient 12 is
also a factor of 24.

Is the number a factor of 30?

13. 5   14. 6   15. 7   16. 10   17. 2   18. 15

Is the number a factor of 28?

19. 4   20. 8   21. 1   22. 7   23. 14   24. 28

Is the number a factor of 48?

25. 4   26. 6   27. 3   28. 7   29. 24   30. 48

31. Test the numbers from 1 to 4 for factors of 24.
    List eight factors of 24.

List all factors of the number.

32. 22   33. 32   34. 36   35. 40   36. 45   37. 50

Reviewing Needed Skills

Add.

| 1. 23 $+56$ | 2. 44 $+32$ | 3. 69 $+27$ | 4. 56 $+18$ | 5. 73 $+29$ |

| 6. 57 89 $+63$ | 7. 92 15 $+46$ | 8. 72 9 84 $+21$ | 9. 64 37 8 $+52$ | 10. 43 5 39 $+86$ |

| 11. $\$3.95$ $+4.26$ | 12. $\$2.86$ $+5.97$ | 13. $\$24.87$ $+56.95$ | 14. $\$63.81$ $+58.09$ |

Subtract.

| 15. 98 -53 | 16. 76 -21 | 17. 82 -67 | 18. 53 -14 | 19. 65 -38 |

| 20. 789 -654 | 21. 643 -130 | 22. 927 -798 | 23. 809 -426 | 24. 700 -357 |

| 25. $\$98.52$ -45.76 | 26. $\$83.17$ -35.49 | 27. $\$64.03$ -28.18 | 28. $\$56.70$ -9.86 |

Multiply.

| 29. 32 $\times3$ | 30. 41 $\times2$ | 31. 56 $\times4$ | 32. 78 $\times6$ | 33. 87 $\times5$ |

| 34. 275 $\times8$ | 35. 639 $\times7$ | 36. 58 $\times23$ | 37. 97 $\times34$ | 38. 40 $\times56$ |

| 39. $\$4.27$ $\times35$ | 40. $\$9.38$ $\times56$ | 41. $\$8.07$ $\times43$ | 42. $\$7.63$ $\times84$ |

UNIT 12

Shapes in Space

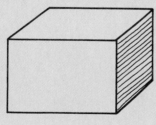

Box

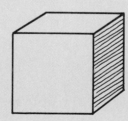

Cube

Sphere

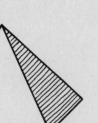

Pyramid

Cone

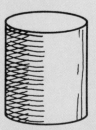

Cylinder

Geometry

a Name the shapes you see.

1.

2.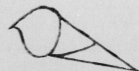

3.

4.

5.

6.

7.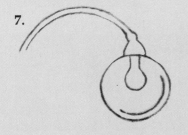

8.

9.

263

Shapes

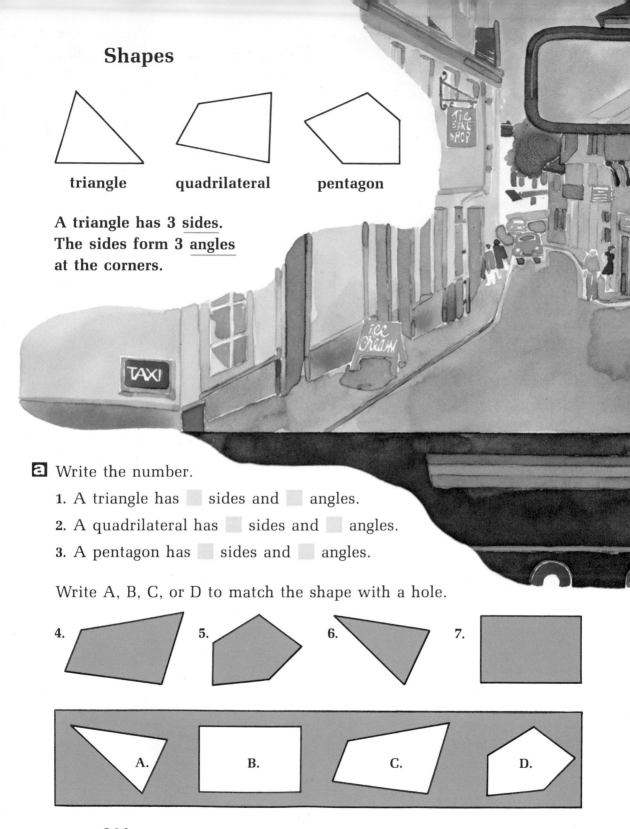

triangle   quadrilateral   pentagon

A triangle has 3 sides.
The sides form 3 angles
at the corners.

a Write the number.

1. A triangle has ▨ sides and ▨ angles.

2. A quadrilateral has ▨ sides and ▨ angles.

3. A pentagon has ▨ sides and ▨ angles.

Write A, B, C, or D to match the shape with a hole.

4.   5.   6.   7.

A.   B.   C.   D.

b How many sides and how many angles does the shape have?

8.

9.

STOP

SPEED LIMIT 50

10.

NO PASSING ZONE

c Name the shape of the sign.

11.

YIELD

12.

ROCKY MOUNTAIN NAT'L PARK 6 KM

13.

14.

Lines and Points

The sides of a triangle are parts of lines.
We may call them <u>lines</u>. Two sides of
a triangle meet in a <u>point</u>.

We may use letters to name
shapes and their parts.
Triangle **ABC** is shown.
Angle **B** is formed by
line **AB** and line **BC**.

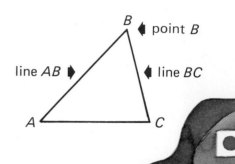

line *AB* ▶ ◀ point *B*

◀ line *BC*

 Write A, B, C, or D to match the picture with a name.

1.
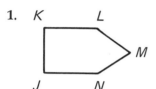

2.
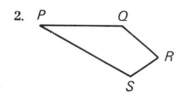

3.
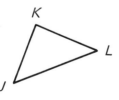

4.
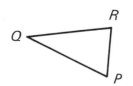

A. triangle *PQR*

B. quadrilateral *PQRS*

C. pentagon *JKLMN*

D. triangle *JKL*

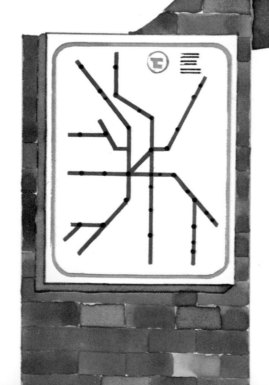

b Write A, B, C, or D to match the name with a picture.

5. triangle *RST*

6. point *M*

7. angle *Q*

8. line *NP*

A. 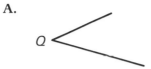 Q

B.  R S T

C. • *M*

D. N ———— P

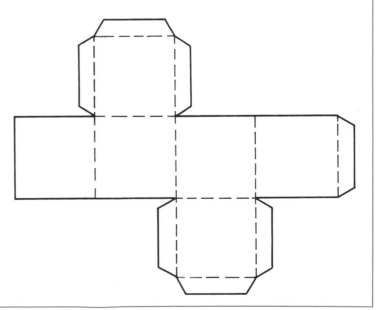

Boxes

Use the pattern to make a box shaped like a cube. Fold along dashed lines.

Can you hold the box so that all you see is one side?

Set the box down so that you see three sides. Draw it.

267

Angles

We can compare the sizes of two angles by comparing their openings.
Angle A is greater than angle B.

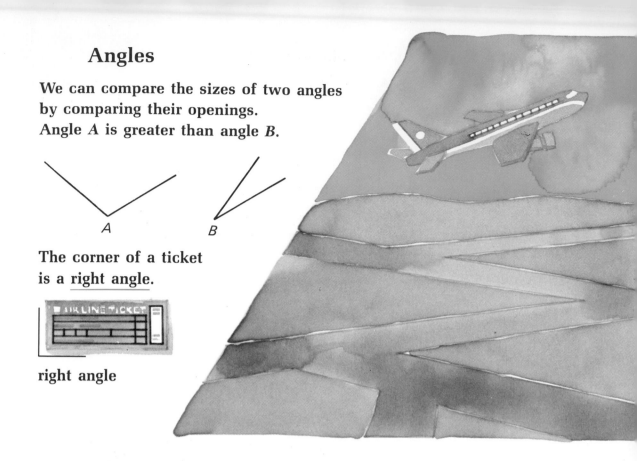

A   B

The corner of a ticket
is a <u>right angle.</u>

right angle

a Which angle is greater?

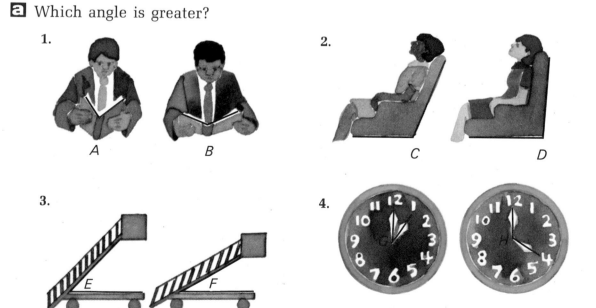

1.

A   B

2.

C   D

3.

E   F

4.

b Is it a right angle? Test with the corner of a card.

5.   6.   7.   8.

How many right angles are in the shape?

9.   10.   11.   12.

How many angles are greater than a right angle?

13.   14.   15.   16.

How many angles are less than a right angle?

17.   18.   19.   20.

How many angles are right?

What is the greatest number of right angles a triangle can have?
Make some drawings to help you answer.

Triangles

All triangles have 3 sides and 3 angles, but not all triangles have the same size and shape.

a Do the triangles have the same size and shape?

1.

2.

3.

4.

5.

6.

b Write A, B, or C for the triangle with these parts.

7. all sides the same length

8. no sides the same length

9. only 2 sides the same length

10. one right angle

11. one angle greater than a right angle

12. all angles less than a right angle

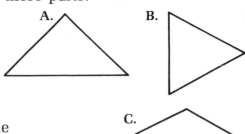

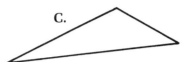

Review A   (pages 262–271)

Name the shape in space.

1.   2.   3.   4.

Write the number.

5. A triangle has ▦ sides and ▦ angles.

6. A quadrilateral has ▦ sides and ▦ angles.

Write A, B, C, or D to match the name with a picture.

7. point *P*   8. angle *F*   9. line *ST*   10. triangle *PQR*

A. *S* _____ *T*   B. *P* ▽ *Q*   C. ● *P*   D. ——⟍ *F*
                         R

Is it a right angle?

11.   12.   13.   14.

Do the triangles have the same size and shape?

15.   16.   17.    18.

Extra practice on p. 332

Lines

The road and the train track cross <u>at right angles.</u>

The rails of the track never cross. They are <u>parallel.</u>

lines at right angles

parallel lines

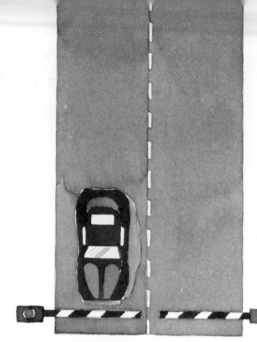

a Write P if you see parallel lines and R for right angles.

1.

2.

3.

4.

5.

6.

7.

8.

9.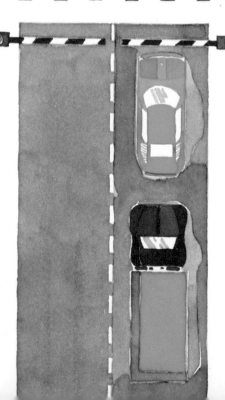

b Write P if you see parallel lines and R for right angles.

10.

11.

12.

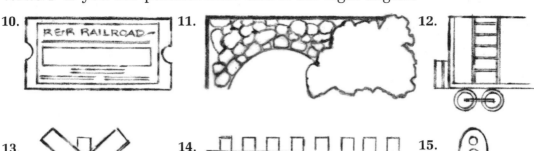

13.

14.

15.

c 16. Use a ruler to draw two parallel lines.

A ———————————————— B

C ———————————————— D

17. Use the corner of a card to draw two lines at right angles.

X

E ———————————————— F

Y

18. Use what you learned in Exercises 16 and 17 to draw a shape like this.

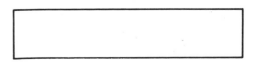

Rectangles and Squares

Some quadrilaterals have special names.

rectangle   square

A **rectangle** has four right angles. Its opposite sides are parallel.

A **square** is a rectangle with all sides the same length.

a Is the shape a rectangle?

1.

2.

3.

4.

Is the shape a square?

5.

6.

7.

8.

b Complete for rectangle ABCD.

9. Side *AB* is opposite side ▧.

10. Side *AB* is parallel to side ▧.

11. Side *AB* is ▧ cm long.

12. Side *CD* is ▧ cm long.

13. Side *AB* is the same length as side ▧.

14. Side *AD* is opposite side ▧.

15. Side *AD* is parallel to side ▧.

16. Side *AD* is ▧ cm long.

17. Side *BC* is ▧ cm long.

18. Side *AD* is the same length as side ▧.

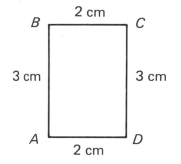

Shapes in your world

Bring to class pictures which remind you of the shapes you have studied.
Outline and label each shape.

Maps

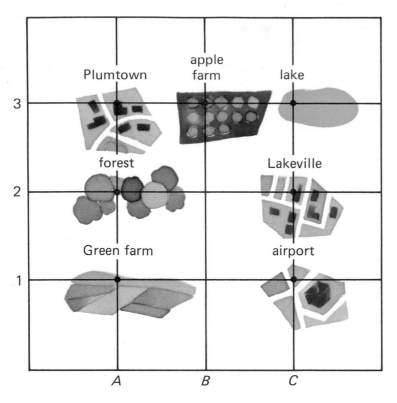

We may use parallel lines and lines at right angles to find a point on a map. Lakeville is at the point where the line from *C* crosses the line from 2. We may name this point (*C*, 2).

a Complete.

1. The airport is at (*C*,).

2. The lake is at (, 3).

3. The apple farm is at (*B*,).

4. Plumtown is at (, 3).

5. The forest is at (*A*,).

6. Green farm is at (, 1).

276

b Complete.

7. book store at (A, ■)

8. RR station at (■, 5)

9. movies at (■, ■)

10. library at (■, ■)

11. hospital at (■, ■)

12. park at (■, ■)

13. market at (■, ■)

14. drug store at (■, ■)

15. bank at (■, ■)

16. post office at (■, ■)

17. school at (■, ■)

18. fire station at (■, ■)

19. hotel at (■, ■)

20. gas station at (■, ■)

21. diner at (■, ■)

	A	B	C
5	hospital	gas station	RR station
4	drug store	fire station	park
3	bank	library	school
2	market	post office	hotel
1	book store	movies	diner

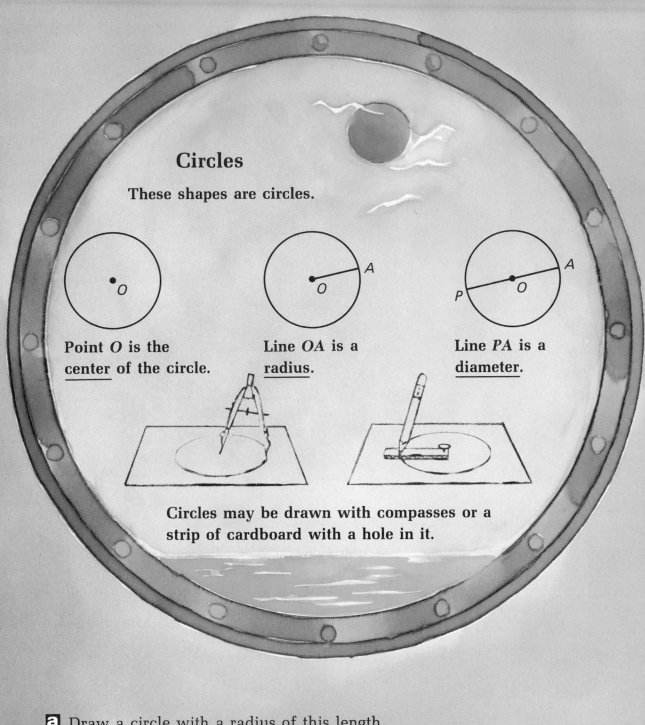

Circles

These shapes are circles.

Point *O* is the
center of the circle.

Line *OA* is a
radius.

Line *PA* is a
diameter.

Circles may be drawn with compasses or a
strip of cardboard with a hole in it.

a Draw a circle with a radius of this length.

1. 5 cm   2. 4 cm   3. 2 cm   4. 1 cm

5. Draw a circle with a radius 3 cm long.
   Label the center O. Draw a radius OA.

D Measure the diameter of the circle.

6.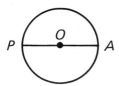

7.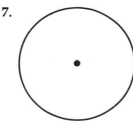

8.

C Complete.

9. Radius *AB* is ▢ cm long.

10. Diameter *CD* is ▢ cm long.

11. The diameter of the circle is ▢ times as long as the radius.

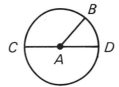

Review B   (pages 272–279)

Write P if you see parallel lines and R for right angles.

1.
2.
3.
4.

Is the shape a rectangle?

5.
6.
7.
8.

Write the missing letter or number.

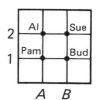

9. Al (A, ▢)   10. Sue (B, ▢)

11. Pam (▢, 1)   12. Bud (▢, ▢)

13. Draw a circle with a radius 2 cm long. Label the center *Q*. Draw a radius *QR*. Draw a diameter *ST*.

Extra practice on p. 333   **279**

Problem Solving   Problem • Plan • Arithmetic • Answer

| 2 | Make a plan. | What do you do to solve the problem? |

Sometimes we need to picture the parts of a shape to solve a problem.

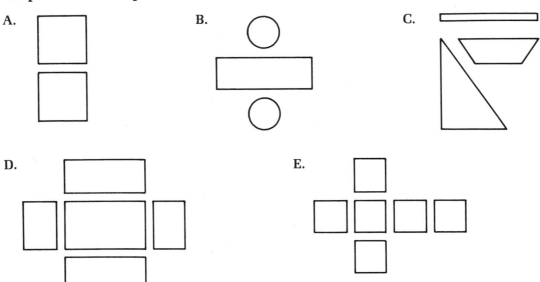

A.   B.   C.

D.   E.

Write A, B, C, D, or E to answer the question.

1. Which pieces are a pattern for covering a coffee can with wallpaper?

2. Which pieces can be nailed together to make a cube of wood?

3. Which pieces are a pattern for making a cut-paper picture of a sail boat?

4. Which pieces are a pattern for nailing together an open wooden box for a turtle?

5. Which pieces are a pattern for sewing a simple square pillow cover?

Unit Test

Name the shape in space.   (pages 262–263)

1.
2.
3.
4.
5.

Write A, B, C, or D to match the name with a picture.   (pages 264–267)

6. angle *G*   **7.** line *LM*   **8.** triangle *RST*   **9.** point *Q*

A. •*Q*   **B.** *G*   **C.** *L* ——————— *M*   **D.** *R* *S*
                                                                                                          T

Write A, B, or C for the triangle with these parts.   (pages 268–271)

10. one right angle   **11.** all sides the same length

12. one angle greater than a right angle

A. 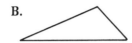   **B.**   **C.**

Complete for the rectangle.   (pages 272–275)

13. Side *BC* is opposite side ▨.

14. Side *BC* is parallel to side ▨.

Write the missing letter or number.
(pages 276–277)

15. Ed (*B*, ▨)   **16.** Joe (▨, 2)

17. Ida (▨, 1)   **18.** Al (▨, ▨)

Complete for the circle.   (pages 278–279)

19. Radius *AB* is ▨ cm long.

20. Diameter *CD* is ▨ cm long.

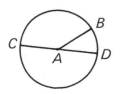

Solve.   (page 280)

21. If you use a drinking glass as a cookie cutter,
what is the shape of the cookie you cut?

Taking Another Look

Pages 262–263

Shapes in space

- box
- cube
- sphere
- pyramid
- cone
- cylinder

Name the shape.

1.

2.

3.

4.

5.

6. (cone)

Pages 264–267

triangle

quadrilateral

pentagon

Write A, B, C, D, E, or F to match the name with a picture.

1. triangle *NOP*   2. angle *S*   3. pentagon

4. point *W*   5. quadrilateral   6. line *CD*

A. *S*   B. • *W*   C. *C* ——— *D*

D. (pentagon)   E. *N* (triangle) *O* *P*   F. (quadrilateral)

Pages 268–271

right angle

**less than
a right angle**

**greater than
a right angle**

Write A, B, or C for the triangle with these parts.

1. one right angle   2. no sides the same length

3. all sides the same length

4. one angle greater than a right angle

5. only 2 sides the same length

A.   B.   C. (triangle)

Pages 272–275

Pages 272–275

parallel lines

lines at
right angles

Complete for rectangle *MNOP*.

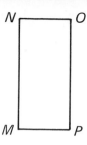

1. Side *MN* is opposite side ▩.

2. Side *MN* is parallel to side ▩.

3. Side *NO* is the same length as side ▩.

4. Side *OP* is the same length as side ▩.

Pages 276–277

The letter comes first. The number comes second.

Write the missing letter or number.

1. Amy (▩, 1)   2. Pat (*B*, ▩)

3. Dan (▩, ▩)   4. Bob (*A*, ▩)

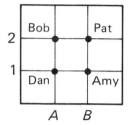

Pages 278–279

Circle with radius *OA*

Write A, B, or C to match the parts.

1. the center   A. line *EF*

2. a radius   B. point *C*

3. a diameter   C. line *CD*

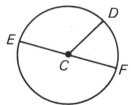

Page 280

1. **Problem**
2. **Plan**
3. **Arithmetic**
4. **Answer**

Write A or B to answer the question.

A.

B.

1. Which pieces are a pattern for making a pyramid?

2. Which pieces are a pattern for making an open box?

Something Extra • SYMMETRY

If we fold this shape along the dashed line,
one half fits on the other exactly.
The shape has <u>symmetry</u>.
The dashed line is a <u>line of symmetry</u>.

Is the dashed line a line of symmetry?

1.    2. 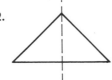   3.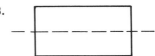

Does the shape have symmetry?

4.    5.    6.

7.    8.    9.

Trace the shape. Draw all the lines of symmetry.

10.   11.   12.   13.

Reviewing Needed Skills

Add or subtract.

1. $\begin{array}{r} 22 \\ +36 \\ \hline \end{array}$
2. $\begin{array}{r} 18 \\ +41 \\ \hline \end{array}$
3. $\begin{array}{r} 95 \\ -54 \\ \hline \end{array}$
4. $\begin{array}{r} 89 \\ -36 \\ \hline \end{array}$
5. $\begin{array}{r} 57 \\ +24 \\ \hline \end{array}$

6. $\begin{array}{r} 69 \\ +16 \\ \hline \end{array}$
7. $\begin{array}{r} 72 \\ -37 \\ \hline \end{array}$
8. $\begin{array}{r} 64 \\ -29 \\ \hline \end{array}$
9. $\begin{array}{r} 48 \\ + 5 \\ \hline \end{array}$
10. $\begin{array}{r} 76 \\ + 8 \\ \hline \end{array}$

11. $\begin{array}{r} 91 \\ - 7 \\ \hline \end{array}$
12. $\begin{array}{r} 85 \\ - 8 \\ \hline \end{array}$
13. $\begin{array}{r} 329 \\ +486 \\ \hline \end{array}$
14. $\begin{array}{r} 107 \\ +588 \\ \hline \end{array}$
15. $\begin{array}{r} 523 \\ -106 \\ \hline \end{array}$

16. $\begin{array}{r} 864 \\ -379 \\ \hline \end{array}$
17. $\begin{array}{r} 5743 \\ +2279 \\ \hline \end{array}$
18. $\begin{array}{r} 4108 \\ +3979 \\ \hline \end{array}$
19. $\begin{array}{r} 6903 \\ -4921 \\ \hline \end{array}$
20. $\begin{array}{r} 9002 \\ -7145 \\ \hline \end{array}$

Complete.

21. $\frac{1}{2} = \frac{\blacksquare}{8}$
22. $\frac{2}{5} = \frac{\blacksquare}{10}$
23. $\frac{1}{3} = \frac{\blacksquare}{12}$
24. $\frac{3}{8} = \frac{\blacksquare}{16}$

25. $\frac{8}{10} = \frac{\blacksquare}{5}$
26. $\frac{6}{14} = \frac{\blacksquare}{7}$
27. $\frac{6}{8} = \frac{\blacksquare}{4}$
28. $\frac{2}{6} = \frac{\blacksquare}{3}$

29. $\frac{2}{3} = \frac{\blacksquare}{9}$
30. $\frac{5}{6} = \frac{\blacksquare}{12}$
31. $\frac{5}{7} = \frac{\blacksquare}{14}$
32. $\frac{2}{3} = \frac{\blacksquare}{12}$

33. $\frac{10}{16} = \frac{\blacksquare}{8}$
34. $\frac{6}{9} = \frac{\blacksquare}{3}$
35. $\frac{4}{6} = \frac{\blacksquare}{3}$
36. $\frac{2}{14} = \frac{\blacksquare}{7}$

Write the decimal.

37. 6 tenths
38. 2 tenths
39. 43 hundredths
40. 8 hundredths

41. $\frac{4}{10}$
42. $\frac{1}{10}$
43. $\frac{68}{100}$
44. $\frac{3}{100}$

45. $\frac{14}{100}$
46. $\frac{9}{10}$
47. $\frac{5}{100}$
48. $\frac{84}{100}$

UNIT 13

Simplifying Fractions

$\frac{8}{12}$ and $\frac{2}{3}$ are equal fractions.

$$\frac{8}{12} = \frac{8 \div 4}{12 \div 4} = \frac{2}{3}$$

We simplify $\frac{8}{12}$ when we write it as $\frac{2}{3}$. We cannot simplify $\frac{2}{3}$. It is a fraction in <u>simplest form</u>.

The simplest form of $\frac{3}{3}$ is 1.

The simplest form of $\frac{0}{3}$ is 0.

Fractions and Decimals

a Complete.

1. $\frac{2}{4} = \frac{1}{\blacksquare}$ 2. $\frac{2}{6} = \frac{1}{\blacksquare}$ 3. $\frac{2}{8} = \frac{1}{\blacksquare}$ 4. $\frac{2}{10} = \frac{1}{\blacksquare}$ 5. $\frac{2}{12} = \frac{1}{\blacksquare}$

6. $\frac{3}{12} = \frac{\blacksquare}{4}$ 7. $\frac{4}{12} = \frac{\blacksquare}{3}$ 8. $\frac{6}{12} = \frac{\blacksquare}{2}$ 9. $\frac{8}{12} = \frac{\blacksquare}{3}$ 10. $\frac{9}{12} = \frac{\blacksquare}{4}$

b Is the fraction in simplest form?

11. $\frac{12}{24}$ 12. $\frac{6}{12}$ 13. $\frac{4}{8}$ 14. $\frac{3}{6}$ 15. $\frac{2}{4}$ 16. $\frac{1}{2}$

17. $\frac{8}{16}$ 18. $\frac{7}{16}$ 19. $\frac{6}{16}$ 20. $\frac{5}{16}$ 21. $\frac{4}{16}$ 22. $\frac{3}{16}$

Write the fraction in simplest form.

23. $\frac{4}{8}$ 24. $\frac{4}{6}$ 25. $\frac{3}{9}$ 26. $\frac{4}{16}$ 27. $\frac{6}{8}$ 28. $\frac{4}{4}$

29. $\frac{5}{10}$ 30. $\frac{12}{16}$ 31. $\frac{0}{2}$ 32. $\frac{4}{10}$ 33. $\frac{10}{10}$ 34. $\frac{10}{15}$

Addition of Fractions

$\frac{2}{4}$ of the garden has beans. $\frac{1}{4}$ has carrots.

$\frac{3}{4}$ of the garden has beans or carrots.

We add the numerators
when the denominators
are the same.

$$\frac{2}{4} + \frac{1}{4} = \frac{3}{4}$$

$$\begin{array}{r} \frac{2}{4} \\ + \frac{1}{4} \\ \hline \frac{3}{4} \end{array}$$

a Add.

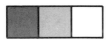 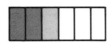

1. $\frac{1}{3} + \frac{1}{3}$ 2. $\frac{1}{4} + \frac{1}{4}$ 3. $\frac{1}{5} + \frac{1}{5}$ 4. $\frac{1}{6} + \frac{1}{6}$

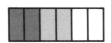 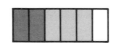 

5. $\frac{2}{6} + \frac{1}{6}$ 6. $\frac{2}{6} + \frac{2}{6}$ 7. $\frac{2}{6} + \frac{3}{6}$ 8. $\frac{2}{6} + \frac{4}{6}$

9. $\frac{1}{8} + \frac{1}{8}$ 10. $\frac{2}{8} + \frac{1}{8}$ 11. $\frac{3}{8} + \frac{1}{8}$ 12. $\frac{4}{8} + \frac{1}{8}$

13. $\frac{3}{5} + \frac{1}{5}$ 14. $\frac{2}{5} + \frac{1}{5}$ 15. $\frac{2}{5} + \frac{2}{5}$ 16. $\frac{2}{5} + \frac{3}{5}$

b Add.

17. $\frac{4}{6} + \frac{1}{6}$ 18. $\frac{1}{9} + \frac{1}{9}$ 19. $\frac{5}{8} + \frac{2}{8}$ 20. $\frac{3}{7} + \frac{2}{7}$ 21. $\frac{2}{10} + \frac{1}{10}$

22. $\frac{4}{8} + \frac{3}{8}$ 23. $\frac{3}{10} + \frac{4}{10}$ 24. $\frac{2}{8} + \frac{3}{8}$ 25. $\frac{1}{9} + \frac{3}{9}$ 26. $\frac{3}{12} + \frac{2}{12}$

27. $\begin{array}{r} \frac{1}{7} \\ + \frac{1}{7} \\ \hline \end{array}$ 28. $\begin{array}{r} \frac{2}{4} \\ + \frac{1}{4} \\ \hline \end{array}$ 29. $\begin{array}{r} \frac{1}{8} \\ + \frac{4}{8} \\ \hline \end{array}$ 30. $\begin{array}{r} \frac{3}{12} \\ + \frac{4}{12} \\ \hline \end{array}$ 31. $\begin{array}{r} \frac{2}{10} \\ + \frac{5}{10} \\ \hline \end{array}$

c Add. Write the answer in simplest form.

32. $\frac{1}{6} + \frac{2}{6}$ 33. $\frac{2}{10} + \frac{3}{10}$ 34. $\frac{5}{8} + \frac{1}{8}$ 35. $\frac{2}{9} + \frac{1}{9}$ 36. $\frac{4}{6} + \frac{2}{6}$

37. $\frac{4}{8} + \frac{2}{8}$ 38. $\frac{1}{2} + \frac{1}{2}$ 39. $\frac{4}{9} + \frac{2}{9}$ 40. $\frac{4}{12} + \frac{2}{12}$ 41. $\frac{3}{10} + \frac{3}{10}$

42. $\begin{array}{r} \frac{1}{4} \\ + \frac{1}{4} \\ \hline \end{array}$ 43. $\begin{array}{r} \frac{1}{6} \\ + \frac{3}{6} \\ \hline \end{array}$ 44. $\begin{array}{r} \frac{2}{8} \\ + \frac{2}{8} \\ \hline \end{array}$ 45. $\begin{array}{r} \frac{1}{8} \\ + \frac{3}{8} \\ \hline \end{array}$ 46. $\begin{array}{r} \frac{1}{4} \\ + \frac{3}{4} \\ \hline \end{array}$

Subtraction of Fractions

Joe has $\frac{4}{8}$ of the pizza.

He eats $\frac{1}{8}$ of the pizza.

He has $\frac{3}{8}$ left.

We subtract the numerators when the denominators are the same.

$$\frac{4}{8} - \frac{1}{8} = \frac{3}{8}$$

$$\begin{array}{r} \frac{4}{8} \\ -\frac{1}{8} \\ \hline \frac{3}{8} \end{array}$$

a Subtract.

1. $\frac{5}{8} - \frac{1}{8}$ 2. $\frac{5}{8} - \frac{2}{8}$ 3. $\frac{5}{8} - \frac{3}{8}$

4. $\frac{7}{8} - \frac{1}{8}$ 5. $\frac{7}{8} - \frac{2}{8}$ 6. $\frac{7}{8} - \frac{3}{8}$ 7. $\frac{7}{8} - \frac{4}{8}$ 8. $\frac{7}{8} - \frac{5}{8}$

9. $\frac{2}{8} - \frac{1}{8}$ 10. $\frac{2}{6} - \frac{1}{6}$ 11. $\frac{2}{5} - \frac{1}{5}$ 12. $\frac{2}{4} - \frac{1}{4}$ 13. $\frac{2}{3} - \frac{1}{3}$

14. $\frac{5}{6} - \frac{1}{6}$ 15. $\frac{5}{6} - \frac{2}{6}$ 16. $\frac{5}{6} - \frac{3}{6}$ 17. $\frac{5}{6} - \frac{4}{6}$ 18. $\frac{5}{6} - \frac{5}{6}$

b Subtract.

19. $\frac{3}{5} - \frac{1}{5}$ 20. $\frac{3}{4} - \frac{2}{4}$ 21. $\frac{4}{6} - \frac{3}{6}$ 22. $\frac{3}{6} - \frac{2}{6}$ 23. $\frac{4}{8} - \frac{3}{8}$

24. $\frac{4}{6} - \frac{1}{6}$ 25. $\frac{4}{5} - \frac{3}{5}$ 26. $\frac{6}{7} - \frac{2}{7}$ 27. $\frac{4}{5} - \frac{2}{5}$ 28. $\frac{7}{10} - \frac{4}{10}$

29. $\frac{4}{5}$ 30. $\frac{5}{7}$ 31. $\frac{9}{10}$ 32. $\frac{6}{12}$ 33. $\frac{7}{9}$
$-\frac{1}{5}$ $-\frac{4}{7}$ $-\frac{2}{10}$ $-\frac{5}{12}$ $-\frac{2}{9}$

c Subtract. Write the answer in simplest form.

34. $\frac{4}{8}$ 35. $\frac{3}{4}$ 36. $\frac{5}{6}$ 37. $\frac{7}{9}$ 38. $\frac{6}{8}$ 39. $\frac{6}{6}$
$-\frac{2}{8}$ $-\frac{1}{4}$ $-\frac{3}{6}$ $-\frac{1}{9}$ $-\frac{2}{8}$ $-\frac{2}{6}$

40. $\frac{5}{9}$ 41. $\frac{4}{4}$ 42. $\frac{5}{8}$ 43. $\frac{6}{8}$ 44. $\frac{5}{6}$ 45. $\frac{7}{9}$
$-\frac{2}{9}$ $-\frac{2}{4}$ $-\frac{1}{8}$ $-\frac{4}{8}$ $-\frac{2}{6}$ $-\frac{4}{9}$

Solve.

46. Jeff's share is $\frac{3}{8}$ of a pizza. He eats $\frac{2}{8}$.
What part of the pizza does he have left?

47. A pizza is cut into 8 equal parts. The children eat $\frac{5}{8}$ of the
pizza and bring the rest home. What part of the pizza do
they bring home?

Different Denominators

$\frac{1}{2}$ of the papers are for Robin Road.

$\frac{1}{4}$ of the papers are for Oak Drive.

What part of the papers is that in all?

$$\frac{1}{2} = \frac{2}{4}$$
$$+\frac{1}{4} = +\frac{1}{4}$$
$$\overline{\qquad\qquad \frac{3}{4}}$$

Write $\frac{1}{2}$ as $\frac{2}{4}$ to make the denominators the same.

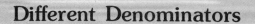

 **Complete.**

1. $\frac{1}{2} = \frac{}{6}$

    $+\frac{1}{6} = +\frac{1}{6}$

    $\frac{}{6}$

2. $\frac{1}{2} = \frac{}{8}$

    $+\frac{1}{8} = +\frac{1}{8}$

    $\frac{}{8}$

3. $\frac{1}{2} = \frac{}{10}$

    $+\frac{1}{10} = +\frac{1}{10}$

    $\frac{}{10}$

4. $\frac{5}{12} = \frac{5}{12}$

    $+\frac{1}{2} = +\frac{}{12}$

    $\frac{}{12}$

5. $\frac{5}{12} = \frac{5}{12}$

    $+\frac{1}{3} = +\frac{}{12}$

    $\frac{}{12}$

6. $\frac{5}{12} = \frac{5}{12}$

    $+\frac{1}{4} = +\frac{}{12}$

    $\frac{}{12}$

292

b Add.

7. $\dfrac{1}{2}$
$+\dfrac{3}{8}$

8. $\dfrac{3}{5}$
$+\dfrac{1}{10}$

9. $\dfrac{1}{6}$
$+\dfrac{1}{3}$

10. $\dfrac{1}{12}$
$+\dfrac{1}{2}$

11. $\dfrac{3}{10}$
$+\dfrac{2}{5}$

12. $\dfrac{1}{4}$
$+\dfrac{1}{8}$

13. $\dfrac{1}{4}$
$+\dfrac{3}{8}$

14. $\dfrac{1}{12}$
$+\dfrac{1}{3}$

15. $\dfrac{1}{3}$
$+\dfrac{1}{9}$

16. $\dfrac{1}{5}$
$+\dfrac{1}{10}$

17. $\dfrac{2}{3}$
$+\dfrac{1}{6}$

18. $\dfrac{1}{12}$
$+\dfrac{1}{6}$

19. $\dfrac{1}{16}$
$+\dfrac{3}{8}$

20. $\dfrac{2}{10}$
$+\dfrac{1}{5}$

21. $\dfrac{3}{4}$
$+\dfrac{1}{12}$

22. $\dfrac{1}{9}$
$+\dfrac{2}{3}$

23. $\dfrac{3}{16}$
$+\dfrac{1}{4}$

24. $\dfrac{3}{4}$
$+\dfrac{1}{8}$

25. $\dfrac{2}{3}$
$+\dfrac{1}{15}$

26. $\dfrac{2}{9}$
$+\dfrac{1}{3}$

27. $\dfrac{2}{10}$
$+\dfrac{3}{5}$

28. $\dfrac{1}{8}$
$+\dfrac{1}{16}$

29. $\dfrac{1}{12}$
$+\dfrac{1}{4}$

30. $\dfrac{2}{3}$
$+\dfrac{1}{12}$

c Solve.

31. Rosa works on her paper route records $\frac{1}{2}$ hour before dinner and $\frac{1}{4}$ hour after dinner. What part of an hour is that in all?

32. $\frac{3}{10}$ of the people pay Rosa on Friday. $\frac{1}{2}$ of the people pay Rosa on Saturday. What part of the people pay Rosa on these two days?

33. John delivers $\frac{1}{6}$ of his papers on Tree Street and $\frac{1}{3}$ on Pomo Road. Is this $\frac{1}{2}$ of his papers?

34. Do $\frac{1}{4}$ hour and $\frac{3}{4}$ hour make one hour?

293

Different Denominators

$\frac{1}{2}$ full before the sale

$\frac{1}{4}$ full after the sale

What part was sold?

$$\frac{1}{2} = \frac{2}{4}$$
$$-\frac{1}{4} = -\frac{1}{4}$$
$$\overline{\frac{1}{4}}$$

Write $\frac{1}{2}$ as $\frac{2}{4}$ to make the denominators the same.

a Complete.

1. $\frac{1}{2} = \frac{\blacksquare}{6}$
$-\frac{1}{6} = -\frac{1}{6}$
$\overline{\frac{\blacksquare}{6}}$

2. $\frac{1}{2} = \frac{\blacksquare}{8}$
$-\frac{1}{8} = -\frac{1}{8}$
$\overline{\frac{\blacksquare}{8}}$

3. $\frac{1}{2} = \frac{\blacksquare}{10}$
$-\frac{1}{10} = -\frac{1}{10}$
$\overline{\frac{\blacksquare}{10}}$

4. $\frac{1}{4} = \frac{\blacksquare}{8}$
$-\frac{1}{8} = -\frac{1}{8}$
$\overline{\frac{\blacksquare}{8}}$

5. $\frac{2}{4} = \frac{\blacksquare}{8}$
$-\frac{1}{8} = -\frac{1}{8}$
$\overline{\frac{\blacksquare}{8}}$

6. $\frac{3}{4} = \frac{\blacksquare}{8}$
$-\frac{1}{8} = -\frac{1}{8}$
$\overline{\frac{\blacksquare}{8}}$

b Subtract.

7. $\dfrac{1}{2}$ $-\dfrac{3}{8}$

8. $\dfrac{1}{5}$ $-\dfrac{1}{10}$

9. $\dfrac{3}{4}$ $-\dfrac{1}{2}$

10. $\dfrac{1}{6}$ $-\dfrac{1}{12}$

11. $\dfrac{5}{6}$ $-\dfrac{1}{2}$

12. $\dfrac{7}{12}$ $-\dfrac{1}{3}$

13. $\dfrac{2}{3}$ $-\dfrac{1}{6}$

14. $\dfrac{7}{12}$ $-\dfrac{1}{2}$

15. $\dfrac{7}{10}$ $-\dfrac{1}{5}$

16. $\dfrac{5}{8}$ $-\dfrac{1}{16}$

17. $\dfrac{1}{4}$ $-\dfrac{1}{12}$

18. $\dfrac{3}{8}$ $-\dfrac{1}{4}$

19. $\dfrac{1}{8}$ $-\dfrac{1}{16}$

20. $\dfrac{5}{6}$ $-\dfrac{1}{3}$

21. $\dfrac{1}{3}$ $-\dfrac{1}{12}$

22. $\dfrac{3}{4}$ $-\dfrac{5}{8}$

23. $\dfrac{7}{10}$ $-\dfrac{3}{5}$

24. $\dfrac{7}{12}$ $-\dfrac{1}{6}$

Review A   (pages 286–295)

Write the fraction in simplest form.

1. $\dfrac{5}{10}$

2. $\dfrac{5}{5}$

3. $\dfrac{6}{8}$

4. $\dfrac{0}{4}$

Add or subtract.

5. $\dfrac{3}{6} + \dfrac{2}{6}$

6. $\dfrac{1}{8} + \dfrac{2}{8}$

7. $\dfrac{1}{7} + \dfrac{1}{7}$

8. $\dfrac{3}{10} + \dfrac{4}{10}$

9. $\dfrac{3}{6} - \dfrac{2}{6}$

10. $\dfrac{8}{8} - \dfrac{3}{8}$

11. $\dfrac{6}{10} - \dfrac{3}{10}$

12. $\dfrac{5}{7} - \dfrac{2}{7}$

13. $\dfrac{1}{4}$ $+\dfrac{1}{2}$

14. $\dfrac{5}{10}$ $+\dfrac{1}{5}$

15. $\dfrac{1}{4}$ $+\dfrac{5}{8}$

16. $\dfrac{1}{6}$ $+\dfrac{2}{3}$

17. $\dfrac{5}{8}$ $-\dfrac{1}{4}$

18. $\dfrac{2}{5}$ $-\dfrac{1}{10}$

19. $\dfrac{2}{3}$ $-\dfrac{1}{9}$

20. $\dfrac{5}{6}$ $-\dfrac{2}{3}$

Mixed Numbers

$$\frac{2}{2} + \frac{1}{2} = \frac{3}{2}$$

$$\frac{2}{2} + \frac{1}{2} = 1 + \frac{1}{2}$$

We may write $1 + \frac{1}{2}$ as $1\frac{1}{2}$.

We may write $\frac{3}{2}$ as $1\frac{1}{2}$.

$1\frac{1}{2}$ is called a <u>mixed number</u>.

a Complete.

1. $\frac{4}{3} = 1\frac{\boxed{}}{3}$ 2. $\frac{5}{3} = 1\frac{\boxed{}}{3}$ 3. $\frac{7}{3} = 2\frac{\boxed{}}{3}$

4. $\frac{5}{4} = 1\frac{\boxed{}}{4}$ 5. $\frac{6}{4} = 1\frac{\boxed{}}{4}$ 6. $\frac{7}{4} = 1\frac{\boxed{}}{4}$

7. $\frac{7}{6} = 1\frac{\boxed{}}{6}$ 8. $\frac{8}{6} = 1\frac{\boxed{}}{6}$ 9. $\frac{9}{6} = 1\frac{\boxed{}}{6}$

10. $\dfrac{5}{5} = 1$ 11. $\dfrac{6}{6} = 1$ 12. $\dfrac{8}{8} = 1$ 13. $\dfrac{10}{10} = 1$

$\dfrac{6}{5} = 1\dfrac{\square}{5}$ $\dfrac{10}{6} = 1\dfrac{\square}{6}$ $\dfrac{13}{8} = 1\dfrac{\square}{8}$ $\dfrac{15}{10} = 1\dfrac{\square}{10}$

14. $\dfrac{4}{2} = 2$ 15. $\dfrac{6}{3} = 2$ 16. $\dfrac{8}{4} = 2$ 17. $\dfrac{10}{5} = 2$

$\dfrac{5}{2} = 2\dfrac{\square}{2}$ $\dfrac{8}{3} = 2\dfrac{\square}{3}$ $\dfrac{9}{4} = 2\dfrac{\square}{4}$ $\dfrac{12}{5} = 2\dfrac{\square}{5}$

c Add. Write the answer as a mixed number.

18. $\dfrac{2}{3}$ 19. $\dfrac{3}{5}$ 20. $\dfrac{3}{4}$ 21. $\dfrac{5}{8}$ 22. $\dfrac{2}{6}$ 23. $\dfrac{6}{7}$

$+\dfrac{2}{3}$ $+\dfrac{4}{5}$ $+\dfrac{3}{4}$ $+\dfrac{7}{8}$ $+\dfrac{5}{6}$ $+\dfrac{3}{7}$

24. $\dfrac{3}{4}$ 25. $\dfrac{5}{6}$ 26. $\dfrac{5}{8}$ 27. $\dfrac{1}{2}$ 28. $\dfrac{6}{10}$ 29. $\dfrac{11}{12}$

$+\dfrac{1}{2}$ $+\dfrac{1}{3}$ $+\dfrac{3}{4}$ $+\dfrac{5}{6}$ $+\dfrac{1}{2}$ $+\dfrac{1}{6}$

Decimals Greater than 1

0.3 is the decimal for $\frac{3}{10}$.

1.3 is the decimal for $1\frac{3}{10}$.

We read 1.3 as *one point three* or *one and three tenths.*

0.35 is the decimal for $\frac{35}{100}$.

2.35 is the decimal for $2\frac{35}{100}$.

We read 2.35 as *two point three five* or *two and 35 hundredths.*

a Complete.

1. 2.6   = 2 and ▢ tenths
2. 2.65 = 2 and ▢ hundredths
3. 7.4   = 7 and ▢ tenths
4. 7.48 = 7 and ▢ hundredths
5. 15.9   = 15 and ▢ tenths
6. 15.98 = 15 and ▢ hundredths
7. 3.5   = 3 and ▢ tenths
8. 3.50 = 3 and ▢ hundredths
9. 3.05 = 3 and ▢ hundredths
10. 6.4   = ▢ and ▢ tenths
11. 6.43 = ▢ and ▢ hundredths
12. 31.2   = ▢ and ▢ tenths
13. 31.20 = ▢ and ▢ hundredths
14. 31.02 = ▢ and ▢ hundredths

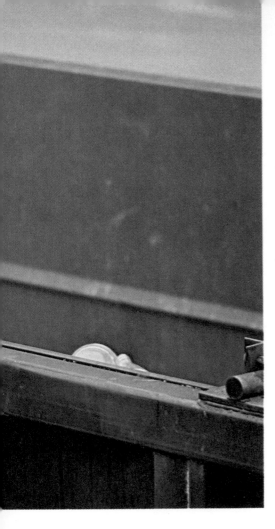

b Write the decimal.

15. one and five tenths

16. six and nine tenths

17. 31 and 26 hundredths

18. 10 and 53 hundredths

19. 24 and 50 hundredths

20. 99 and 9 hundredths

21. $1\frac{6}{10}$　　22. $3\frac{58}{100}$　　23. $17\frac{4}{10}$

24. $7\frac{63}{100}$　　25. $21\frac{12}{100}$　　26. $3\frac{6}{100}$

27. $5\frac{70}{100}$　　28. $13\frac{3}{10}$　　29. $13\frac{3}{100}$

30. $34\frac{7}{100}$　　31. $98\frac{6}{10}$　　32. $99\frac{44}{100}$

33. $10\frac{1}{10}$　　34. $1\frac{1}{100}$　　35. $20\frac{30}{100}$

36. $9\frac{99}{100}$　　37. $235\frac{7}{10}$　　38. $68\frac{75}{100}$

Decimals for fractions

$\frac{2}{5}$ and $\frac{4}{10}$ are equal fractions. The decimal for $\frac{4}{10}$ is 0.4.
$\frac{2}{5}$ may be written as the decimal 0.4.

Complete.

1. $\frac{1}{5} = \frac{\blacksquare}{10}$　　2. $\frac{1}{5} = 0.\blacksquare$　　3. $\frac{3}{5} = \frac{\blacksquare}{10}$　　4. $\frac{3}{5} = 0.\blacksquare$

5. $\frac{4}{5} = \frac{\blacksquare}{10}$　　6. $\frac{4}{5} = 0.\blacksquare$　　7. $\frac{1}{2} = \frac{\blacksquare}{10}$　　8. $\frac{1}{2} = 0.\blacksquare$

9. $1\frac{1}{5} = 1.\blacksquare$　　10. $1\frac{3}{5} = 1.\blacksquare$　　11. $2\frac{4}{5} = 2.\blacksquare$　　12. $3\frac{1}{2} = 3.\blacksquare$

299

Tenths, Addition and Subtraction

Compare these examples.

```
   8        0.8       1.1              48        4.8       12.1
  +3       +0.3      -0.3             +73       +7.3      - 7.3
  ──       ────      ────             ───       ────      ─────
  11        1.1       0.8             121       12.1       4.8
```

When we add or subtract decimals, we keep the
decimal points in line.

a Add or subtract.

1.
```
   6        0.6
  +3       +0.3
```

2.
```
   6        0.6
  +4       +0.4
```

3.
```
   6        0.6
  +5       +0.5
```

4.
```
  23        2.3
  + 8      +0.8
```

5.
```
  23        2.3
  +48      +4.8
```

6.
```
  23        2.3
  +98      +9.8
```

7.
```
   7        0.7
  -4       -0.4
```

8.
```
  17        1.7
  - 4      -0.4
```

9.
```
  17        1.7
  - 9      -0.9
```

10.
```
  98        9.8
 -47       -4.7
```

11.
```
  92        9.2
 -47       -4.7
```

12.
```
  92        9.2
 -87       -8.7
```

b Add or subtract.

13.	0.4 +0.5	14.	6.3 +0.2	15.	1.6 +2.8	16.	0.9 +0.5	17.	8.2 +7.3
18.	0.9 −0.7	19.	8.1 −2.5	20.	3.6 −2.8	21.	1.8 −0.8	22.	7.7 −4.3
23.	16.3 −12.2	24.	35.7 +10.3	25.	10.6 − 7.3	26.	63.4 +49.2	27.	56.1 −49.7
28.	0.3 0.4 +0.5	29.	1.7 0.9 +3.6	30.	3.6 8.5 +6.4	31.	21.3 0.6 + 8.9	32.	45.6 30.2 +28.7

c Solve.

33. A board is 0.8 m long. Flora needs a piece 0.5 m long. How long is the piece that is not needed?

34. Tony has 2.5 ℓ of paint in one can and 1.5 ℓ of paint in another can. How many liters is that in all?

35. Mike needs a strip of wood 0.5 m long and another strip 0.8 m long. He takes both from a strip 1.5 m long. How long is the piece that is left?

Hundredths, Addition and Subtraction

Compare these examples.

48	0.48	1.21		648	6.48	9.21
+73	+0.73	−0.73		+273	+2.73	−2.73
121	1.21	0.48		921	9.21	6.48

When we add or subtract decimals, we keep the decimal points in line.

a Add or subtract.

1.
32	0.32
+45	+0.45

2.
82	0.82
+45	+0.45

3.
182	1.82
+ 45	+0.45

4.
763	7.63
+225	+2.25

5.
783	7.83
+225	+2.25

6.
1783	17.83
+ 225	+ 2.25

7.
45	0.45
−21	−0.21

8.
145	1.45
− 21	−0.21

9.
145	1.45
− 61	−0.61

10.
436	4.36
−115	−1.15

11.
436	4.36
−145	−1.45

12.
436	4.36
−345	−3.45

b Add or subtract.

13. $\begin{array}{r} 0.35 \\ +0.26 \\ \hline \end{array}$	**14.** $\begin{array}{r} 1.75 \\ +0.65 \\ \hline \end{array}$	**15.** $\begin{array}{r} 3.06 \\ +2.88 \\ \hline \end{array}$	**16.** $\begin{array}{r} 0.98 \\ +0.64 \\ \hline \end{array}$	**17.** $\begin{array}{r} 5.27 \\ +8.35 \\ \hline \end{array}$
18. $\begin{array}{r} 6.98 \\ -3.76 \\ \hline \end{array}$	**19.** $\begin{array}{r} 0.84 \\ -0.27 \\ \hline \end{array}$	**20.** $\begin{array}{r} 3.50 \\ -1.75 \\ \hline \end{array}$	**21.** $\begin{array}{r} 8.02 \\ -2.64 \\ \hline \end{array}$	**22.** $\begin{array}{r} 4.75 \\ -3.79 \\ \hline \end{array}$
23. $\begin{array}{r} 13.45 \\ +14.79 \\ \hline \end{array}$	**24.** $\begin{array}{r} 20.59 \\ -12.58 \\ \hline \end{array}$	**25.** $\begin{array}{r} \$25.95 \\ +10.88 \\ \hline \end{array}$	**26.** $\begin{array}{r} \$25.00 \\ -24.89 \\ \hline \end{array}$	**27.** $\begin{array}{r} \$16.75 \\ +\ 5.99 \\ \hline \end{array}$
28. $\begin{array}{r} 0.21 \\ 0.37 \\ +0.68 \\ \hline \end{array}$	**29.** $\begin{array}{r} 1.98 \\ 1.98 \\ +1.98 \\ \hline \end{array}$	**30.** $\begin{array}{r} \$18.89 \\ 6.28 \\ +\ 4.99 \\ \hline \end{array}$	**31.** $\begin{array}{r} \$10.98 \\ 15.01 \\ +25.76 \\ \hline \end{array}$	**32.** $\begin{array}{r} \$12.27 \\ 23.95 \\ +14.78 \\ \hline \end{array}$

Review B (pages 296–303)

Complete.

1. $\dfrac{3}{3} = 1$ 2. $\dfrac{8}{8} = 1$ 3. $\dfrac{4}{4} = 1$ 4. $\dfrac{6}{3} = 2$

$\dfrac{4}{3} = 1\dfrac{\blacksquare}{3}$ $\dfrac{9}{8} = 1\dfrac{\blacksquare}{8}$ $\dfrac{7}{4} = 1\dfrac{\blacksquare}{4}$ $\dfrac{7}{3} = 2\dfrac{\blacksquare}{3}$

Write the decimal.

5. six and five tenths

6. one and two tenths

7. 35 and 46 hundredths

8. 12 and 5 hundredths

Add or subtract.

9. $\begin{array}{r} 0.2 \\ +0.7 \\ \hline \end{array}$	**10.** $\begin{array}{r} 7.5 \\ +3.8 \\ \hline \end{array}$	**11.** $\begin{array}{r} 0.9 \\ -0.7 \\ \hline \end{array}$	**12.** $\begin{array}{r} 7.5 \\ -2.8 \\ \hline \end{array}$
13. $\begin{array}{r} 0.32 \\ +0.28 \\ \hline \end{array}$	**14.** $\begin{array}{r} \$5.98 \\ +6.89 \\ \hline \end{array}$	**15.** $\begin{array}{r} 0.82 \\ -0.56 \\ \hline \end{array}$	**16.** $\begin{array}{r} \$6.25 \\ -5.75 \\ \hline \end{array}$

Problem Solving   Problem • Plan • Arithmetic • Answer

1. 5 lights turned on
   3 lights turned off
   How many lights on?

2. 16 bags of trash
   9 bags of cans
   How many bags in all?

3. $50 fine for littering
   2 fines paid
   How much paid?

4. 5 people in each car pool
   65 people
   How many car pools?

5. 58 students and 19 parents meet to plan a paper drive.
   About how many people is that in all?

6. They collect 128 bundles of papers the first week.
   They collect 119 bundles of papers the second week.
   How many more bundles do they collect the first week?

7. It takes 21 days to clean up the parks.
   How many weeks is that?

8. The local dairy pays 20¢ for each milk bottle returned.
   Luis returns 3 bottles.
   What does the dairy pay him?

9. Liz is paid 2 dollars in quarters for cleaning up a yard.
   How many quarters is she paid?

10. There are 6 winners in the Clean Town Poster Contest.
    $\frac{1}{3}$ of them win blue ribbons.
    How many win blue ribbons?

11. The Garden Club has 8 dozen maple trees and 20 oaks.
    How many trees is that in all?

12. The Garden Club sells small trees for $1.75 each.
    Ricardo pays for 3 trees with 10 dollars.
    What is his change?

13. 58 people volunteer to paint the railroad station.
    How many teams of 10 painters can be made?
    How many extra people are not on a team?

304

Unit Test

Write the fraction in simplest form.   (pages 286–287)

1. $\frac{7}{14}$ 2. $\frac{6}{9}$ 3. $\frac{8}{8}$ 4. $\frac{8}{12}$ 5. $\frac{0}{3}$

Add or subtract.   (pages 288–291)

6. $\frac{3}{9} + \frac{1}{9}$ 7. $\frac{4}{5} - \frac{2}{5}$ 8. $\frac{2}{8} + \frac{3}{8}$ 9. $\frac{5}{6} - \frac{4}{6}$ 10. $\frac{9}{10} - \frac{6}{10}$

Add or subtract.   (pages 292–295)

11. $\frac{1}{6}$ 12. $\frac{5}{9}$ 13. $\frac{3}{8}$ 14. $\frac{1}{3}$ 15. $\frac{4}{5}$

$+\frac{2}{3}$ $-\frac{1}{3}$ $+\frac{1}{4}$ $+\frac{3}{12}$ $-\frac{5}{10}$

Complete.   (pages 296–297)

16. $\frac{4}{4} = 1$ 17. $\frac{7}{7} = 1$ 18. $\frac{5}{5} = 1$ 19. $\frac{4}{2} = 2$

$\frac{5}{4} = 1\frac{}{4}$ $\frac{9}{7} = 1\frac{}{7}$ $\frac{8}{5} = 1\frac{}{5}$ $\frac{5}{2} = 2\frac{}{2}$

Write the decimal.   (pages 298–299)

20. one and eight tenths   21. 56 and 14 hundredths

22. $18\frac{2}{10}$ 23. $23\frac{5}{100}$

Add or subtract.   (pages 300–303)

24.   23.8   25.   9.1   26.   0.49   27. $2.89   28. $34.08
    +19.7   −5.6   +0.35   +6.47   −16.79

Solve.   (page 304)

29. 3.5 ℓ in a jug   30. $3.25 to spend
    1.4 ℓ poured out $1.70 spent
    How much is left in the jug?   How much is left?

Taking Another Look

Pages 286–287

$$\frac{9}{12} = \frac{9 \div 3}{12 \div 3} = \frac{3}{4}$$

$$\frac{4}{4} = 1 \qquad \frac{0}{4} = 0$$

Write the fraction in simplest form.

1. $\frac{3}{9}$ 2. $\frac{6}{9}$ 3. $\frac{4}{8}$ 4. $\frac{6}{8}$

5. $\frac{4}{12}$ 6. $\frac{8}{10}$ 7. $\frac{12}{16}$ 8. $\frac{10}{15}$

Pages 288–291

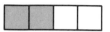

$$\frac{1}{4} + \frac{1}{4} = \frac{2}{4}$$

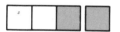

$$\frac{2}{4} - \frac{1}{4} = \frac{1}{4}$$

Add or subtract.

1. $\frac{1}{5} + \frac{1}{5}$ 2. $\frac{1}{5} + \frac{2}{5}$ 3. $\frac{3}{5} - \frac{2}{5}$

4. $\frac{2}{8} + \frac{3}{8}$ 5. $\frac{4}{6} + \frac{1}{6}$ 6. $\frac{4}{10} + \frac{3}{10}$

7. $\frac{7}{9} - \frac{2}{9}$ 8. $\frac{11}{12} - \frac{4}{12}$ 9. $\frac{7}{8} - \frac{4}{8}$

10. $\frac{6}{7} - \frac{3}{7}$ 11. $\frac{8}{12} + \frac{3}{12}$ 12. $\frac{9}{10} - \frac{6}{10}$

Pages 292–295

$$\begin{array}{rcr} \frac{1}{2} &=& \frac{5}{10} \\[4pt] +\frac{2}{10} &=& +\frac{2}{10} \\ \hline &=& \frac{7}{10} \end{array}$$

$$\begin{array}{rcr} \frac{7}{12} &=& \frac{7}{12} \\[4pt] -\frac{1}{6} &=& -\frac{2}{12} \\ \hline &=& \frac{5}{12} \end{array}$$

Add or subtract.

1.
$$\begin{array}{rcr} \frac{1}{16} &=& \frac{1}{16} \\[4pt] +\frac{3}{8} &=& +\frac{\blacksquare}{16} \\ \hline &=& \frac{\blacksquare}{16} \end{array}$$

2.
$$\begin{array}{rcr} \frac{2}{3} &=& \frac{\blacksquare}{9} \\[4pt] -\frac{1}{9} &=& -\frac{1}{9} \\ \hline &=& \frac{\blacksquare}{9} \end{array}$$

3. $\begin{array}{r} \frac{1}{2} \\ +\frac{1}{8} \\ \hline \end{array}$ 4. $\begin{array}{r} \frac{1}{10} \\ +\frac{3}{5} \\ \hline \end{array}$ 5. $\begin{array}{r} \frac{2}{12} \\ +\frac{1}{4} \\ \hline \end{array}$ 6. $\begin{array}{r} \frac{2}{3} \\ +\frac{1}{6} \\ \hline \end{array}$

7. $\begin{array}{r} \frac{7}{10} \\ -\frac{2}{5} \\ \hline \end{array}$ 8. $\begin{array}{r} \frac{3}{4} \\ -\frac{5}{8} \\ \hline \end{array}$ 9. $\begin{array}{r} \frac{5}{8} \\ -\frac{1}{16} \\ \hline \end{array}$ 10. $\begin{array}{r} \frac{4}{6} \\ -\frac{1}{2} \\ \hline \end{array}$

Pages 296–297

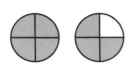

$\frac{7}{4} = 1\frac{3}{4}$

Complete.

1. $\frac{5}{5} = 1$

$\frac{6}{5} = 1\frac{\blacksquare}{5}$

2. $\frac{5}{5} = 1$

$\frac{7}{5} = 1\frac{\blacksquare}{5}$

3. $\frac{5}{5} = 1$

$\frac{8}{5} = 1\frac{\blacksquare}{5}$

4. $\frac{8}{8} = 1$

$\frac{11}{8} = 1\frac{\blacksquare}{8}$

5. $\frac{3}{3} = 1$

$\frac{5}{3} = 1\frac{\blacksquare}{3}$

6. $\frac{8}{4} = 2$

$\frac{9}{4} = 2\frac{\blacksquare}{4}$

Pages 298–299

12 and 87 hundredths

$12\frac{87}{100} = 12.87$

Write the decimal.

1. two and seven tenths

2. eight and one tenth

3. 63 and 40 hundredths

4. 89 and 4 hundredths

5. $5\frac{4}{10}$

6. $24\frac{75}{100}$

7. $52\frac{2}{10}$

8. $39\frac{20}{100}$

Pages 300–303

$$\begin{array}{r} 72.81 \\ -46.85 \\ \hline 25.96 \end{array}$$

Add or subtract.

1. $\begin{array}{r} 37 \\ +48 \\ \hline \end{array}$ $\quad$ $\begin{array}{r} 3.7 \\ +4.8 \\ \hline \end{array}$

2. $\begin{array}{r} 256 \\ -\;\;79 \\ \hline \end{array}$ $\quad$ $\begin{array}{r} 2.56 \\ -0.79 \\ \hline \end{array}$

3. $\begin{array}{r} 62.9 \\ +35.3 \\ \hline \end{array}$

4. $\begin{array}{r} 20.2 \\ -\;\;8.6 \\ \hline \end{array}$

5. $\begin{array}{r} 7.84 \\ +9.37 \\ \hline \end{array}$

6. $\begin{array}{r} \$59.06 \\ -43.39 \\ \hline \end{array}$

Page 304

1. **Problem**
2. **Plan**
3. **Arithmetic**
4. **Answer**

Solve.

1. Sam spends $5.25, $1.75, and $2.88. What is his change from $10.00?

2. We need $\frac{1}{3}$ of the paint for the door and $\frac{1}{3}$ for trim. What part of the paint do we need in all for the door and trim?

Something Extra • SECONDS

An hour is 60 minutes.
A minute is 60 seconds.
Some digital clocks show hours, minutes, and seconds.
03: 24: 17 means 3 hours 24 minutes 17 seconds.

Complete.

1. 11: 32: 48 means ▨ hours ▨ minutes ▨ seconds.
2. 05: 18: 20 means ▨ hours ▨ minutes ▨ seconds.
3. 01: 50: 02 means ▨ hours ▨ minutes ▨ seconds.
4. 10: 06: 20 means ▨ hours ▨ minutes ▨ seconds.
5. 06: 00: 59 means ▨ hours ▨ minutes ▨ seconds.

What time will the clock show 30 seconds later?

6. 02: 18: 17   7. 02: 18: 30   8. 12: 18: 48
9. 01: 58: 38   10. 01: 59: 38   11. 01: 00: 38

What time did the clock show 30 seconds earlier?

12. 11: 28: 42   13. 11: 28: 38   14. 11: 28: 30
15. 01: 01: 31   16. 10: 30: 59   17. 08: 15: 00

Solve.

18. Ramon's time in the long-distance race is 01: 12: 58.
    Jim's time is 3 seconds longer.
    What is Jim's time?

19. Jill wins the cross-country ski race with a time of 01: 32: 24.
    Tina's time is 2 minutes and 16 seconds longer.
    What is Tina's time?

20. The 1937 flight record across the country was 07: 28: 25.
    By 1959 jet time across the country was 04: 04: 00.
    How many hours, minutes, and seconds less was jet time?

Reviewing Needed Skills

Add or subtract.

1. $\begin{array}{r} 56 \\ +28 \\ \hline \end{array}$

2. $\begin{array}{r} 297 \\ +354 \\ \hline \end{array}$

3. $\begin{array}{r} 73 \\ 18 \\ +45 \\ \hline \end{array}$

4. $\begin{array}{r} 64 \\ 9 \\ 27 \\ +32 \\ \hline \end{array}$

5. $\begin{array}{r} 51 \\ 38 \\ 6 \\ +47 \\ \hline \end{array}$

6. $\begin{array}{r} 93 \\ -48 \\ \hline \end{array}$

7. $\begin{array}{r} 85 \\ -69 \\ \hline \end{array}$

8. $\begin{array}{r} 627 \\ -465 \\ \hline \end{array}$

9. $\begin{array}{r} 581 \\ -193 \\ \hline \end{array}$

10. $\begin{array}{r} 6294 \\ -3765 \\ \hline \end{array}$

Multiply or divide.

11. $\begin{array}{r} 38 \\ \times 6 \\ \hline \end{array}$

12. $\begin{array}{r} 629 \\ \times 8 \\ \hline \end{array}$

13. $\begin{array}{r} 74 \\ \times 36 \\ \hline \end{array}$

14. $\begin{array}{r} 87 \\ \times 53 \\ \hline \end{array}$

15. $\begin{array}{r} 928 \\ \times 47 \\ \hline \end{array}$

16. $4\overline{)98}$

17. $9\overline{)295}$

18. $2\overline{)739}$

19. $3\overline{)916}$

20. $36\overline{)523}$

Add or subtract.

21. $\begin{array}{r} \frac{2}{10} \\ +\frac{5}{10} \\ \hline \end{array}$

22. $\begin{array}{r} \frac{3}{9} \\ +\frac{4}{9} \\ \hline \end{array}$

23. $\begin{array}{r} \frac{2}{3} \\ +\frac{1}{6} \\ \hline \end{array}$

24. $\begin{array}{r} \frac{1}{8} \\ +\frac{3}{4} \\ \hline \end{array}$

25. $\begin{array}{r} \frac{3}{5} \\ +\frac{3}{10} \\ \hline \end{array}$

26. $\begin{array}{r} \frac{6}{7} \\ -\frac{4}{7} \\ \hline \end{array}$

27. $\begin{array}{r} \frac{9}{12} \\ -\frac{4}{12} \\ \hline \end{array}$

28. $\begin{array}{r} \frac{5}{8} \\ -\frac{3}{16} \\ \hline \end{array}$

29. $\begin{array}{r} \frac{4}{6} \\ -\frac{1}{2} \\ \hline \end{array}$

30. $\begin{array}{r} \frac{5}{7} \\ -\frac{5}{14} \\ \hline \end{array}$

Add or subtract.

31. $\begin{array}{r} 0.9 \\ +0.5 \\ \hline \end{array}$

32. $\begin{array}{r} 8.6 \\ +3.7 \\ \hline \end{array}$

33. $\begin{array}{r} 2.54 \\ +6.73 \\ \hline \end{array}$

34. $\begin{array}{r} \$18.09 \\ +54.64 \\ \hline \end{array}$

35. $\begin{array}{r} \$32.95 \\ +46.83 \\ \hline \end{array}$

36. $\begin{array}{r} 0.8 \\ -0.3 \\ \hline \end{array}$

37. $\begin{array}{r} 24.2 \\ -16.9 \\ \hline \end{array}$

38. $\begin{array}{r} 8.36 \\ -5.47 \\ \hline \end{array}$

39. $\begin{array}{r} \$57.29 \\ -19.36 \\ \hline \end{array}$

40. $\begin{array}{r} \$92.46 \\ -57.83 \\ \hline \end{array}$

Extra practice · Unit 1 (A)

(For use with pages 2–9)

Pages
2–3

1. 3 +1	2. 8 +1	3. 3 +2	4. 3 +5	5. 4 +3
6. 6 −1	7. 8 −2	8. 7 −4	9. 6 −2	10. 8 −4
11. 5 +2	12. 9 −3	13. 3 +3	14. 5 −3	15. 4 +5

Pages
4–5

16. 8 +3	17. 5 +5	18. 6 +5	19. 7 +5	20. 6 +7
21. 13 − 5	22. 10 − 6	23. 12 − 5	24. 12 − 8	25. 11 − 4
26. 5 +8	27. 13 − 7	28. 9 +4	29. 11 − 6	30. 6 +6

Pages
6–7

31. 7 +7	32. 9 +8	33. 6 +9	34. 9 +9	35. 8 +8
36. 15 − 8	37. 14 − 6	38. 18 − 9	39. 16 − 7	40. 17 − 9

Pages
8–9

41. 7 +3	42. 8 +6	43. 9 +3	44. 7 +8	45. 1 +1
46. 15 − 6	47. 17 − 8	48. 11 − 9	49. 14 − 8	50. 16 − 9
51. 4 +4	52. 13 − 9	53. 9 +7	54. 4 −2	55. 5 +9

Extra practice · Unit 1 (B)

(For use with pages 10–15)

Pages 10–11

1. 11 + 7	2. 15 + 4	3. 10 + 4	4. 12 + 6	5. 18 + 1
6. 15 + 2	7. 10 + 9	8. 13 + 5	9. 17 + 2	10. 12 + 5
11. 15 + 3	12. 14 + 4	13. 12 + 3	14. 11 + 8	15. 14 + 5

Pages 12–13

16. 16 + 7	17. 15 + 8	18. 12 + 9	19. 14 + 7	20. 13 + 9
21. 17 + 5	22. 14 + 8	23. 18 + 8	24. 19 + 4	25. 17 + 8
26. 16 + 6	27. 15 + 9	28. 13 + 8	29. 12 + 8	30. 17 + 7

Pages 14–15

31. 5 2 +4	32. 9 7 +6	33. 5 3 +7	34. 4 7 +6	35. 8 9 +2
36. 1 4 5 +2	37. 9 2 6 +4	38. 3 5 8 +2	39. 6 3 4 +6	40. 7 8 3 +2
41. 5 7 2 2 +3	42. 4 8 1 5 +6	43. 1 2 3 4 +5	44. 9 4 4 1 +7	45. 6 5 4 3 +9

Extra practice · Unit 2 (A)

(For use with pages 22–31)

Pages
22–23

Write < or > for ▦.

1. 50 ▦ 90   2. 58 ▦ 98   3. 60 ▦ 50   4. 65 ▦ 56

5. 80 ▦ 60   6. 87 ▦ 64   7. 60 ▦ 10   8. 61 ▦ 16

9. 30 ▦ 40   10. 32 ▦ 48   11. 90 ▦ 30   12. 93 ▦ 39

Pages
24–25

Write the standard form.

13. 300 + 50 + 7   14. one hundred eighty-five

15. 2 hundreds 5 tens 8 ones   16. 500 + 8

17. seven hundred five   18. 5 hundreds 6 tens

Write < or > for ▦.

19. 300 ▦ 500   20. 700 ▦ 400   21. 300 ▦ 400
    380 ▦ 580   726 ▦ 426   360 ▦ 410

22. 611 ▦ 600   23. 255 ▦ 252   24. 368 ▦ 413

Pages
26–27

Write the numbers that are between the given numbers.

25. 5634 ▦▦ 5637   26. 7119 ▦▦ 7122   27. 5998 ▦▦ 6001

Write the standard form.

28. 5000 + 200 + 40   29. six thousand fifty-eight

30. 8 thousand 132   31. 4 thousand 306

Pages
28–29

Write the numbers that are between the given numbers.

32. 350,009 ▦▦ 350,012   33. 89,998 ▦▦ 90,001

34. 16,084 ▦▦ 16,087   35. 60,059 ▦▦ 60,062

Pages
30–31

Round to the nearest ten.

36. 218   37. 691   38. 85   39. 727   40. 333

Round to the nearest hundred.

41. 808   42. 556   43. 97   44. 728   45. 678

Extra practice · Unit 2 (B)

(For use with pages 32–39)

Pages 32–33

Use a dollar sign and a point to show the amount.

1. 4 dollars and 67 cents
2. 12 dollars and 75 cents
3. 307¢
4. 2 dollars 1 nickel
5. 6 dollars 2 dimes
6. 89¢
7. 11 dollars and 5 cents
8. 7 dollars 1 dime 1 nickel

What is the amount to the nearest dollar?

9. $.95   10. $7.29   11. $3.88   12. $2.05   13. $8.59

14. $.75   15. $5.99   16. $4.25   17. $1.19   18. $19.98

Pages 34–35

Write cm, m, or km for ▓.

19. My door is 2 ▓ high.
20. A pen is 14 ▓ long.
21. A sandwich is 10 ▓ wide.
22. We drove 50 ▓ today.
23. Kim ran the 50 ▓ dash.
24. The paper is 20 ▓ wide.
25. My book is 24 ▓ long.
26. My desk is 60 ▓ wide.

Pages 36–37

Write g or kg to name the better unit to measure each.

27. a paperclip
28. a piano
29. a baby
30. an elephant
31. an apple
32. a stick of butter
33. a suitcase
34. a pencil
35. a hen's egg
36. a couch
37. a worm
38. a horse

Pages 38–39

Name the best United States unit to measure each.

39. length of a caterpillar
40. distance to London
41. weight of a person
42. length of a football field
43. distance walked in a week
44. weight of an ant
45. length of a pencil
46. weight of a turkey
47. weight of an ocean liner
48. depth of a swimming pool

Extra practice · Unit 3 (A)

(For use with pages 46–55)

Pages 46–47

1. 52
   +46

2. 61
   +33

3. 27
   +51

4. 34
   +63

5. 44
   +25

6. 40
   23
   +10

7. 27
   50
   +12

8. 61
   17
   +20

9. 36
   31
   +21

10. 25
    43
    +30

Pages 48–49

11. 36
    +25

12. 48
    +24

13. 57
    +34

14. 88
    +13

15. 29
    +66

16. 45
    +28

17. 36
    +36

18. 74
    +16

19. 52
    +18

20. 63
    +29

Pages 50–51

21. 47
    6
    + 5

22. 65
    7
    + 2

23. 53
    9
    + 8

24. 72
    8
    + 4

25. 29
    7
    + 3

26. 28
    3
    + 5

27. 56
    3
    + 9

28. 37
    8
    + 4

29. 52
    7
    + 5

30. 45
    2
    + 6

Pages 52–53

31. 257
    +115

32. 578
    +118

33. 799
    + 21

34. 378
    + 86

35. 553
    +337

36. 644
    +276

37. 524
    +188

38. 897
    +108

39. 346
    +279

40. 431
    +469

Pages 54–55

41. 6678
    +1119

42. 4534
    +2238

43. 2765
    +4117

44. 5133
    +1639

45. 6312
    +2168

46. 9514
    +2185

47. 4281
    +7187

48. 6245
    +7298

49. 2840
    +7396

50. 8457
    +3907

Extra practice · Unit 3 (B)

(For use with pages 56–65)

Pages
56–57

1.   87
  − 8

2.   57
  −19

3.   77
  − 8

4.   48
  −39

5.   56
  −28

6.   22
  −17

7.   57
  −38

8.   73
  −59

9.   44
  −19

10.   70
  −34

Pages
58–59

11.   381
  −194

12.   604
  −298

13.   868
  −299

14.   770
  −394

15.   526
  −479

16.   746
  −667

17.   830
  −681

18.   467
  −389

19.   963
  −386

20.   505
  −479

Pages
60–61

21.   9840
  −8170

22.   7480
  −5297

23.   6408
  −4189

24.   4000
  −1634

25.   5128
  −3149

26.   4500
  −2178

27.   6513
  −3386

28.   7822
  −4665

29.   5870
  −1495

30.   3018
  −1296

Pages
62–63

31. $.64
  +.28

32. $.83
  +.29

33. $.37
  −.19

34. $3.89
  −1.56

35. $3.22
  +2.68

36. $23.77
  +11.88

37. $5.52
  −3.98

38. $15.25
  − 4.59

Pages
64–65

Round each number. Then estimate the answer.

39.   74
  +17

40.   67
  +15

41.   45¢
  +58¢

42.   86¢
  +62¢

43.   46¢
  +44¢

44.   52
  −39

45.   82
  −23

46.   75¢
  −38¢

47.   59¢
  −12¢

48.   71¢
  −19¢

Extra practice · Unit 4 (A)

(For use with pages 72–81)

Pages
72–73

1. $1 + 1$ 2. 2×1 3. $1 + 1 + 1$ 4. 3×1

5. $4 + 4$ 6. 2×4 7. $5 + 5 + 5$ 8. 3×5

9. $5 + 5$ 10. 2×5 11. $7 + 7 + 7$ 12. 3×7

Pages
74–75

○ ○ ○ ○ ○ ○ ○   ○ ○ ○ ○ ○ ○ ○ ○
○ ○ ○ ○ ○ ○ ○   ○ ○ ○ ○ ○ ○ ○ ○

13. 2×7 14. 7×2 15. 2×8 16. 8×2

Pages
76–77

17. 2×2 18. $4 \div 2$ 19. 2×6 20. $12 \div 6$

21. 3×3 22. $9 \div 3$ 23. 1×6 24. $6 \div 6$

25. 1×8 26. $8 \div 8$ 27. 2×9 28. $18 \div 9$

Pages
78–79

29. $\begin{array}{r} 2 \\ \times 6 \\ \hline \end{array}$ 30. $\begin{array}{r} 2 \\ \times 3 \\ \hline \end{array}$ 31. $\begin{array}{r} 2 \\ \times 5 \\ \hline \end{array}$ 32. $\begin{array}{r} 4 \\ \times 2 \\ \hline \end{array}$ 33. $\begin{array}{r} 2 \\ \times 8 \\ \hline \end{array}$

34. $\begin{array}{r} 2 \\ \times 9 \\ \hline \end{array}$ 35. $\begin{array}{r} 7 \\ \times 2 \\ \hline \end{array}$ 36. $\begin{array}{r} 2 \\ \times 1 \\ \hline \end{array}$ 37. $\begin{array}{r} 3 \\ \times 2 \\ \hline \end{array}$ 38. $\begin{array}{r} 9 \\ \times 2 \\ \hline \end{array}$

39. $2\overline{)16}$ 40. $2\overline{)6}$ 41. $2\overline{)12}$ 42. $2\overline{)14}$ 43. $2\overline{)18}$

44. $2\overline{)2}$ 45. $8\overline{)16}$ 46. $2\overline{)10}$ 47. $7\overline{)14}$ 48. $2\overline{)8}$

Pages
80–81

49. $\begin{array}{r} 3 \\ \times 8 \\ \hline \end{array}$ 50. $\begin{array}{r} 3 \\ \times 5 \\ \hline \end{array}$ 51. $\begin{array}{r} 3 \\ \times 4 \\ \hline \end{array}$ 52. $\begin{array}{r} 3 \\ \times 7 \\ \hline \end{array}$ 53. $\begin{array}{r} 3 \\ \times 9 \\ \hline \end{array}$

54. $\begin{array}{r} 6 \\ \times 3 \\ \hline \end{array}$ 55. $\begin{array}{r} 3 \\ \times 1 \\ \hline \end{array}$ 56. $\begin{array}{r} 9 \\ \times 3 \\ \hline \end{array}$ 57. $\begin{array}{r} 8 \\ \times 3 \\ \hline \end{array}$ 58. $\begin{array}{r} 7 \\ \times 3 \\ \hline \end{array}$

59. $3\overline{)27}$ 60. $3\overline{)21}$ 61. $3\overline{)24}$ 62. $8\overline{)24}$ 63. $6\overline{)18}$

64. $3\overline{)15}$ 65. $4\overline{)12}$ 66. $9\overline{)27}$ 67. $3\overline{)18}$ 68. $7\overline{)21}$

316

Extra practice · Unit 4 (B)

(For use with pages 82–87)

Pages
82–83

1. 4
    ×5

2. 4
    ×7

3. 9
    ×4

4. 4
    ×4

5. 6
    ×4

6. 4
    ×9

7. 4
    ×6

8. 8
    ×4

9. 2
    ×4

10. 4
     ×3

11. 4)24   12. 8)32   13. 3)12   14. 4)36   15. 7)28

16. 9)36   17. 5)20   18. 4)16   19. 4)32   20. 4)12

Pages
84–85

21. 3
     ×6

22. 2
     ×7

23. 3
     ×4

24. 2
     ×2

25. 3
     ×2

26. 2
     ×8

27. 3
     ×5

28. 3
     ×7

29. 3
     ×8

30. 2
     ×6

31. 4
     ×2

32. 4
     ×8

33. 2
     ×5

34. 5
     ×4

35. 9
     ×3

36. 2)10   37. 3)6   38. 3)15   39. 2)16   40. 4)8

41. 4)28   42. 2)14   43. 8)16   44. 3)24   45. 2)12

46. 3)27   47. 3)18   48. 2)8   49. 2)18   50. 4)20

Pages
86–87

51. 1
     ×1

52. 3
     ×1

53. 0
     ×3

54. 3
     ×2

55. 5
     ×3

56. 2
     ×9

57. 4
     ×0

58. 6
     ×1

59. 3
     ×3

60. 4
     ×2

61. 2)2   62. 2)0   63. 3)3   64. 3)21   65. 3)6

66. 7)21   67. 9)27   68. 4)0   69. 5)15   70. 6)24

317

Extra practice · Unit 5 (A)

(For use with pages 94–103)

Pages 94–95

1. 3×5 2. 5×5 3. 5×4 4. 6×5

5. $20 \div 5$ 6. $30 \div 6$ 7. $15 \div 5$ 8. $30 \div 5$

9. $10 \div 5$ 10. $15 \div 3$ 11. $5 \div 5$ 12. $20 \div 4$

Pages 96–97

13. $\begin{array}{r} 5 \\ \times 6 \\ \hline \end{array}$ 14. $\begin{array}{r} 8 \\ \times 5 \\ \hline \end{array}$ 15. $\begin{array}{r} 5 \\ \times 7 \\ \hline \end{array}$ 16. $\begin{array}{r} 9 \\ \times 5 \\ \hline \end{array}$ 17. $\begin{array}{r} 5 \\ \times 5 \\ \hline \end{array}$

18. $5 \overline{)30}$ 19. $9 \overline{)45}$ 20. $5 \overline{)5}$ 21. $4 \overline{)20}$ 22. $5 \overline{)45}$

23. $5 \overline{)35}$ 24. $5 \overline{)40}$ 25. $3 \overline{)15}$ 26. $6 \overline{)30}$ 27. $8 \overline{)40}$

Pages 98–99

28. $\begin{array}{r} 6 \\ \times 6 \\ \hline \end{array}$ 29. $\begin{array}{r} 7 \\ \times 6 \\ \hline \end{array}$ 30. $\begin{array}{r} 6 \\ \times 5 \\ \hline \end{array}$ 31. $\begin{array}{r} 8 \\ \times 6 \\ \hline \end{array}$ 32. $\begin{array}{r} 6 \\ \times 9 \\ \hline \end{array}$

33. $6 \overline{)12}$ 34. $9 \overline{)54}$ 35. $6 \overline{)48}$ 36. $6 \overline{)36}$ 37. $4 \overline{)24}$

38. $7 \overline{)42}$ 39. $6 \overline{)6}$ 40. $3 \overline{)18}$ 41. $6 \overline{)42}$ 42. $6 \overline{)54}$

Pages 100–101

43. $\begin{array}{r} 0 \\ \times 8 \\ \hline \end{array}$ 44. $\begin{array}{r} 4 \\ \times 6 \\ \hline \end{array}$ 45. $\begin{array}{r} 8 \\ \times 1 \\ \hline \end{array}$ 46. $\begin{array}{r} 5 \\ \times 0 \\ \hline \end{array}$ 47. $\begin{array}{r} 4 \\ \times 4 \\ \hline \end{array}$

48. $3 \overline{)27}$ 49. $5 \overline{)0}$ 50. $6 \overline{)18}$ 51. $1 \overline{)5}$ 52. $4 \overline{)28}$

53. $2 \overline{)10}$ 54. $6 \overline{)24}$ 55. $3 \overline{)3}$ 56. $4 \overline{)0}$ 57. $2 \overline{)12}$

Pages 102–103

58. $\begin{array}{r} 7 \\ \times 3 \\ \hline \end{array}$ 59. $\begin{array}{r} 6 \\ \times 7 \\ \hline \end{array}$ 60. $\begin{array}{r} 7 \\ \times 5 \\ \hline \end{array}$ 61. $\begin{array}{r} 4 \\ \times 7 \\ \hline \end{array}$ 62. $\begin{array}{r} 7 \\ \times 7 \\ \hline \end{array}$

63. $8 \overline{)56}$ 64. $7 \overline{)49}$ 65. $7 \overline{)28}$ 66. $7 \overline{)63}$ 67. $7 \overline{)35}$

68. $7 \overline{)21}$ 69. $7 \overline{)7}$ 70. $9 \overline{)63}$ 71. $2 \overline{)14}$ 72. $7 \overline{)56}$

Extra practice · Unit 5 (B)

(For use with pages 104–111)

Pages
104–105

1. 8
    ×2

2. 5
    ×8

3. 8
    ×0

4. 8
    ×6

5. 8
    ×3

6. 7
    ×8

7. 8
    ×4

8. 1
    ×8

9. 8
    ×8

10. 8
     ×9

11. 5)40   12. 8)48   13. 8)64   14. 3)24   15. 4)32

16. 8)0   17. 8)56   18. 8)8   19. 8)32   20. 8)72

Pages
106–107

21. 6
     ×0

22. 6
     ×5

23. 4
     ×6

24. 1
     ×7

25. 3
     ×9

26. 4)16   27. 7)42   28. 3)21   29. 5)35   30. 6)54

31. 4)36   32. 8)24   33. 3)27   34. 6)36   35. 5)25

Pages
108–109

36. 9
     ×3

37. 0
     ×9

38. 9
     ×6

39. 4
     ×9

40. 7
     ×9

41. 9
     ×9

42. 1
     ×9

43. 9
     ×7

44. 9
     ×8

45. 9
     ×5

46. 9)54   47. 5)45   48. 9)18   49. 9)63   50. 9)81

Pages
110–111

51. 6
     ×6

52. 4
     ×5

53. 3
     ×7

54. 0
     ×0

55. 5
     ×5

56. 8
     ×5

57. 3
     ×5

58. 9
     ×2

59. 5
     ×9

60. 7
     ×7

61. 7)28   62. 6)18   63. 5)15   64. 4)20   65. 6)30

66. 9)45   67. 7)49   68. 6)42   69. 2)14   70. 9)72

Extra practice · Unit 6 (A)

(For use with pages 118–127)

Pages
118–119

Measure the length to the nearest centimeter.

1. _____   2. _____

3. _____   4. _____

Pages
120–121

What is the perimeter?

5.

2 cm

1 cm   1 cm

2 cm

6.

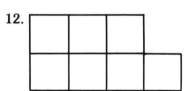

3 cm

2 cm   1 cm

3 cm

Pages
122–123

Measure the length to the nearest inch.

7. _____   8. _____

9. _____   10. _____

Pages
124–125

What is the area?

11.

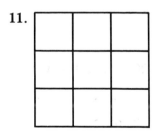

12.

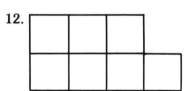

Pages
126–127

What is the volume?

13.

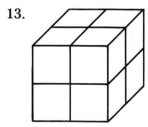

14.

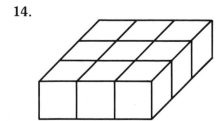

320

Extra practice · Unit 6 (B)

(For use with pages 128–133)

Pages
128–129

Write ml or l to name the better unit for ▒.

1. 200 ▒ of cocoa in a cup

2. 12 ▒ of gasoline in a tank

3. 30 ▒ of juice in a lemon

4. 20 ▒ of milk in a case

5. 5 ▒ of water in a fish bowl

6. 2 ▒ of water in a spoon

7. 1 ▒ of cooking oil sold

8. 500 ▒ of syrup in a bottle

9. 2 ▒ of cream in a spoon

10. 1 ▒ of cola in a bottle

11. 1 ▒ of medicine in a dose

12. 300 ▒ of punch in a glass

Pages
130–131

How many?

13. cups in 2 pints

14. pints in 2 quarts

15. cups in 3 pints

16. pints in 3 quarts

17. cups in 1 quart

18. quarts in 2 gallons

19. pints in 2 gallons

20. quarts in 3 gallons

21. cups in 2 quarts

22. pints in 3 gallons

23. cups in 1 gallon

24. cups in 2 gallons

25. quarts in 1 gallon

26. cups in 1 pint

Pages
132–133

How many?

27. hours in 1 day

28. months in 1 year

29. days in 1 week

30. weeks in 1 year

31. minutes in 1 hour

32. days in 2 weeks

33. days in 5 weeks

34. seconds in 1 minute

35. months in 2 years

36. days in 3 weeks

37. days in 8 weeks

38. weeks in 2 years

39. minutes in 2 hours

40. hours in 3 days

41. days in 4 weeks

42. days in 7 weeks

43. days in 6 weeks

44. hours in 2 days

45. seconds in 2 minutes

46. days in 9 weeks

Extra practice · Unit 7 (A)

(For use with pages 140–149)

Pages
140–141

1. 30
   ×2

2. 10
   ×8

3. 400
   ×2

4. 3000
   ×3

5. 1000
   ×7

6. 30
   ×3

7. 20
   ×3

8. 100
   ×6

9. 2000
   ×4

10. 300
    ×2

Pages
142–143

11. 80
    ×6

12. 70
    ×3

13. 600
    ×5

14. 800
    ×4

15. 3000
    ×8

16. 50
    ×9

17. 80
    ×5

18. 700
    ×4

19. 5000
    ×7

20. 6000
    ×6

Pages
144–145

21. 34
    ×2

22. 61
    ×5

23. 53
    ×3

24. 72
    ×3

25. 91
    ×5

26. 21
    ×9

27. 71
    ×8

28. 83
    ×2

29. 61
    ×7

30. 93
    ×3

Pages
146–147

31. 56
    ×2

32. 78
    ×3

33. 18
    ×9

34. 75
    ×4

35. 64
    ×4

36. 82
    ×8

37. 38
    ×7

38. 26
    ×3

39. 55
    ×5

40. 77
    ×4

Pages
148–149

Estimate. Then figure the exact cost.

41. 39¢
    ×4

42. 57¢
    ×5

43. 63¢
    ×9

44. 42¢
    ×5

45. 64¢
    ×8

46. 99¢
    ×2

47. 88¢
    ×4

48. 33¢
    ×7

49. 27¢
    ×6

50. 53¢
    ×5

Extra practice · Unit 7 (B)

(For use with pages 150–157)

Pages
150–151

1. 137
×2

2. 115
×6

3. 118
×3

4. 223
×4

5. 437
×2

6. 336
×2

7. 617
×4

8. 318
×5

9. 816
×6

10. 519
×4

11. 302
×3

12. 103
×6

13. 205
×7

14. 604
×5

15. 909
×9

Pages
152–153

16. 167
×7

17. 389
×2

18. 143
×9

19. 365
×5

20. 186
×8

21. 388
×6

22. 526
×7

23. 294
×6

24. 357
×3

25. 863
×4

Pages
154–155

26. 2152
×6

27. 6205
×3

28. 2033
×8

29. 6564
×2

30. 5560
×7

31. 9398
×8

32. 6868
×3

33. 9724
×8

34. 6035
×7

35. 5672
×5

Pages
156–157

36. $4.48
×6

37. $8.65
×9

38. $7.42
×5

39. $3.18
×7

40. $1.99
×2

41. $5.25
×4

42. $3.04
×5

43. $2.87
×4

44. $46.72
×4

45. $56.68
×3

46. $93.12
×3

47. $11.99
×2

48. $75.02
×6

49. $11.22
×7

50. $52.53
×2

51. $18.50
×6

Extra practice · Unit 8 (A)

(For use with pages 164–173)

Pages
164–165

○ ○ ○
○ ○
○ ○

1. How many threes in 7?
2. How many extra?

3. How many twos in 7?
4. How many extra?

○ ○ ○ ○
○ ○ ○ ○
○ ○ ○

5. How many threes in 11?
6. How many extra?

7. How many fours in 11?
8. How many extra?

Pages
166–167

9. 5)$\overline{12}$ 10. 7)$\overline{24}$ 11. 3)$\overline{14}$ 12. 6)$\overline{25}$ 13. 8)$\overline{36}$

14. 6)$\overline{33}$ 15. 5)$\overline{42}$ 16. 9)$\overline{57}$ 17. 6)$\overline{47}$ 18. 8)$\overline{52}$

19. 4)$\overline{23}$ 20. 8)$\overline{65}$ 21. 7)$\overline{30}$ 22. 2)$\overline{5}$ 23. 3)$\overline{17}$

24. 9)$\overline{75}$ 25. 4)$\overline{29}$ 26. 6)$\overline{28}$ 27. 3)$\overline{26}$ 28. 2)$\overline{19}$

Pages
168–169

29. 2)$\overline{20}$ 30. 2)$\overline{80}$ 31. 6)$\overline{180}$ 32. 3)$\overline{120}$ 33. 5)$\overline{250}$

34. 9)$\overline{90}$ 35. 3)$\overline{60}$ 36. 8)$\overline{320}$ 37. 7)$\overline{350}$ 38. 6)$\overline{540}$

39. 4)$\overline{80}$ 40. 8)$\overline{80}$ 41. 9)$\overline{270}$ 42. 6)$\overline{420}$ 43. 5)$\overline{450}$

44. 3)$\overline{30}$ 45. 5)$\overline{50}$ 46. 9)$\overline{810}$ 47. 9)$\overline{720}$ 48. 2)$\overline{100}$

Pages
170–171

49. 3)$\overline{33}$ 50. 4)$\overline{84}$ 51. 6)$\overline{66}$ 52. 2)$\overline{64}$ 53. 7)$\overline{77}$

54. 4)$\overline{48}$ 55. 3)$\overline{39}$ 56. 2)$\overline{24}$ 57. 3)$\overline{93}$ 58. 5)$\overline{55}$

Pages
172–173

59. 3)$\overline{81}$ 60. 5)$\overline{60}$ 61. 3)$\overline{48}$ 62. 6)$\overline{72}$ 63. 5)$\overline{85}$

64. 4)$\overline{96}$ 65. 7)$\overline{84}$ 66. 8)$\overline{96}$ 67. 2)$\overline{30}$ 68. 4)$\overline{64}$

Extra practice · Unit 8 (B)

(For use with pages 174–181)

Pages
174–175

1. 3)86   2. 7)95   3. 6)79   4. 5)63   5. 6)81

6. 4)57   7. 3)43   8. 7)89   9. 5)82   10. 4)63

11. 2)75   12. 6)94   13. 8)94   14. 3)52   15. 3)77

16. 2)35   17. 2)31   18. 4)69   19. 8)95   20. 7)93

21. 5)76   22. 3)49   23. 7)85   24. 6)92   25. 2)33

Pages
176–177

26. 4)328   27. 7)637   28. 5)355   29. 5)255

30. 6)306   31. 7)497   32. 9)819   33. 7)217

34. 6)486   35. 8)568   36. 8)728   37. 6)546

38. 8)648   39. 6)426   40. 3)246   41. 2)102

Pages
178–179

42. 9)297   43. 8)192   44. 5)225   45. 9)198

46. 8)120   47. 7)322   48. 8)288   49. 9)144

50. 5)215   51. 3)132   52. 6)312   53. 6)456

54. 4)304   55. 8)360   56. 7)504   57. 2)110

58. 3)255   59. 6)234   60. 2)190   61. 2)172

Pages
180–181

62. 7)220   63. 5)379   64. 7)246   65. 6)215

66. 7)397   67. 6)569   68. 7)512   69. 7)463

70. 8)214   71. 6)166   72. 5)487   73. 9)389

74. 8)349   75. 8)620   76. 8)331   77. 3)220

Extra practice · Unit 9 (A)   (For use with pages 188–197)

Pages 188–189

Write the fraction for the shaded part.

1. 2. 3. 4.

5. 6. 7. 8.

Pages 190–191

Write the fraction.

9. 1 of the 5 books

10. 1 of the 8 people

11. 2 of the 5 apples

12. 3 of the 8 cartons

13. 2 of the 9 pencils

14. 7 of the 9 cookies

15. 1 of the 10 bags

16. 3 of the 10 classes

17. 9 of the 10 teachers

18. 3 of the 100 students

Pages 192–193

Complete.

19. $\dfrac{1}{3} = \dfrac{\blacksquare}{6}$

20. $\dfrac{2}{4} = \dfrac{\blacksquare}{8}$

21. $\dfrac{2}{3} = \dfrac{\blacksquare}{9}$

22. $\dfrac{1}{2} = \dfrac{\blacksquare}{8}$

Pages 194–195

23. $\dfrac{3}{8} = \dfrac{\blacksquare}{16}$
24. $\dfrac{1}{2} = \dfrac{\blacksquare}{12}$
25. $\dfrac{3}{4} = \dfrac{\blacksquare}{12}$
26. $\dfrac{2}{5} = \dfrac{\blacksquare}{10}$

27. $\dfrac{5}{7} = \dfrac{\blacksquare}{14}$
28. $\dfrac{3}{5} = \dfrac{\blacksquare}{15}$
29. $\dfrac{5}{6} = \dfrac{\blacksquare}{12}$
30. $\dfrac{1}{3} = \dfrac{\blacksquare}{9}$

Pages 196–197

31. $\dfrac{4}{8} = \dfrac{\blacksquare}{2}$
32. $\dfrac{6}{9} = \dfrac{\blacksquare}{3}$
33. $\dfrac{8}{12} = \dfrac{\blacksquare}{6}$
34. $\dfrac{6}{10} = \dfrac{\blacksquare}{5}$

35. $\dfrac{3}{12} = \dfrac{\blacksquare}{4}$
36. $\dfrac{12}{15} = \dfrac{\blacksquare}{5}$
37. $\dfrac{2}{14} = \dfrac{\blacksquare}{7}$
38. $\dfrac{4}{16} = \dfrac{\blacksquare}{4}$

39. $\dfrac{8}{16} = \dfrac{1}{\blacksquare}$
40. $\dfrac{8}{10} = \dfrac{4}{\blacksquare}$
41. $\dfrac{7}{14} = \dfrac{1}{\blacksquare}$
42. $\dfrac{6}{18} = \dfrac{2}{\blacksquare}$

Extra practice · Unit 9 (B)

(For use with pages 198–207)

Pages 198–199

Write < or > for ▨.

1. $\frac{4}{8}$ ▨ $\frac{7}{8}$ 2. $\frac{4}{5}$ ▨ $\frac{3}{5}$ 3. $\frac{1}{6}$ ▨ $\frac{3}{6}$ 4. $\frac{7}{8}$ ▨ $\frac{5}{8}$

5. $\frac{1}{4}$ ▨ $\frac{3}{4}$ 6. $\frac{6}{10}$ ▨ $\frac{8}{10}$ 7. $\frac{3}{7}$ ▨ $\frac{4}{7}$ 8. $\frac{2}{5}$ ▨ $\frac{4}{5}$

9. $\frac{6}{8}$ ▨ $\frac{2}{8}$ 10. $\frac{6}{7}$ ▨ $\frac{1}{7}$ 11. $\frac{5}{12}$ ▨ $\frac{6}{12}$ 12. $\frac{1}{10}$ ▨ $\frac{9}{10}$

Pages 200–201

Write the number.

13. $\frac{1}{2}$ of 8 14. $\frac{1}{5}$ of 20 15. $\frac{1}{4}$ of 16 16. $\frac{1}{3}$ of 3

17. $\frac{1}{5}$ of 45 18. $\frac{1}{2}$ of 14 19. $\frac{1}{4}$ of 12 20. $\frac{1}{12}$ of 12

21. $\frac{1}{2}$ of 6 22. $\frac{1}{6}$ of 30 23. $\frac{1}{8}$ of 32 24. $\frac{1}{3}$ of 27

Pages 202–203

25. $\frac{2}{6}$ of 12 26. $\frac{2}{7}$ of 14 27. $\frac{5}{8}$ of 8 28. $\frac{2}{3}$ of 24

29. $\frac{5}{6}$ of 18 30. $\frac{2}{8}$ of 16 31. $\frac{2}{5}$ of 20 32. $\frac{7}{8}$ of 16

33. $\frac{2}{3}$ of 21 34. $\frac{4}{5}$ of 20 35. $\frac{3}{4}$ of 40 36. $\frac{2}{3}$ of 30

Pages 204–205

Write the decimal.

37. $\frac{1}{10}$ 38. $\frac{8}{10}$ 39. $\frac{5}{10}$ 40. $\frac{2}{10}$ 41. $\frac{6}{10}$

42. 9 out of 10 brands 43. 3 of the 10 winners

44. 7 out of 10 doctors 45. 4 of the 10 classes

Pages 206–207

46. 72 hundredths 47. 28 hundredths 48. 65 hundredths

49. 99 hundredths 50. 90 hundredths 51. 9 hundredths

52. $\frac{36}{100}$ 53. $\frac{75}{100}$ 54. $\frac{51}{100}$ 55. $\frac{40}{100}$ 56. $\frac{1}{100}$

57. 88 out of 100 answers 58. 20 of the 100 points

59. 53 out of 100 voters 60. 6 of the 100 pennies

Extra practice · Unit 10 (A)

(For use with pages 214–223)

Pages
214–215

1. 19
×3

2. 37
×7

3. 16
×5

4. 23
×4

5. 12
×9

6. 43
×4

7. 35
×3

8. 63
×5

9. 27
×3

10. 21
×5

Pages
216–217

11. 226
×3

12. 517
×4

13. 488
×3

14. 1562
×8

15. 2604
×7

16. 356
×4

17. 638
×6

18. 219
×8

19. 1319
×6

20. 3702
×8

Pages
218–219

21. 42
×10

22. 37
×30

23. 31
×80

24. 40
×40

25. 52
×30

26. 22
×90

27. 78
×50

28. 83
×10

29. 28
×60

30. 81
×70

Pages
220–221

31. 48
×12

32. 62
×18

33. 43
×15

34. 78
×13

35. 57
×15

36. 74
×11

37. 29
×16

38. 65
×14

39. 53
×16

40. 91
×12

Pages
222–223

41. 21
×35

42. 82
×23

43. 52
×63

44. 67
×28

45. 28
×38

46. 64
×52

47. 91
×34

48. 76
×24

49. 58
×53

50. 37
×62

51. 71
×48

52. 36
×42

53. 19
×98

54. 83
×84

55. 55
×55

Extra practice · Unit 10 (B)

(For use with pages 224–231)

Pages 224–225

1. 215
×40

2. 620
×10

3. 656
×30

4. 567
×50

5. 119
×80

6. 724
×30

7. 491
×40

8. 862
×60

9. 672
×30

10. 295
×70

Pages 226–227

11. 235
×18

12. 716
×12

13. 592
×14

14. 527
×16

15. 336
×13

16. 352
×17

17. 628
×14

18. 475
×15

19. 215
×19

20. 198
×13

Pages 228–229

21. 719
×24

22. 552
×32

23. 362
×41

24. 329
×36

25. 131
×67

26. 459
×62

27. 618
×56

28. 872
×25

29. 696
×37

30. 790
×63

31. 403
×32

32. 509
×26

33. 608
×49

34. 303
×98

35. 805
×64

Pages 230–231

36. $1.78
×10

37. $8.99
×10

38. $6.03
×10

39. $2.50
×10

40. $1.99
×20

41. $6.32
×50

42. $9.06
×40

43. $2.50
×80

44. $3.67
×54

45. $2.29
×46

46. $9.43
×22

47. $7.18
×32

48. $2.98
×26

49. $6.60
×34

50. $3.08
×52

51. $4.99
×30

Extra practice · Unit 11 (A)

(For use with pages 238–247)

Pages
238–239

1. 2)42 2. 2)45 3. 2)46 4. 2)49

5. 9)876 6. 5)339 7. 7)689 8. 8)681

9. 2)159 10. 4)332 11. 6)431 12. 7)624

13. 7)268 14. 6)252 15. 6)498 16. 8)387

Pages
240–241

17. 8)888 18. 3)669 19. 2)246 20. 3)663

21. 2)664 22. 2)462 23. 2)826 24. 3)966

25. 5)555 26. 6)666 27. 2)448 28. 9)999

29. 3)639 30. 2)488 31. 3)366 32. 2)628

Pages
242–243

33. 2)236 34. 6)726 35. 8)896 36. 7)784

37. 3)378 38. 3)729 39. 4)524 40. 5)655

41. 3)846 42. 4)496 43. 5)855 44. 4)924

Pages
244–245

45. 2)350 46. 2)590 47. 8)976 48. 8)944

49. 2)570 50. 2)974 51. 7)973 52. 6)804

53. 5)720 54. 4)512 55. 6)756 56. 7)994

57. 4)756 58. 5)675 59. 3)741 60. 3)858

Pages
246–247

61. 3)736 62. 2)533 63. 6)760 64. 4)918

65. 5)768 66. 4)579 67. 7)937 68. 3)797

69. 2)353 70. 2)779 71. 7)880 72. 3)875

330

Extra practice · Unit 11 (B)

(For use with pages 248–255)

Pages
248–249

1. 3)618   2. 6)642   3. 3)906   4. 3)317

5. 5)536   6. 4)423   7. 7)762   8. 2)807

9. 4)819   10. 5)542   11. 2)609   12. 7)728

13. 8)875   14. 5)529   15. 9)972   16. 5)504

17. 6)603   18. 7)721   19. 3)323   20. 3)330

Pages
250–251

21. 20)85   22. 30)73   23. 20)47   24. 40)92

25. 60)180   26. 50)267   27. 70)372   28. 30)249

29. 50)380   30. 40)334   31. 60)522   32. 20)164

33. 80)792   34. 70)393   35. 50)348   36. 90)181

Pages
252–253

37. 27)65   38. 38)88   39. 25)90   40. 17)42

41. 36)92   42. 42)73   43. 27)80   44. 19)55

45. 45)89   46. 33)94   47. 29)95   48. 48)90

49. 35)81   50. 18)46   51. 27)73   52. 34)65

53. 57)62   54. 13)22   55. 29)46   56. 18)89

Pages
254–255

57. 26)328   58. 55)761   59. 38)922   60. 62)715

61. 36)849   62. 48)930   63. 54)626   64. 35)833

65. 28)719   66. 18)461   67. 28)440   68. 48)618

69. 39)916   70. 48)839   71. 27)510   72. 89)927

Extra practice · Unit 12 (A)

(For use with pages 262–271)

Pages
262–263

Match the picture with a name.

1.

2.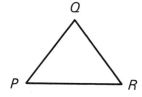

3.

4.

A. sphere   B. cube   C. cylinder   D. cone

Pages
264–265

Match the shape with its parts.

5. quadrilateral   A. exactly 3 angles

6. pentagon   B. exactly 4 sides

7. triangle   C. exactly 5 angles

Pages
266–267

Complete for triangle PQR.

8. Triangle PQR has angle P, angle Q, and angle ▨.

9. Triangle PQR has side PQ, side QR, and side ▨.

10. Line PQ and line QR form angle ▨.

11. Line QR and line PR meet in point ▨.

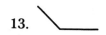

Pages
268–269

Match the angle with its size.

12. 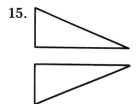   A. a right angle

13.   B. less than a right angle

14.   C. greater than a right angle

Pages
270–271

Do the triangles have the same size and shape?

15. 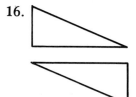   16. 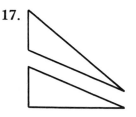   17.

332

Extra practice · Unit 12 (B)   (For use with pages 272–279)

Pages 272–273

Write P if you see parallel lines and R for right angles.

1.
2.
3.
4.

Pages 274–275

Complete for rectangle *PQRS*.

5. Side *PQ* is parallel to side ▨.

6. Side *QR* is parallel to side ▨.

7. Side *RS* is the same length as side ▨.

8. Side *PS* is the same length as side ▨.

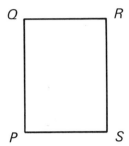

Is the shape a square?

9.
10.
11.
12.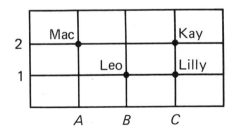

Pages 276–277

Complete.

13. Lilly (*C*, ▨)

14. Mac (*A*, ▨)

15. Leo (▨, 1)

16. Kay (▨, 2)

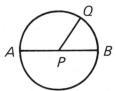

Pages 278–279

Match the part of the circle with its name.

17. point *P*   A. radius

18. line *PQ*   B. diameter

19. line *AB*   C. center

Extra practice · Unit 13 (A)

(For use with pages 286–295)

Pages
286–287

Write the fraction in simplest form.

1. $\frac{2}{4}$ 2. $\frac{2}{10}$ 3. $\frac{2}{8}$ 4. $\frac{2}{6}$ 5. $\frac{3}{6}$

6. $\frac{4}{12}$ 7. $\frac{8}{12}$ 8. $\frac{9}{12}$ 9. $\frac{6}{9}$ 10. $\frac{6}{10}$

11. $\frac{10}{16}$ 12. $\frac{10}{12}$ 13. $\frac{6}{15}$ 14. $\frac{6}{6}$ 15. $\frac{0}{5}$

Pages
288–289

16. $\frac{1}{3} + \frac{1}{3}$ 17. $\frac{1}{5} + \frac{1}{5}$ 18. $\frac{1}{5} + \frac{3}{5}$ 19. $\frac{3}{7} + \frac{3}{7}$

20. $\frac{1}{4} + \frac{2}{4}$ 21. $\frac{3}{8} + \frac{2}{8}$ 22. $\frac{2}{6} + \frac{3}{6}$ 23. $\frac{6}{10} + \frac{1}{10}$

24. $\frac{2}{7}$ 25. $\frac{2}{5}$ 26. $\frac{4}{10}$ 27. $\frac{3}{8}$ 28. $\frac{3}{5}$
$+ \frac{1}{7}$ $+ \frac{2}{5}$ $+ \frac{3}{10}$ $+ \frac{4}{8}$ $+ \frac{2}{5}$

Pages
290–291

29. $\frac{3}{5} - \frac{2}{5}$ 30. $\frac{6}{7} - \frac{1}{7}$ 31. $\frac{5}{8} - \frac{4}{8}$ 32. $\frac{8}{10} - \frac{5}{10}$

33. $\frac{2}{6} - \frac{1}{6}$ 34. $\frac{6}{9} - \frac{4}{9}$ 35. $\frac{4}{7} - \frac{2}{7}$ 36. $\frac{4}{4} - \frac{1}{4}$

37. $\frac{2}{3}$ 38. $\frac{4}{5}$ 39. $\frac{6}{7}$ 40. $\frac{5}{8}$ 41. $\frac{9}{10}$
$- \frac{1}{3}$ $- \frac{3}{5}$ $- \frac{4}{7}$ $- \frac{2}{8}$ $- \frac{8}{10}$

Pages
292–293

42. $\frac{1}{6}$ 43. $\frac{1}{6}$ 44. $\frac{2}{4}$ 45. $\frac{3}{10}$ 46. $\frac{3}{8}$
$+ \frac{1}{2}$ $+ \frac{1}{12}$ $+ \frac{1}{8}$ $+ \frac{1}{5}$ $+ \frac{3}{16}$

47. $\frac{3}{5}$ 48. $\frac{5}{6}$ 49. $\frac{1}{16}$ 50. $\frac{1}{3}$ 51. $\frac{1}{5}$
$+ \frac{3}{10}$ $+ \frac{1}{12}$ $+ \frac{5}{8}$ $+ \frac{3}{6}$ $+ \frac{1}{15}$

Pages
294–295

52. $\frac{1}{2}$ 53. $\frac{1}{3}$ 54. $\frac{3}{4}$ 55. $\frac{7}{10}$ 56. $\frac{3}{5}$
$- \frac{1}{12}$ $- \frac{1}{6}$ $- \frac{1}{8}$ $- \frac{2}{5}$ $- \frac{1}{10}$

Extra practice · Unit 13 (B)

(For use with pages 296–303)

Pages
296–297

Complete.

1. $\frac{2}{2} = 1$ 2. $\frac{3}{3} = 1$ 3. $\frac{4}{4} = 1$ 4. $\frac{5}{5} = 1$

$\frac{3}{2} = 1\frac{\blacksquare}{2}$ $\frac{5}{3} = 1\frac{\blacksquare}{3}$ $\frac{5}{4} = 1\frac{\blacksquare}{4}$ $\frac{7}{5} = 1\frac{\blacksquare}{5}$

5. $\frac{6}{6} = 1$ 6. $\frac{10}{10} = 1$ 7. $\frac{8}{4} = 2$ 8. $\frac{10}{5} = 2$

$\frac{11}{6} = 1\frac{\blacksquare}{6}$ $\frac{11}{10} = 1\frac{\blacksquare}{10}$ $\frac{11}{4} = 2\frac{\blacksquare}{4}$ $\frac{11}{5} = 2\frac{\blacksquare}{5}$

Pages
298–299

Write the decimal.

9. one and six tenths   10. five and three tenths

11. 13 and 86 hundredths   12. 20 and 65 hundredths

13. $2\frac{1}{10}$ 14. $7\frac{8}{10}$ 15. $18\frac{9}{10}$ 16. $95\frac{4}{10}$ 17. $10\frac{2}{10}$

18. $1\frac{82}{100}$ 19. $7\frac{56}{100}$ 20. $12\frac{27}{100}$ 21. $18\frac{50}{100}$ 22. $26\frac{5}{100}$

Pages
300–301

23.	24.	25.	26.
0.4 +0.3	0.9 +0.7	12.6 + 3.5	23.8 +89.7

27.	28.	29.	30.
0.8 −0.5	5.7 −3.2	18.2 − 2.9	78.1 −39.5

Pages
302–303

31.	32.	33.	34.
0.24 +0.53	0.45 +0.87	8.02 +6.19	26.35 + 5.88

35.	36.	37.	38.
0.77 −0.53	0.55 −0.19	5.63 −2.79	32.46 − 2.55

39.	40.	41.	42.
$1.25 .75 +3.88	$5.98 5.98 +5.98	$12.35 8.79 5.67 + 1.88	$23.00 14.98 12.49 +10.89

Table of Measures

TIME

1 minute (min) = 60 seconds (s)
1 hour (h) = 60 minutes
1 day = 24 hours
1 week = 7 days

1 year = 52 weeks
1 year = 12 months
1 century = 100 years

Metric

LENGTH

1 centimeter (cm) = 10 millimeters (mm)
1 meter (m) = 100 centimeters
1 kilometer (km) = 1000 meters

WEIGHT (Mass)

1 kilogram (kg) = 1000 grams (g)

CAPACITY

1 liter (ℓ) = 1000 milliliters (ml)

United States Customary

LENGTH

1 foot (ft) = 12 inches (in.)
1 yard (yd) = 3 feet
1 mile (mi) = 5280 feet
1 mile = 1760 yards

WEIGHT

1 pound (lb) = 16 ounces (oz)
1 ton = 2000 pounds

CAPACITY

1 pint (pt) = 2 cups
1 quart (qt) = 2 pints
1 gallon (gal) = 4 quarts

Glossary

angle (p. 264) A figure formed when two lines meet.

area (p. 124) The number of square units that fit inside a shape.

average (p. 186) The sum of the given numbers divided by the number of numbers.

box (p. 262) A shape in space with six sides, all rectangles.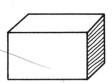

circle (p. 278) A round shape like this. Point *O* is the center of the circle.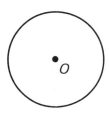

cone (p. 262) A shape in space like this.

cube (p. 262) A shape in space with six sides, all squares of the same size.

cylinder (p. 262) A shape in space like this.

decimal (p. 204) A number which uses a decimal point to show tenths and hundredths, like 0.2 and 1.76.

denominator (p. 190) 3 is the denominator in the fraction $\frac{2}{3}$.

diameter (p. 278) Line *PA* is a diameter of the circle. It goes through the center 0.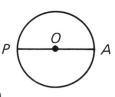

difference (p. 2) The answer in subtraction.

digit (p. 24) The symbol 0, 1, 2, 3, 4, 5, 6, 7, 8, or 9.

equal fractions (p. 192) Fractions that have the same value. $\frac{2}{4}$ and $\frac{1}{2}$ are equal fractions.

estimate (p. 64) To guess a likely answer by rounding the numbers before doing the arithmetic.

even number (p. 92)   A number with 0, 2, 4, 6, or 8 in the ones' place.

factors (p. 260)   Numbers to be multiplied. 2 and 6 are factors of 12 since 2 × 6 = 12.

fraction   (p. 188)   A number such as $\frac{1}{2}$, $\frac{6}{10}$, and $\frac{5}{3}$.

graph (p. 5)   A picture that is used to show information.

line of symmetry (p. 284)   A line along which a shape can be folded so that one half fits on the other half exactly.

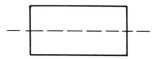

mixed number (p. 296)   A whole number plus a fraction. $2\frac{1}{3}$ is a mixed number.

numerator (p. 190)   2 is the numerator in the fraction $\frac{2}{3}$.

odd number (p. 92)   A number with 1, 3, 5, 7, or 9 in the ones' place.

parallel lines (p. 272)   Lines that never meet.

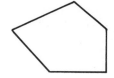

pentagon (p. 264) A shape with five sides.

perimeter (p. 120)   The distance around a shape.

product (p. 72)   The answer in multiplication.

pyramid (p. 262) A shape in space like this.

quadrilateral (p. 264)   A shape with four sides.

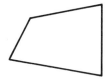

quotient (p. 76)   The answer in division.

radius (p. 278) Line OA is a radius of the circle whose center is O.

rectangle (p. 274)   A quadrilateral with four right angles.

remainder (p. 166)
The number left over
when a division
is complete.

```
      2
6) 15
  -12
remainder ▶ 3
```

right angle
(p. 268)   An angle
that looks like the
corner of a page.

Roman numeral (p. 44)   A
numeral written with the symbols I,
V, X, L, C, D, or M.

round (p. 30)   To write the ten
or hundred nearest a number. 58
rounded to the nearest ten is 60.

simplest form (p. 286)   A
fraction is in simplest form when
its numerator and denominator
cannot be divided by the same
number. $\frac{1}{2}$ is the simplest form
of $\frac{4}{8}$.

solve (p. 16)   Answer the
question asked in a problem.

sphere (p. 262)   A
round shape in space
like this.

square (p. 274)   A
rectangle with all sides
the same length.

standard form (p. 24)   The
usual, short form of a number. 573
is the standard form for 5 hundreds
7 tens 3 ones.

sum (p. 2)   The answer in
addition.

triangle (p. 264)
A shape with
three sides.

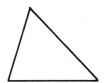

volume (p. 126)   The number of
cubic units that fit inside a shape in
space.

Index

Addition
of decimals, 300–303
estimating in, 64–66
facts, 2–9
four-place, 54
of fractions, 288,
  292, 297
with money, 62–65
one number greater
  than ten, 10–13, 50
three or more
  numbers, 14, 46
three-place, 52
two-place, 46–51
Angles, 264–271
comparing, 268, 271
right, 268–271, 272,
  274, 276
Applications
estimating, 64–66,
  69, 116, 151, 157,
  158, 161, 169, 253
measurement
  metric, 35, 37, 40,
    43, 53, 121,
    129, 133, 134,
    138, 177, 182,
    236, 253, 301,
    308
  U.S. Customary,
    38, 123, 131,
    133, 182, 236,
    308
money, 32, 62–65,
  97, 99, 101, 105,
  112, 115, 116,
  157, 158, 161,
  162, 167, 169,
  217, 227, 229,
  231, 232, 235,
  241, 243, 256,
  301, 304, 307

See also Word
  problems
Area, 124
Average, 186

Capacity, 128–131
Celsius, 138
Center of a circle, 278
Centimeter, 34, 118
Circle, 278
Circle graph, 212
Coins, 32, 51, 63, 112
Compasses, 278
Cone, 262
Cube, 128, 262, 267
Cubic unit, 126, 128
Cylinder, 262

Decimal point, 204
Decimals, 204–207, 298,
  300–303
Denominator, 190
Diameter, 278
Difference, 2
Digit, 24
Division
estimating in, 250–
  255
facts, 76–87, 94–111
fractions and, 200–
  203
meaning of, 76
with remainders,
  164–167, 174,
  179, 180, 238,
  246–255
by tens, 250
by tens and ones,
  252–255
with tens as quotients,
  168

with three-place
  quotients, 240–249
with two-place
  quotients, 168–181,
  238, 254
zero in, 100, 248
Dollars and cents, *see*
  Money
Drawing and
  construction
circle, 278
lines at right angles,
  273
parallel lines, 273

Enrichment
average, 186
calculator, 151
charts and tables,
  162, 236
comparison, 177, 199
division, 179, 245,
  249, 253
games and puzzles,
  13, 20, 59, 125,
  171
geometry, 267, 269,
  275, 284
graphs, 5, 212
measurement, 35,
  138
mental arithmetic, 49,
  107, 241
money, 51, 63, 116
numbers, 44, 92,
  260, 299
shortcut, 221
Something Extra, 20,
  44, 70, 92, 116,
  138, 162, 186,
  212, 236, 260,
  284, 308

Number pairs, 276
Number pattern, 8, 86, 108, 140–142
Numbers
  comparing, 22, 25, 177
  even, 92
  to a million, 22–29
  mixed, 296–299
  odd, 92
  in order, 22, 25, 27, 29
  rounding, 30, 64–66, 148, 252, 254
  in standard form, 24–28
  See also Decimals *and* Fractions
Numerator, 190

Odd number, 92
Order
  of fractions, 198
  of numbers to millions, 22, 25, 27, 29
Ordinal number, 193

Parallel lines, 272–277
Pentagon, 264
Perimeter, 120, 123
Place value, 24–29
Point, 266, 276
Practice
  Extra practice, 310–335
  See also Reviews
Problem Solving
  giving the answer, 134, 232
  four-step method, 16, 40, 66, 304

making a plan, 88, 112, 256, 280
understanding the problem, 158, 182, 208
See also Word problems
Product, 72
Pyramid, 262

Quadrilateral, 264, 274
Quotient, 76, 166

Radius, 278
Rectangle, 274
Rectangular box, 262
Remainder, 166
Reviews
  Review A, 9, 31, 55, 81, 103, 127, 149, 172, 197, 223, 247, 271, 295
  Review B, 15, 39, 65, 87, 111, 133, 157, 181, 207, 231, 255, 279, 303
  Reviewing Needed Skills, 21, 45, 71, 93, 117, 139, 163, 187, 213, 237, 261, 285, 309
  Taking Another Look, 18, 42, 68, 90, 114, 136, 160, 184, 210, 234, 258, 282, 306
Right angle, 268–274, 276
Roman numerals, 44
Rounding, 30, 64–66, 252, 254
  money, 31, 33, 64, 148, 157

Simplest form of a fraction, 286
Sphere, 262
Square, 274
Square unit, 124
Standard form, 24
Subtraction
  checking, 58
  of decimals, 300–303
  estimating in, 64
  facts, 2–9
  four-place, 60, 62
  of fractions, 290, 294
  with money, 62–65, 116
  three-place, 58, 62
  two-place, 56, 62
Sum, 2
Symmetry, 284

Table of Measures, 336
Temperature, 138
Tenth, 204, 298–301
Tests, Unit, 17, 41, 67, 89, 113, 135, 159, 183, 209, 233, 257, 281, 305
Time, 29, 70, 96, 132, 182, 236, 308
Triangle, 264–267, 270

United States
  Customary system of measurement, 38, 122, 130, 336
Units of measurement, *see* Measurement

Volume, 126

Weight (mass), 36, 38

Credits

Illustrations

ANCO/Boston Technical Art
Ginger Brown 29, 118, 119, 132, 188,
  190, 192
Lynne Cherry 46–66, 214–232
Christine Czernota 18–21 (repeated
  between all units)
Mark Kelley 140–158
Amy Myers 2–16, 164–182
Diane Shapiro 72–88, 238–255
Dorothea Sierra 24
Susan Swan 94–112, 262–278, 284

Cover, Title Page:
  Susan Swan

Photography

Marion Bernstein 36 (monkey), 188–
  89, 192, 193, 199–201
John Hamilton Burke 34, 36, 202,
  203, 290
Don Dietz 206–7
Walter Chandoha 22–23

BRUCE COLEMAN INC:
  Daniel J. Lyons 37
  Norman Myers 25
  Oxford Scientific Foundation 26
  Hans Reinhard 36 (elephant)
  Norman Owen Tomalin 35 (bottom)
  Dieter Zingel 35 (top)
Dr. Harold E. Edgerton 198
Grant Heilman 27
Ken Heyman 205
Martucci Studio 32
PHOTO RESEARCHERS: National
  Audubon Society Collection, William
  Curtsinger 40
  Ruth Orkin 196
Hakim Raquib 122–23, 128, 129
Jonathan Rawle 286–289, 291–302
George Sheng 30, 33 (Living World®
  Habitrail® equipment courtesy of the
  Metaframe Corporation, Elmwood
  Park, N.J.; 39 (exhibit courtesy of the
  Museum of Science, Boston)
STOCK BOSTON: Denley Karlson 204
  Frank Siteman 38, 191
Bonnie Unsworth 118–121, 125, 126,
  130–134, 194–95